Professional Hockey
in Philadelphia

# Professional Hockey in Philadelphia
## *A History*

### Alan Bass

McFarland & Company, Inc., Publishers
*Jefferson, North Carolina*

Unless otherwise noted, photographs belong to the author.

ISBN (print) 978-1-4766-8269-3
ISBN (ebook) 978-1-4766-4064-8

LIBRARY OF CONGRESS AND BRITISH LIBRARY
CATALOGUING DATA ARE AVAILABLE

Library of Congress Control Number 2020036976

© 2020 Alan Bass. All rights reserved

*No part of this book may be reproduced or transmitted in any form or by any means, electronic or mechanical, including photocopying or recording, or by any information storage and retrieval system, without permission in writing from the publisher.*

Front cover: The Philadelphia Firebirds team photograph from the 1976–77 season (Bruce "Scoop" Cooper)

Printed in the United States of America

*McFarland & Company, Inc., Publishers
Box 611, Jefferson, North Carolina 28640
www.mcfarlandpub.com*

# Table of Contents

*Acknowledgments* vii

*Preface* 1

*Introduction: Philadelphia Professional Hockey* 5

1. Quaker City Hockey Club: American Amateur Hockey League, 1900–01 — 11

2. The Arrows: Canadian-American Hockey League (CAHL), 1927–35 — 22

3. The Quakers: National Hockey League (NHL), 1930–31 — 42

4. The Comets: Tri-State Hockey League (T-SHL), 1932–33 — 57

5. The Ramblers: Canadian-American Hockey League (CAHL), 1935–36; International-American Hockey League (I-AHL), 1936–40; American Hockey League (AHL), 1940–41 — 64

6. The Rockets/Falcons: American Hockey League (AHL), 1941–42; Eastern Amateur Hockey League (EAHL), 1942–46; American Hockey League, 1946–49; Eastern Amateur Hockey League, 1951 — 79

7. The Ramblers: Eastern Hockey League (EHL), 1955–64 — 93

8. The Flyers: National Hockey League (NHL), 1967–Present — 106

9. The Blazers: World Hockey Association (WHA), 1972–73 — 130

**10.** The Firebirds: North American Hockey League
   (NAHL), 1974–77; American Hockey League (AHL),
   1977–79                                                150

**11.** The Phantoms: American Hockey League (AHL),
   1996–2009                                              178

*Epilogue*                                                197

*Appendix: The History of the Philadelphia Arena*         199

*Chapter Notes*                                           211

*Bibliography*                                            221

*Index*                                                   225

# Acknowledgments

Any nonfiction book, especially one covering more than a century of history, is never a solo project. Rather, it requires the help and support of many, both personally and professionally. Since the vast majority of the teams featured in this book played their final game before I was born, I was reliant on a plethora of people and resources to create what you now hold in your hands.

First and foremost, I want to thank everyone who took time out of their busy schedules to speak with me about their knowledge and experiences in or around any of these Philadelphia hockey teams, including Peter Luukko, Nick "Rocky" Rukavina, Gregg Pilling, Reggie Lemelin, Gord Brooks, Mark Hebscher, Lou Scheinfeld, Frank Miceli, Bill Barber, Sidney Brown, Bob Kitrinos, Dave Andrews, Derek Sanderson, and many more. Thank you also to Karen Wonoski of Boston Bruins Alumni, who got me in touch with multiple former players that helped contribute to this book.

A hearty thanks goes to Stuart McComish of the National Hockey League. Stuart dealt with my constant emails for many months, seeking information from the NHL Archives. He would regularly take a list of a dozen or more questions, riffle through the league's archives, and provide me with as much information as he could find—including newspaper articles, if he couldn't find the answer within the league office. His information helped confirm or deny many rumors that were reported in other books, news sources, and by people I spoke to.

The chapter on the Philadelphia Quakers would certainly not have been as complete as it was without the help of Paul Christman. His extensive research and writing on the NHL's Pittsburgh Pirates and Quakers laid the groundwork for the chapter and much of the knowledge we have today about those two franchises. If anyone were to write a full book on the Pirates and Quakers, he would be the one—and I would be first in line to read it.

In my search for archival information outside of the newspapers,

I came upon Jim Rhodes, the grandson of Philadelphia hockey coach and Hockey Hall of Famer Herb Gardiner. Jim proudly and generously shared his grandfather's life with me, providing an incredible amount of information, memorabilia, and stories that have been passed down through his family. Gardiner's life is arguably fascinating enough to merit his own biography one day, but we wouldn't even know half of that life without Jim and his family's care in keeping the history alive. Thanks also to *The Hockey News*' Brian Costello for putting me in touch with Jim.

Through the book, I regularly used various resources that may not otherwise be cited in the bibliography: the Newspapers.com archive provided a bulk of the newspaper articles that laid the groundwork for the entirety of the book. This book would not have been remotely possible without it. HockeyDB.com has been my go-to source for hockey statistics from the moment I began writing many years ago. My visits to the site were hourly throughout this project, as I gathered and confirmed statistics for each player and team. The Pennsylvania Department of State Business Database provided me with excellent documentation on nearly all of the Philadelphia hockey teams, from ownership records to miscellaneous business filings. TheEHL.com was also a treasure trove of information about the Eastern Hockey League, and although nothing in the book was specifically sourced from the site, the resource provided fantastic background and a great foundation with which to understand the EHL.

One of the biggest thank-yous for this book goes to Bruce "Scoop" Cooper, a Philadelphia hockey historian who has attended thousands of professional hockey games in his lifetime and makes it a point to mentor young, aspiring writers with his fountain of knowledge of the game. Scoop took me under his wing for the first time back in 2010, when I wrote my first book, *The Great Expansion: The Ultimate Risk That Changed the NHL Forever*, and his tutelage has been irreplaceable ever since. Not only did he spend many hours on the phone and in person with me throughout this entire process, but his archive of photographs, memorabilia, and knowledge is prominently featured throughout this book. The final version would not be nearly as complete without him.

Another major acknowledgment goes to my dad, who, in essence, created this beast when he first took me to a Philadelphia Flyers game against the Pittsburgh Penguins in November 1996 where I immediately fell in love with the sport (they won, 7–3!). Through countless Flyers and Phantoms games in my early life, I developed a deeper love for hockey than just simply being a fan of the teams—I constantly yearned to learn more about the sport, how it works, how it grew, and how it became what it is today. Although it certainly wasn't his intention when he shared his love of hockey with his son one night in the 1990s, it was his introduction of the game that can easily be correlated with the publication of this book. His support during this writing process and critiques of the manuscript helped shape it into the final copy. To both of my parents, thank you for your constant support of my writing.

Most importantly, my wife, Emily, has been ever-present from the start of this project. When you tell someone that you want to write a book, many tilt their head like a confused dog, boggled at why you would do something so unusual. Emily was not only supportive from the beginning, but enthusiastic about the potential for this project. Emily, who is far from a sports fan, sat with open ears and with pen and paper as I read aloud to her the entirety of the book, looking for feedback on form, content, and the big picture of what I tried to achieve with this work. Her encouragement when I hit a wall, along with her genuine excitement for all of my writing, makes every project worthwhile.

Lastly, I feel the need to make a special mention of the Philadelphia newspapers of the 20th century. This book could not have been written were it not for the incredible work done by the beat writers for the teams featured, from the Arrows all the way to the Phantoms. Whether it was Stan Baumgartner and Frank Dolson of the *Philadelphia Inquirer*, Jay Greenberg and Bill Fleischman of the *Philadelphia Daily News*, or any unnamed writer that published without a byline in the early days of Philadelphia hockey, their contribution to the history of the sport is incalculable. A full list of the newspapers utilized can be seen by perusing the book's notes and bibliography, but it was well over 30 different news sources, compounded by the number of daily issues each one published. Flipping through each day's paper was as close as one can get to living through each team's life without having personally lived through it as much as 90 years earlier. My biggest hope for this book is that, years from now, someone can look upon it the same way I looked upon the work of these dedicated newspapermen, and bring the stories of these teams and players to life yet again.

# Preface

Philadelphia is, when you get right down to it, a hockey town. When the Flyers are performing well or making a deep run into the playoffs, the city transforms in a way that is unparalleled. When the Flyers won their first Stanley Cup in 1974, an estimated two million fans attended the parade, nearly triple the number that attended the Eagles' Super Bowl parade in 2018. This is not to take away from the accomplishments of the other sports teams that call South Philadelphia their home. Rather, it is a comment on the importance of ice hockey to the culture of Philadelphia. Among all the sports that the city has hosted over the years, hockey perhaps has the most illustrious history and the largest number of professional teams to reside in Philadelphia since the turn of the 20th century. The sport's history within the city goes all the way back to 1897.

It was with that in mind that I realized the sports fans of the region were missing a crucial piece of the hockey history of this city. Numerous books have been written about the Flyers while other books have touched lightly on the other teams to grace the ice here, but no one had yet taken the time to delve into the memorable, and sometimes tenuous, history of the teams that paved the way for hockey's now successful hold on the hearts of Philadelphians today. As someone who grew up with ice in his veins, like millions of other Philadelphians, I believe the history of these squads merits a place on the bookshelves of hockey fans throughout the region. That's why I initially set out to write this book.

Rather than discuss the history of hockey solely chronologically, I have chosen instead to focus each chapter on the entire lifespan of each organization. Because of that, scant pieces of certain chapters may overlap. Yet, I felt the best way to tell the story of these teams was by separating them as they are in this book. Each team has such a unique story that it did not feel fair to me to merge and weave the teams together and risk missing out on the personality of each one. The players, coaches, and fans of each team were often so memorable that they each deserved their own chapter.

For the purpose of this book, a team is defined by an organization whose bones remain the same. For example, the Ramblers of the 1930s could be considered a continuation of the Arrows franchise, but with a different roster, different ownership, and different management structure, they are treated here as a separate franchise. The Rockets and Falcons, on the other hand, were teams of different names in different leagues, but had the same makeup, the same ownership, and similar rosters. They simply bounced around between leagues. Likewise, the Firebirds took the same ownership and management structure and a majority of their roster from the NAHL to the AHL. Both of these franchises are considered a single team and are therefore discussed within the same chapter.

On top of the grey area of teams that jumped between leagues, the term "professional" hockey can be subjective, especially when going back over a century to a time when media coverage was spotty, at best. Many teams of that era were called "amateur" teams, but this simply meant that they played under the guidance of the Amateur Hockey Association of the United States, the organization which is known today as USA Hockey. These amateur teams generally still paid the players, recruited them to their teams, and otherwise were treated like professional teams. For the purpose of this book, some of the "amateur" teams described will be classified as "professional" teams, in order to more accurately portray the players and their relationship with the game and the leagues in which they played.

This book essentially started during the writing process for my first book, *The Great Expansion: The Ultimate Risk That Changed the NHL Forever*, which was published in 2011. With the Flyers having a heavy presence within that project, the wheels began turning for this project, whose image was not fully clear until a few years ago. Over the course of many conversations with the hockey historians that populate the press room at Flyers games each night, along with my own preliminary research into the specific teams detailed here, this manuscript very quickly became a reality. Through dozens of interviews, the picture became even clearer. Some of those I spoke with played for, worked in, or even coached some of the later Philadelphia teams—the Ramblers, Flyers, Blazers, Firebirds, and Phantoms. Others have done extensive research into the history of certain teams and were happy to share their knowledge, such is the case with the Quakers and the Quaker City Hockey Club.

Most importantly, the newspaper archives from the 1890s through present day were of the utmost importance, since even those that lived through the respective team's existence may not have remembered everything with 100 percent accuracy. Only those writers who were covering these teams on a nightly basis had the full story to share, which helped this book take shape.

One of the issues that arose during the research process was, in fact, the accuracy of some of the newspaper accounts. Sometimes it was as simple as a misspelling of a player's name; other times it was a complete disagreement on a fact from the game. More often than not, multiple sources were utilized in order to state a fact or story with confidence. If a fact or story was not demonstrably accurate, I stated within the chapter alternative news sources, so as to provide the reader with all the information possible so that their own conclusions could be drawn. As a side note, some quotes from the newspaper sources throughout the book have been altered to reflect proper spelling or modern grammar, for ease of reading. The content of these quotes, however, is never altered.

After compiling all of the research, the stories of these hockey franchises essentially told themselves over the course of a year. The fodder from the newspapers, mixed with the first- or second-hand knowledge from those that I spoke with, helped weave together an illustrious narrative of the history of the sport in Philadelphia. Fortunately, as any hockey fan will attest, former players, hockey historians and media members love to talk about the game. The conversations were endless, took curvy roads around the actual topics of discussion, as most hockey conversations do, yet ultimately provided a fantastic foundation for this project.

The book is written to be read from start to finish, so that one can truly appreciate the evolution of the sport into what it is today. However, there is no doubt that certain readers, for a variety of reasons, will want to jump directly to a certain team, like a fan flipping through the pages of *The Hockey News* to see what was written about their home team. And while that will certainly have its merit, be it a direct connection to those teams or an avid fan of those teams years ago, I implore you to also read about the rest of the teams that entertained Philadelphia hockey fans, for better or for worse, over the course of the last hundred-plus years. Whether the team existed for one year or ten years, all of them contributed greatly to what is now an elite hockey culture in the city of Philadelphia.

# Introduction: Philadelphia Professional Hockey

Since 1967, Philadelphia hockey has been synonymous with the Flyers. With a *Forbes* valuation of $800 million in 2018 and one of the most successful National Hockey League organizations in the league's 100-year-plus history, they have rightfully earned their place high above anyone else in Philadelphia hockey lore. As long as there is NHL hockey, there will be NHL hockey in Philadelphia.

But the success of the Flyers organization and the spell it casts on its fans each year is not independent of the sport's history in this city. As early as 1927, professional hockey had a presence in the City of Brotherly Love. In fact, in the forty years before the Flyers even iced a team, Philadelphia had seen seven professional hockey organizations present the world's fastest sport to the region, with varying degrees of success. Even after the Flyers inaugural season, three additional professional teams showed their faces in the city, with the American League's Phantoms being the last.

Unbeknownst to many diehard Flyers fans, the Flyers were not even the city's first NHL team. Philadelphia's first shot at NHL hockey came in 1930. Just one year after receiving an NHL franchise in 1925, the Pittsburgh Pirates became rampant with reports that the team was going to relocate, with Cleveland and Philadelphia as the potential markets. A rumor in 1930 even suggested the team would move to Atlantic City as a temporary fix while Cleveland prepared an NHL arena. But when that plan seemed destined to fail, Philadelphia was granted control of the Pirates and renamed them the Philadelphia Quakers. Unfortunately, the Quakers had arguably the worst season in NHL history and the team was shuttered in 1931, after just one season.

Philadelphia held claim to numerous minor-pro hockey teams over the past 100 years as well. The Canadian-American League's Philadelphia Arrows existed from 1927 to 1935, without ever winning a league championship. The Philadelphia Comets of the Tri-State League existed for just four months between 1932 and 1933, but failed to win a single game in 16 contests.

The New York Rangers took control of the Arrows in 1935, and the team was rebranded the Ramblers for the 1935–36 season, immediately rising to the top and winning the Frank Fontaine Cup as the league's champions. The organization existed until the 1941–42 season, when it gave way to the Philadelphia Rockets of the American League. They quickly became the Philadelphia Falcons and joined the Eastern Amateur League in 1942. At the time, the Falcons were the only professional hockey team in Philadelphia.

But the Falcons folded in 1946, giving way to the return of the AHL's Philadelphia Rockets. This team was even worse than the Quakers, finishing 5–52–7 for a .133 winning percentage. That team would end its operations in 1949. The Falcons returned for one season in 1951–52, but would stop playing in the middle of the season and fold at the conclusion of the campaign. The Philadelphia Ramblers were reborn in 1955, this time in the Eastern League. The team had more longevity than any other Philadelphia hockey team before them, as they lasted nine years before folding after the 1963–64 season.

The Flyers, of course, were added to the NHL circuit for the 1967–68 season in what became known as "The Great Expansion," when the league doubled in size. The Flyers era also saw the Philadelphia Blazers of the World Hockey Association compete for one season, along with the Philadelphia Firebirds for five years in the North American League and the AHL. And in 1996, the AHL's Phantoms were born, enjoying a lengthy life in Philadelphia before finding their permanent home in Allentown, Pennsylvania, a short ride north of the city.

Even outside of the Quakers and the Flyers, Philadelphia had legitimate other attempts to bring NHL hockey to the city. In 1924, Jules Mastbaum, owner of the Philadelphia Arena (which housed every hockey team until 1967), applied to the NHL for a major league franchise in Philadelphia. His letter to the league, according to Board of Governors minutes, "was put aside for further consideration." In 1928, with the Pittsburgh Pirates franchise in limbo, Irwin Wener of the Philadelphia Arena made a pitch to the league to move the team to Philadelphia.*

After the NHL's Montreal Maroons franchise went dormant in 1938, multiple attempts were made to revive the organization. In the

---

*The eventual relocation of the Pirates to Philadelphia as the Quakers was done through different owners, rather than through Wener, as you will read about in Chapter 3.

mid–1940s, a man named Leonard A. Peto moved to Philadelphia after experiencing success as an NHL executive. A member of the Board of Directors of the Canadian Arena Company, he served with the Maroons before their demise and with the Canadiens afterwards, winning the Stanley Cup with the latter franchise in 1944. After establishing himself in Philadelphia in 1946, he promised to construct a $2.5 million arena at the site of the old Baker Bowl, located between Broad and 15th streets, acquire the defunct Maroons franchise, and relocate them to Philadelphia as the NHL's seventh team.

The attempt was met with open arms and a smile by the league's front office. "We'll be glad to welcome Philadelphia into the National League," said NHL President Mervyn "Red" Dutton to the *Philadelphia Evening Bulletin* in January 1946. According to Canadiens GM Tommy Gorman, the Board of Governors was willing to approve the transaction, even going so far as to suggest the move would be approved a month later.[1]

However, Peto ran into some barriers and the process began to slog. There was pushback from the AHL's Philadelphia Rockets, who opposed professional competition to their franchise. The city of Philadelphia also gave Peto a hard time with his arena plans (you can read more about this in the appendix on the history of the Philadelphia Arena). At the February 14, 1946, NHL Board of Governors meeting, Peto made his pitch to the league, outlining his arena plans, financial arrangements, and tried to sell the Board on his all-around plan to bring major league hockey to Philadelphia. Dutton told the *Times* publicly that a decision would not be made at that time,[2] though privately it seemed the league made an agreement with Peto, so long as he fulfilled the conditions that were laid out, including a new arena.[3]

The process dragged into 1947, at which point Peto still held optimism that his plan would succeed, even going so far as to place an ad in a Winnipeg newspaper seeking players for the "Maroon Hockey Club" for the 1948 season. At a June 3, 1947, meeting, he requested and was granted an extension by the Board to continue securing plans for the new building. Despite the setbacks, the *Times* reported, "if a rink can be built by the fall of 1948, the new Maroons will begin play then."[4] In 1946, according to Charles Coleman in the league-sponsored publication *The Trail of the Stanley Cup*, "the league governors were prepared to approve of such a transfer providing satisfactory evidence was produced of the financial capability of these interests."[5]

Throughout 1947, league notes show that Peto was unable to secure the proper funding, endangering his proposal. A year later, the league expressed a continued hope from the Board of Governors, describing the potential Philadelphia franchise as "a continuing obligation which the league was committed to fulfill, subject to the Philadelphia applicants complying with the conditions laid down." But at the June 2, 1948, Board of Governors meeting, the owners instructed league president Clarence Campbell to terminate the agreement with Peto and reject his request to establish a player reserve list for the Maroons franchise, claiming that he had "not fulfilled the requirements necessary for the approval of this franchise transfer." At this point, the league had had enough, demanding that the Canadian Arena Company return Peto's payment for the franchise, and officially terminated the Maroons organization. Philadelphia would have to wait another two decades for NHL hockey to make its return.[6]

Despite having just one season of NHL action before 1967, professional hockey's presence in Philadelphia was illustrious at worst and impressive at best. Even at its lowest points, the various teams that graced the ice throughout the city provided not only an introduction to the game of hockey for Philadelphia's blue-collar residents, but planted

**Despite only one year of NHL hockey under its belt before 1967, Philadelphia had developed a keen interest in hockey, evident by the numerous pickup games cropping up in the street throughout the 1930s (Special Collections Research Center, Temple University Libraries, Philadelphia, PA).**

## Introduction: Philadelphia Professional Hockey    9

the seed that would eventually blossom into Philadelphia's falling in love with the sport.

When the ships in Governor William Penn's "Welcome" fleet dropped anchor in the Delaware River on October 28, 1682, not far from the current Philadelphia Sports Complex, none of the settlers who had just made the hard eight weeks' passage from Deal, England, to help populate Penn's new "Greene Countrie Towne" had any idea what the Philadelphia they had come to build would be like three centuries later. What eventually grew from the labors they began, among other things, was a hard-working city populated by millions of proud blue-collar sports fans. Over the past hundred years they have been entertained by the exploits of professional hockey teams which have—regardless of on-ice success—provided them with thousands of nights of exactly the kind of intense, hard-nosed sports action that the city loves the most.

The almost 100-year history of professional hockey in Philadelphia has often been one of stark contrasts. To be sure, over the past half century Philadelphia has been home to many truly great hockey exploits—the NHL Flyers' frequent regular season division and conference titles, eight trips to the final, and two Stanley Cups; their incredible defeat of the Soviet Central Red Army team in 1976; the unprecedented 35-game unbeaten streak in 1979–80; the Hall of Fame playing careers of Bob Clarke, Bernie Parent, Bill Barber, Mark Howe, Eric Lindros, and others; and of course, the consistent success of the Phantoms between 1996 and their exit in 2009, especially their AHL-record 17-game winning streak in 2004–2005 and their two Calder Cup-winning seasons.

With a few exceptions, however, the history of the game's earlier years in Philadelphia was a much more colorful—and perhaps more interesting—story. That history is both distinguished and filled with proud moments, from the original Ramblers' 1936 Fontaine Cup championship to the Firebirds winning the NAHL crown in 1976, from the Flyers' defeat of the Soviets to the Eastern League's Ramblers battling the Soviet team nearly twenty years earlier and getting public praise from legendary coach Anatoli Tarasov amidst a hard-fought tie.

Philadelphia has seen six professional hockey championships from their ten teams. About 1,400 players have tugged on a Philadelphia hockey jersey as of the start of the 2019–20 season, including 18 who ultimately ended up in the Hockey Hall of Fame: Parent, Barber, Clarke, Lindros, Mark Howe, Adam Oates, Chris Pronger, Mark Recchi, Allan Stanley, Darryl Sittler, Dale Hawerchuk, Paul Coffey, and Peter Forsberg of the Flyers. Jaromir Jagr will be added to the list when he becomes eligible. Others who played parts of their Hall of Fame career in Philadelphia included Babe Pratt of the CAHL's Ramblers, Bryan Hextall of the

I-AHL's Ramblers, Marty Barry of the CAHL's Arrows, Art Coulter of the Arrows, and Syd Howe of the NHL's Quakers. The Flyers also have seven additional members in the Hockey Hall of Fame: Ed Snider, Bud Poile, Keith Allen, Roger Neilson, Fred Shero, and Pat Quinn in the builder category and Gene Hart as a member of the media. Herb Gardiner, a Hall of Famer from his playing days with the Montreal Canadiens, coached for many years in Philadelphia.

The city has seen five hockey arenas house the teams discussed in this book: the West Park Ice Palace, the Philadelphia Arena, the Philadelphia Convention Hall and Civic Center, the Spectrum, and the Wells Fargo Center.

While the Flyers rightfully headline the marquee of professional hockey in Philadelphia, the city's hockey history outside the Flyers organization is extensive and just as important to understand. The beginnings of the sport throughout the city helped set the stage for the eventual success of the NHL club. Through team histories, anecdotes, and player profiles, this book will take you through the ups, downs, and characters that have paraded across Philadelphia ice. From the sport's 19th century beginnings in the city in the form of the Quaker City Hockey Club, all the way to the Phantoms and their relocation to Allentown, Pennsylvania, hockey holds a special place in the heart of Philadelphia sports fans. This book chronicles the city's lengthy, illustrious history with the game.

# 1

# Quaker City Hockey Club
*American Amateur Hockey League, 1900–01*

A simple Internet search for the father of Philadelphia hockey brings up endless articles about Ed Snider, the long-time chairman of the NHL's Flyers. And to nearly every Philadelphian, or even hockey fan, that would seem to be accurate. But, as shocking as it may be to most familiar with the sport, Ed Snider was nearly seventy years late to the party and the second Philadelphia resident to earn that distinction.

In 1893, a Strathroy, Ontario native named George Washington Orton was offered a scholarship to the University of Pennsylvania and made his way down to Philadelphia. A student of philosophy and Romance languages (by graduation he was fluent in nine languages), Orton was maimed as a child when he fell out of a tree at age three. With severe damage to his right arm and a blood clot in his brain, he was declared paralyzed and told he would never walk again. Yet, at age ten, he defied the medical odds and took steps for the first time in seven years. Just two years after that, he regained his mobility, despite his right arm being permanently "dead."

By the time he arrived at the University of Pennsylvania, he was already a world-class runner, winning national titles in both Canada and the United States. He set a record by running the mile in 4:21.8, a mark that lasted nearly half a century. His entry to the Ivy League circuit furthered his love for sports, his desire to get more students participating in them, and his dream to get more of the public interested in consuming them. But, despite his love for track and field, his first love, as would be expected of a Canadian, was hockey.

In 1896, he introduced ice hockey to his colleagues in Philadelphia and helped launch Penn's first ice hockey team. Participating as a club sport in the Intercollegiate Hockey League (alongside Yale, Brown, and Columbia), Orton was the coach, captain, and top player on a team comprised mostly of sophomores and other residents from the area. Though

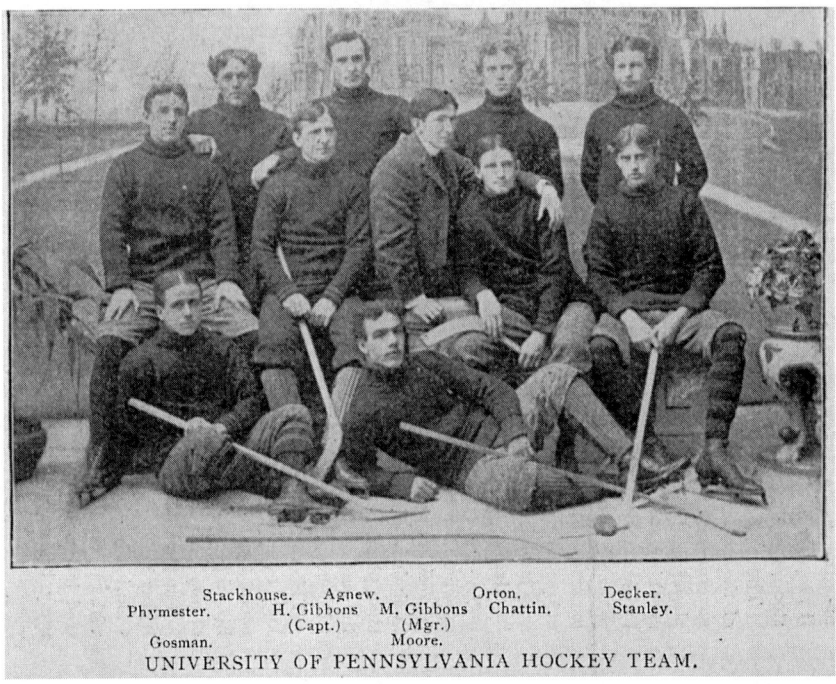

Stackhouse. Agnew. Orton. Decker.
Phymester. H. Gibbons M. Gibbons Chattin. Stanley.
(Capt.) (Mgr.)
Gosman. Moore.
UNIVERSITY OF PENNSYLVANIA HOCKEY TEAM.

The University of Pennsylvania ice hockey team that Orton helped create. His legacy lies within the college's athletic department. L to R: Top row, Arthur Stackhouse, William Agnew, George Orton, Clinton Decker. Middle row, William Phymister, Horace Gibbons, Miles Gibbons, John Chattin, Stanley Willett. Bottom row, John Gosman, Arthur Moore.

the team only played a few games, the city was smitten with Orton, his work ethic, and his passion for the game. "The Quakers won," wrote *The Amateur Athletic* in February 1897, "Due principally to the brilliant individual playing of the four Canadians in the persons of [teammates] Agnew, Phymister, Willett, and Orton. What Orton lacked in the use of an arm, which is crippled and entirely useless, he made up in the agility of his legs and other arm."[1]

Orton quickly became a jack of all trades to the club. "As the manager, travelling secretary, and captain for the University of Pennsylvania Quakers hockey team," wrote Mark Hebscher in his book, *The Greatest Athlete (You've Never Heard Of)*, "Orton had made arrangements for his squad to play games in the new arenas in Baltimore, Washington, and New York during that first season. The Quakers had held daily practices on Philadelphia's Centennial Lake in January and February and were ready to take on all comers."[2]

But, despite its growing popularity, hockey's notoriety seemed to

## 1. Quaker City Hockey Club

hit a ceiling. Orton noticed that the city, one of the largest in the country at the time, was missing a modern, indoor ice arena. Hockey had taken off quickly in Philadelphia, but without a proper facility, it was only able to be played on outdoor rinks a few months out of the year—and that was contingent on the weather cooperating. There was no indoor ice rink that could house the team. After seeking out a suitor, he created a partnership with the West Park Ice Palace and Amusement Company, who presented plans to erect a rink at Jefferson and 52nd streets, just next to the Pennsylvania Railroad station.

The building would house a 225-foot by 55-foot ice surface, along with promenades and a large music area for an orchestra to play. The building also had a cloak room, four reception rooms, a café serving light refreshments, and an amusement hall with kinetoscopes and phonographs. For hockey players, the Ice Palace would have locker rooms and showers behind the rink. It could accommodate up to 1,500 skaters at any given time. The West Park Ice Palace opened on December 14, 1897.[3] The Philadelphia City Archives have no record of the West Park Ice Palace, nor do the Atlases of 1899, 1900, or 1901 show an ice rink at that location. The records do, however, show an ice manufacturing plant that existed from the 1890s to as late as 1910, owned by various ice manufacturing companies including Hestonville Ice Manufacturing Company, York Manufacturing Co., and Franklinville Ice Manufacturing Co. It is believed that the rink was located at the front of the plant.

Mayor Warwick was present for the opening night festivities, along with the Germania band and over two thousand Philadelphians to celebrate the city's first indoor ice arena. Orton split his team into two and the squad played an exhibition game against

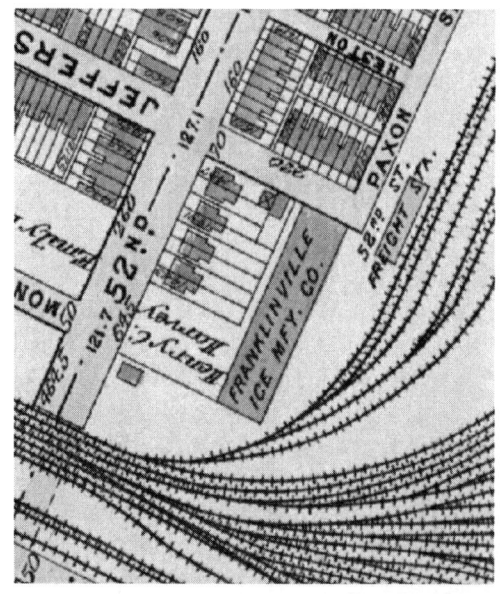

The 1910 Philadelphia City Atlas shows a "Franklinville Ice Manufacturing" plant off 52nd and Jefferson. It is believed that the West Park Ice Palace sat at the front of the plant, on Jefferson.

themselves, with Orton's team defeating the other half of the club by a 1–0 score. After the game, the gates were opened to the public, allowing them to experience the glassy, freshly cleaned ice surface for the first time with a popular two-step playing over the loudspeakers. The building was "beautifully decorated," said the *Philadelphia Inquirer*, and was filled with "attendants in handsome costumes."[4]

At the same time, Orton founded the Quaker City Hockey Club and the Hockey League of Philadelphia. (After exhausting his college eligibility at Penn, Orton wanted to continue playing hockey and running a team.) The league consisted of four teams: Haverford College, Philadelphia Dental School, Wayne, and Quaker City. Orton served as the league's president, while also captaining the Quaker City team. "There was never a mention of conflict of interest," wrote Mark Hebscher. "Everybody knew that Orton was 'Mr. Hockey' in Philly, and without his efforts, the game never would have taken off." The team, with its imported talent from Canada, was exponentially better than any of its competition.[5]

On December 3, 1898, the *Times* of Philadelphia hyped the upcoming schedule. The *Philadelphia Inquirer* called Quaker City "one of the best-known organizations in the country." The team was so talented that, after dominating its league schedule the previous year, the other teams agreed to allow Quaker City to wait for the league winner to emerge, whereupon Quaker City would simply play them for the championship. "Last year," the *Times* wrote, "the Quaker City team defeated every representative hockey team in America, the New York Athletic Club's aggregation excepted.... The Quakers were thus the virtual champions of America."[6] (During this time period, the National Hockey League and its predecessor, the National Hockey Association, were not yet in existence. The Stanley Cup, donated by Lord Stanley of Preston, the Governor General of Canada, in 1892, did not belong to a specific league. Rather, it was a challenge trophy. The team that held it would accept challenges from other senior teams, with the winner laying claim to the Stanley Cup until they lost a future challenge. Amateur teams were not allowed to challenge for the Stanley Cup at the time, leaving only our imaginations to determine whether the Quakers could have possibly obtained Lord Stanley's Holy Grail.)

"The chances of the Quakers are very bright," the *Times* continued, "As they retain their victorious team of last year practically intact." A few weeks later the *Philadelphia Inquirer* ran a pre-season feature on the squad, adding to the heavy expectations that were already laid on the team's shoulders. "The Ice Palace will be the scene of two of the most exciting and interesting hockey matches ever played in Philadelphia," it

## 1. Quaker City Hockey Club

wrote. Yale would play both Penn and Quaker City. "All three teams play fast hockey, and everyone is going in determined to win."[7]

The team's roster was made up of seven players: Moore in goal; Russell at point; Stanley T. Willett, "one of the best-known hockey players in the world," at cover point. "As a hockey player," wrote the *Inquirer*, "Willett has outshone any player ever since upon the ice in Philadelphia. Whether on defense or in attack, he is equally valuable. As a cricketer he has been chosen to represent Canada, while in lacrosse and lawn tennis he is also well known." Dr. Phymister, who played for the Victoria Hockey Club, played rover (a position at the time which utilized all areas of the ice); Neff played left forward; Orton played center forward; and Rogers at right forward. Orton, according to the paper, "is better known as an amateur runner than as a skater or hockey player.... Orton is not such a star hockey player, but he gets in a great deal of extra work and is inexhaustible."[8]

An artists' rendering of the Quaker City Hockey Club printed in the *Times* of Philadelphia in 1899.

As the season progressed, hockey's popularity continued to rise in Philadelphia. What was an unknown attraction as recently as a few years before suddenly became a love of the residents of the nation's former capital. "The game of hockey is interesting," wrote the *Times* on February 12, 1899, "Inasmuch as the spectators are much nearer the players, so that every fine play can be seen by all the spectators, even should they be made at the extreme ends of the rink. There are many opportunities for team work, in which all of these teams have become proficient, and there are also some very fine individual plays, which will bear comparison with some of the most scientific plays in billiards. In fact, it is impossible to give an adequate description of them in print, but they must be seen to be appreciated."[9]

Quaker City was one of the top teams, as expected. On February 19, they beat Johns Hopkins, 5–0, at the Ice Palace, which, according to the newspapers, was possibly six goals lower than what should have been, if not for the acrobatics of Johns Hopkins goaltender Scholl. One week later, the team defeated the Hockey Club of New York in Philadelphia by a 2–1 score in front of a crowd so large that it pushed the rink's accommodations to its limits. A week after that, Montclair became the next victim, losing, 6–1, at the Ice Palace. "The play was fast, but the home team won handily," read the newspaper's game recap.[10]

In March, Orton's squad travelled to New York to play the Brooklyn Skating Club, one of the strongest teams in the country. At that point, Brooklyn, who went undefeated in their league season, was on a thirteen-game winning streak and invited Quaker City, the champions of the Philadelphia league, to the Clermont Avenue Rink for an exhibition match. "It has been recognized that the strong Philadelphia seven was entitled to question Brooklyn's title to the championship of the United States," wrote the *Brooklyn Daily Eagle*. In a game that was described as the fastest and hardest-hitting hockey game that was played in the country all season, the two teams battled for their claim of the best hockey team in the United States.

Orton's team was described as "hard and swift when it came to shooting," and kept up with Brooklyn for the entirety of the match. The game included some breath-taking moments, including a scrum in the front of the net where Moore dropped his goal stick and Brooklyn forward Dobby kicked it away so that it could not be retrieved. Moore then dropped to his knees to stop a shot, which was against the rules at the time. An argument ensued between the two teams before it was broken up and play resumed. Just minutes later, a shot was deflected toward the ceiling, hitting a hanging chandelier and raining glass down onto the ice surface, narrowly missing the players. The Quakers quickly scored two goals, making the game 3–2 in Brooklyn's favor in the midst of the second half. But, with the Quakers pushing to tie the game, Brooklyn's offense took over, scoring three successive goals and defeating the Philadelphia team, 6–2.[11]

Although no detailed statistics were kept for the season, Orton scored regularly, according to the newspapers, and was the star attraction of the team. It is believed the team lost just three games all season, including two losses to the Brooklyn Athletic club.

Outside of the hockey team, he was becoming a star on campus and in the city as well. Philadelphians were invading the Ice Palace for public skates, skating exhibitions, and, of course, hockey games, and they wanted to see Orton. In January 1899, Orton told the media that he was holding a special event to draw attention to the new arena. "This evening," wrote the *Philadelphia Inquirer* on January 19, 1899, "An exhibition of fast skating will be given by George Orton, at the Ice Palace. Orton will endeavor to beat the time made by Le Roy See last Saturday evening [3:51.4]. As See is one of the fastest skaters in New York, Orton will have to skate fast to excel the former's time." That night, Orton didn't disappoint. On a tight-cornered ice surface, in front of about 800 spectators, Orton skated a mile seconds quicker than Le Roy See, to the cheers of the crowd.[12]

In 1900, after realizing his team needed a more competitive schedule, he applied to the New York–based American Amateur Hockey League, one of the toughest leagues in the country at the time. (Some famous players who were part of the AAHL during its tenure include Hobey Baker, the famous collegiate athlete and member of the Hockey Hall of Fame; Sprague Cleghorn, another Hall of Famer; and Odie Cleghorn, who played 179 games in the NHL, along with one season in the predecessor National Hockey Association.)

Founded in 1896, a bulk of the players already came from the Ivy League collegiate circuit. On November 16, 1900, the *New York Tribune* announced that the Montclair Hockey Club tendered its resignation from the league and would be replaced by the Quaker City Hockey Club. Orton would serve on the league's scheduling committee. The league, for the 1900–01 season, consisted of Quaker City, the Brooklyn Crescents, the New York Athletic Club, the St. Nicholas Hockey Club, the Brooklyn Skating Club, and the New York Hockey Club.

"The fact that [Quaker City] will journey to New York to play," wrote the *New York Times* on December 2, "And that the local sevens will go to the Quaker City for some of their games, serves to ensure a broader interest and a greater popularity for this Winter's sports." The team's roster for the new season consisted of Rhodes (in goal), G.S.

**A photograph of the Quaker City Hockey Club, as published in the *Brooklyn Daily Eagle* in January 1901.**

Robertson, Dr. J.H. Gorman, William Jackson "Bill" Clothier, Orton, A. Varney, Menzies, Rogers, Hueston, and J. Devine. (Interestingly enough, Clothier would go on to win tennis' U.S. Open in 1906.) The team played in maroon colors, according to one newspaper report.[13]

Against the highest competition in the amateur circuit, Quaker City failed to dominate their games for the first time in years, but didn't disappoint. On January 11, 1901, the Quakers lost to the New York Hockey Club by an 8–2 score, their second defeat of the young season. However, it wasn't for a lack of talent or effort. "A large crowd was present at the match," wrote the *Inquirer*, "And they saw the fastest hockey that has ever been played in Philadelphia." The score showed a wider spread than the pace of the game suggested. The team, having the speed to keep up with their New York brethren, continued to push aggressively up the ice. When New York countered with strong defense, it left the Quakers wide open to counter-rushes, giving New York an abundance of openings with which to score. "Both sides played grand hockey," the *Inquirer* continued. "It seemed as if the Quakers would even up matters by their fast play." Nonetheless, they could not draw even, eventually giving up numerous goals at the end of the game.[14]

On March 9, the Quakers topped the effort with their first win of the season, defeating the New York Athletic Club, 3–2. "It was the fiercest and most exciting match played in Philadelphia this winter," wrote the *Brooklyn Daily Eagle*. "An extra period of eight minutes was necessary to decide the contest." The recap described a Quakers team that played with determination not seen up to that point in the season. The crowd totaled 2,000, and the game was described as "clean." New York led after the first half, but the second half was controlled by the Quakers. With just a few minutes left, Quakers right winger Devine tied the game. "From this time to the end of the half the playing was terrific on both sides," the *Eagle* wrote. "Both teams played desperately for victory." In the extra frame, the Quakers were pinned down in their own end, before Clothier picked the puck out of a scrum and pushed toward the New York goal. With opposing players closing in on him quickly, he fired a shot over the opposing goalie's shoulder, securing the victory for Quaker City.[15]

Through an eleven-game season, Quaker City finished with two wins, eight losses, and one tie. Orton, despite still playing with one arm, scored eight goals.

The Ice Palace was the center of the Philadelphia hockey world. The city's brass was thrown for a panic when, on January 26, 1898, smoke filled the arena and the patrons were quickly evacuated onto 52nd street. The fire department was called, but the employees were able to extinguish the blaze before it caused any serious damage. The fire, originating in the engine room, confused both the arena's management and the fire department, because it caught fire in a room that had no flammable material present. Nonetheless, the arena continued operating successfully through Orton's playing days.

But a few years later, disaster struck. On March 24, 1901, just one day after the last day of the winter sports season, another fire mysteriously started. By the time the fire department arrived, the building was already engulfed in flames. After the blaze was finally extinguished, all that remained of the structure was a single scorched wall, which would have to be taken down for safety. The Ice Palace, which was only insured for $75,000, took an estimated $130,000 of damage, including $80,000 of machinery and contents. After brief discussion by the York Ice Manufacturing Company, who managed the property, it was determined that the West Park Ice Palace would not be rebuilt. Just a few years after its opening, Philadelphia was again without an indoor hockey arena.[16] There was no investigation into the mysterious fire, which suspiciously

An artists' rendering of the mysterious fire that destroyed the West Park Ice Palace in March 1901.

happened at the end of the season in which it was reported the arena was not profitable. Feel free to develop your own theory or conclusion.

After the demolition of the charred West Park Ice Palace, George Orton and his crew continued to seek out places where they could install a hockey rink to continue their pastime. In the early 1910s, they constructed a small rink on the property adjacent to the former Ice Palace. It wasn't a building, by any means, but instead had a tent covering the ice to protect it from the elements. The plan worked nicely for a while, but when the first major snow storm of the season hit Philadelphia, the weight of the snow collapsed the tent, destroying the ice and rendering their short-term plan useless. Just afterward, Orton put together a company that planned to eventually erect a large building for ice skating, but the plan broke down when World War I started. The hockey magnate would need to wait just a few years more before the building of Philadelphia's dreams could be constructed. Just a couple years after the war ended, the Philadelphia Arena was built. Orton's influence and previous attempts surely set the stage and created the demand that would eventually convince the city to build a new, state-of-the-art building.

His legacy was one that has somehow flown under the radar in the annals of Philadelphia sports. Although there is still much mystery, with records from the era being quite spotty, it can safely be assumed that Orton had as much pull over the powers-to-be of the city as anyone in their generation. To get city support for the West Park Ice Palace, simply promising that there was enough local and business support for hockey would not be enough. As would be proven in the subsequent decades, one had to be in the upper echelon of the Philadelphia sport and political scene. Orton was an Olympic medalist, head of the Penn relays, and at one point the athletic director of the school. He was well-known enough throughout the city to warrant a seat at the table, ultimately resulting in the first indoor hockey arena in Philadelphia history.

Orton remained in Philadelphia for a long time after the loss of the Ice Palace. He remained deeply involved with the Penn hockey team, coaching them and leading them to national fame at the collegiate level. Eventually, he was inducted into Canada's Sports Hall of Fame and, after winning a gold medal in the 2500-meter steeplechase at the 1900 Olympics, was also inducted into the Canadian Olympic Hall of Fame. He later added University of Pennsylvania Hall of Fame and the Philadelphia Sports Hall of Fame to his lengthy credentials. Later in life, he moved to Meredith, New Hampshire, where he rested comfortably until his death at age 85. His tenure in Philadelphia hockey was short, but his pioneering and passion was the spark that ignited Philadelphia's now century-old love of ice hockey.

# 2

# The Arrows

*Canadian-American Hockey League (CAHL), 1927–35*

"Philadelphia is to be represented in professional ice hockey ranks," wrote Stan Baumgartner of the *Philadelphia Inquirer*, announcing the first ever professional team in city history. It was the Fall of 1927 when the nascent Philadelphia Arrows became the sixth member of the Canadian-American Hockey League. CAHL president C.C. Clapp granted Philadelphia entry into the league, authorizing the move of the New Haven club to the City of Brotherly Love, while a new team would begin play in New Haven to increase the league membership. Born in 1926, the CAHL was based in Springfield, Massachusetts, with five teams playing in its inaugural season: the Boston Tigers, the New Haven Eagles, the Providence Reds, the Quebec Castors, and the Springfield Indians. With the addition of the Philadelphia Ice Hockey club, the league was ready for its second season.[1]

Expectations were immediately sky-high for the new squad, which had yet to be named. The previous year, the New Haven team finished in first place, and with many of those players relocating to Philadelphia, there was an assumption that the organization would contend for the league crown in its inaugural season. To meet these expectations, Philadelphia named Norman Shay their manager and head coach. Raised in Parry Sound, Ontario (the town later made famous as Bobby Orr's hometown), the 28-year-old played parts of two seasons in the NHL with the Bruins and the Toronto St. Patricks, before jumping to the new CAHL in 1926 to play for the New Haven Eagles. He was revered for his hockey IQ and, according to the *Inquirer*, "knows the game thoroughly."[2]

The team announced that their games would be played at the Philadelphia Arena. Because the Arena was not yet ready for hockey season, the new club traveled to New Haven for training, giving Shay time to whip the boys into shape and continue building his roster. The media followed him to New Haven to tout the team, whereupon Shay said that "the squad is in great condition and he is very much satisfied with the material on hand. He feels confident he has the proper players to win the championship."[3] Meanwhile, the Arena management held a contest for fans to name the new squad. Offering a cash prize of $100 for the chosen name, thousands of fans sent suggestions to the Arena in hopes of securing themselves a hefty pay day. They announced the team would be outfitted in orange and blue and that the team would be called the Arrows.

The Philadelphia Arrows, CAHL, 1927–35.

At the end of October, Shay announced that he would not be a player-coach. Rather, he would focus his efforts solely on managing and coaching the squad. Still recovering from a fractured ankle suffered the previous season, he was heavily scouting the region, looking for any help he could get. The team hired Percy Fynan, a former New Haven player, as a full-time scout—something that was unheard of at the time. Fynan, known as "Spider" to his colleagues, was tasked with signing any amateur player he found that could help improve the Arrows roster. One of the first finds he made was Dave Campbell, a star defenseman in the Canadian amateur circuit, who he convinced to sign with the Arrows. Upon his signature, he was named team captain.

With the roster quickly taking shape, hockey fans in the city were buzzing. Even those not familiar with the sport were exhilarated by the possibility and intrigued by the new game. The *Inquirer* gave the fans a wonderful introduction to the game, one that had never before been played at the professional level in Philadelphia. "There is more action, more gripping play, in five minutes of hockey," said professional baseball player "Paddy" Smith to the newspaper, "Than in a half hour of baseball or football. You can never tell when a player will come up with a broken nose or a barked shin just because a fellow player decides to do a little 'necking' with his hockey stick. And fast; your eyes can hardly follow the puck as it shoots about the ice." He continued to describe the rule changes for the upcoming season, which included a reduction of the size of goaltenders' equipment, expected to amount to higher-scoring games.[4]

The fans were slowly being introduced to such characters as Earl Robinson, a center for the Arrows. Robinson grew up in Canada, the son of a millionaire mining expert. Robinson Sr., wanted his son to become a lawyer or a businessman with the education he financed. But Robinson was in love with hockey and wanted to make a go of the sport as a career. "You'll have to quit that hockey business," his father told him, "Or I will disinherit you."

"You can keep your money and I will earn my own living," Robinson responded. With that, he packed his bags and left, being forced to make his budding hockey career pay the bills. But, some time later, his father was persuaded to attend a game in which his son was playing. Needing a victory to clinch first place for his team, Robinson went out and tied the game with forty seconds remaining and then scored the game-winning goal on the very next play. According to the *Inquirer*, Robinson was "hoisted to the shoulders of the fans" who had stormed the ice in celebration. His father was so ecstatic that he ran to the locker room, embraced his son, apologized and told him to come home. From then on, the story went, Robinson Sr. demanded that his son do nothing but play hockey during the season.[5] Eventually, the speedy forward would go on to play 417 NHL games with the Maroons, Canadiens and Black Hawks, scoring 83 goals in the process.

Amidst the start of the season, the media continued profiling members of the Arrows organization, as the city began to fall in love with their new team. Fynan was touted as the man who signed some of the team's best players. A recent star on the ice, Fynan was victim of a vicious stick attack in what turned out to be one of his last games. In a battle between the New York Rangers and the Boston Athletic Association, he went in toward the opposing goalie with just one defender in the way, a former Harvard football star. The defender raised his stick and sliced Fynan across the mouth just as the puck was released. Fynan watched the game-winning puck go into the net, but soon after he was bleeding profusely on the ice, eventually needing two front teeth replaced.

Fynan told this story not just to explain why he no longer played, but to showcase the toughness of hockey players, how demanding the game could be, and the pull the sport had on anyone that attended a game. "Hockey takes a great hold in other sports," Fynan said, his eyes lighting up. "When I first started playing the hockey game I lived in the same hotel with [Tris] Speaker and [Les] Nunamaker of the Red Sox. One night I took the backstop to a game. Did he enjoy it. The next day he came up to me and said, 'I would like to try that game.' We fitted him up with shin guards and skates and say in two days we couldn't keep him off the ice."[6]

The scout was also a phenomenal ambassador for the Arrows organization. Just before the home opener at the end of November, he took Baumgartner to ice level to point out the various players on the roster as they walked by, discussing their upbringing, their talent, and their playing experience.

The first player to walk by, Dave Campbell, enjoyed a brief NHL career with the Montreal Canadiens, including a highlight against the Boston Bruins where he and Boston defenseman Billy Coutu tangled while fighting for the puck. Campbell came out of the encounter with a blood-covered face and some missing teeth that had scattered on the ice surface. According to Fynan, he "washed his face and was back in that game ready to go." The two continued to fight throughout the rest of the game, running into each other multiple times and pushing at each other with such ferocity that, at one point, Coutu ended up on his back inside the goal, while Campbell calmly skated off the ice. The two would face each other tonight, for the first time since—Fynan hoped for fireworks.

Fynan also spoke about defenseman Gerold Carson, whose two older brothers played for the Toronto Maple Leafs at the time. Young Gerold was starting his professional hockey career and hoped to follow in their footsteps (he would go on to play 261 NHL games, though none with Toronto).

"Oh, boy, here comes 'Frock' Lowr[e]y, right wing," Fynan said. "Wouldn't he make a great model for a collar advertisement? And the girls think so too. He's the sheik and I don't mean maybe. The boys dubbed him Frock because he wears his clothes to the King's taste. Archie Briden, the left wing comes from Calgary, where they climb an iceberg every morning for an appetizer. He is one of those cold, deep boys who speak only when spoken to but when they speak they say something."[7]

Fynan was both illustrative and enthusiastic about the team he helped put together. The newspapers were equally as excited to introduce the players to the city. Fans were getting on the bandwagon, both curious and exuberant about their new sports team.

The Arrows began their on-ice existence with a promising 5–2 win over Providence, controlling the game from start to finish on the Reds' ice. Right-winger Fred Lowrey scored four of the five goals, including one shorthanded, while goaltender Joe Stark backstopped the team to victory. "The goalie was firm as the rock of Gibraltar," wrote the *Inquirer*,

"And saved the game for his team." Two weeks later, the Arrows played their first game in Philadelphia.[8]

The starting lineup for the home opener against the Boston Tigers was as follows: Joe Stark in net, Campbell and "Stub" Carson on defense, and Robinson centering Lowrey and Briden. Before 6,000 "wildly excited" fans, the Arrows fought hard but fell to the Boston club by a 2–1 score, described as such fast action that "to the untrained eye … it often left but a blur of moving figures." Robinson scored the Arrows' only goal, but the city was stricken. The Arrows had outplayed the league's first-place team for two of the three periods. "In individual brilliance they outshone the Tigers," Baumgartner wrote. And after the game, a few thousand fans were invited to skate on the new Arena ice in celebration of the improved facilities. The fans were enthralled with the players, the sport, and the atmosphere of the games. They were optimistic and hopeful about the team's fortunes for the rest of the season.[9]

Unfortunately, the good news would just about end there for the on-ice product. The city's first professional hockey club finished dead last in its inaugural season with a 13–25–2 record. The team never managed to execute properly on the ice, and mixed with a lengthy injury to Stark, limped their way to the finish line. Nonetheless, there was cause for optimism for the organization. Robinson, just one of many promising players for the Arrows, finished third in the league in goals, with 18, and second in points, with 25, in 34 games. (Unfortunately for the club, Robinson would sign with the NHL's Montreal Maroons that summer, embarking on an NHL career that the Arrows could be proud to have launched.)

Most importantly, the fans had responded positively to the team's efforts, filling the stadium for most home games, despite their terrible record. That was most likely due to the team's continued passion and fight that they showcased, no matter the score. In mid–December, the Arrows took a 4–0 win from Providence, but not before a bench-clearing brawl ensued, leaving two Reds with torn scalps, one with a smashed nose, Lowrey with a torn lip and Briden with torn ligaments in his leg. "The twelve men on the ice forgot they were playing hockey, dropped back to medieval days when jousts between bands of armored knights were a common pastime," wrote Baumgartner. The brawl required policemen to break it up, which proved hilarious when they struggled to walk on the slippery ice. As the fighting escalated, the fans became overly-exuberant, climbing over the rails and joining in the festivities.[10]

One fan, "dressed in his Sunday best," according to the *Inquirer*, grabbed a stick from one of the Providence players sitting on the bench, and ran over to where Lowrey was sitting with the rest of his Arrows teammates. The fan raised the stick over his head, taking aim at the Arrows star, when a teammate caught a glimpse of what was about to happen. With the flick of his wrist, he swiped at the fan, landing his stick directly upon the fan's hat, driving it over his eyes and ears. After the hat had to be ripped off his head in order for him to see, he stormed the Arrows dressing room demanding a new hat at their expense—that is, until one of the players told him that "the only thing we will buy you is a coffin unless you make it snappy getting out of here." The angry young fan obliged.[11]

Eighty dollars' worth of fines were handed down by the league to four Arrows players, but the fans were thrilled with the spectacle. In addition, they were enthralled by Stark's top-notch goaltending and the offensive ability shown by Lowrey in scoring what the newspaper described as "one of the greatest individual goals seen in ice hockey this season."[12]

"Skirmishes of the sort seen Saturday night are not unusual in ice hockey," said Irwin Wener, president of the Arrows and the Arena, letting the fans know he was accepting of the display. "In fact, I was surprised that the two previous games here were as quiet as the Boston and Springfield tiffs."

"That has happened two or three times this season," said Providence president Dubuc, "And as yet none of the boys have been seriously hurt. It just gives them a chance to let off excess energy."

"This is a great hockey town," said Arrows right-winger Stan "Shorty" Veno. "Did you see them climb over the railing when the 'fuss' began? It reminds me of Quebec. You know in the small Canadian rinks each row of seats is divided by a high iron railing from the rows behind and in front. The idea of these railings is to make it harder for the fans to reach each other when they start to fight." The incident would create the first chapter in what would become a lengthy hockey rivalry between Providence and Philadelphia.[13]

Just a few weeks later, Shay made a huge fuss when the Arrows lost to Quebec 4–3, in a game he felt was decided "due to the lax methods of the officials in enforcing the rules of hockey." The coach sent a letter to Clapp in which he listed the four reasons why he felt the Arrows were robbed of a victory. Though the result wasn't changed, the fans applauded Shay's passion and desire to ensure that his team was treated fairly by the league.[14]

On top of the passion, the fans loved the familial feel of the Arrows locker room. The players became more like brothers than teammates, with the crew sticking together on the road and becoming friendly off the ice at home. The "brotherly love" transferred to the fans, who took the team under their wing as their own, returning the favor with a filled Arena most nights.

But perhaps most importantly, the fans were captivated by the passion of team management and their willingness to do whatever it takes to win. Throughout the inaugural season, Wener and Fynan continued to add strength to the Arrows lineup. As the calendar turned to 1928, Wener announced that the team had secured the services of NHLer Leland "Hago" Harrington, property of the Boston Bruins, for a hefty $7,500 fee. "He's just the man we need to carry us to the top of the heap," Wener said. "Philadelphia must have a club which will rank with the best."[15] (Unfortunately, Harrington quickly became involved in a dispute with Boston management, where they claimed he was not eligible to sign with another club. After getting the president of the league involved, it was determined that Boston owned his rights, which prevented Harrington from signing with the club of his choice. The player was then sold to the Providence Reds, where he played for most of the rest of his career.)

Shay mirrored the fans' admiration of their fearless leader. "I know that when his team is concerned money is a secondary matter to Wener," he told the *Inquirer*, "He loves to win; wants to give his fans the best in the game.... Whenever I need a man to bolster up my club I just mentioned the player's name to the president and he gets him. You can't beat a man like that to work for."[16]

Wener would regularly put his money where his mouth was. In the middle of January, amidst a struggling streak, he waltzed into the locker room and threw fifteen one-hundred-dollar bills onto the table. He made the players a deal: if they won six of their next eight games, they could have the money. "You can do it," he told them, looking around the room at each player. "You have one of the best hockey teams in the league and it is only the fact that you have been a bit disorganized which is keeping you down."[17]

At the start of their second season, Wener added left wing Lloyd Andrews, affectionately referred to as "Shrimp" due to his five-foot-four frame. A former NHLer, Andrews was a member of the New Haven Eagles in their first CAHL season. And though he technically signed with the Arrows just before the start of the 1927–28 season, the league required Shay to leave four players with the incoming New Haven team, including Andrews. Before the Arrows' second season commenced, Andrews was allowed to join the squad. Known at the time as one of the best forwards in hockey, the Canadian had previously played four seasons with the NHL's St. Pats, winning the NHL championship in 1922.

His legend was crafted that season when, as a 24-year-old, he became the hero of the championship game. With a deadlocked match progressing late into the third period, Andrews found himself with open space in front of him. As he sped toward the opposing goal, his teammate fired a pass that bounced off his stick and dribbled toward the net. With a defender hot on his tail, both players raised their sticks, swung at each other, and collapsed onto the ice with a thud. As blood gushed from above Andrews' eye, he peered in front of him to see the puck slide into the corner of the goal, clinching the championship for the St. Pats.

His inaugural season in Philadelphia saw him post just 13 points, but the fans cherished the popular player and his potential was noticed. Over the course of the next two seasons, he would become one of the league's top players, scoring 39 goals in 80 games across the 1928–29 and 1929–30 seasons.

But the Arrows' struggles continued. In the 1928–29 campaign they finished with even fewer wins than their inaugural season, winning just 12 and finishing again in last place. The season was overshadowed by off-ice drama in early 1929. At the end of January, Wener made it known that he was making a bold attempt to bring NHL hockey to Philadelphia, imploring league president Frank Calder to grant him the rights to the struggling Ottawa franchise. (This attempt, mixed with others from the region, foreshadowed the eventual arrival of the Philadelphia Quakers NHL team, which you can read more about in Chapter 3.) He swore to Philadelphia that his plan was to operate both the Arrows and the NHL squad simultaneously, and that "this does not mean that we will give up the Arrows' franchise."[18]

Just a few weeks later, with the team continuing to lose games by the barrel-full, Wener fired Shay as the team's head coach and named Fynan his replacement. "Disagreement with Shay over the management, conduct, and style of play of the Arrows was the cause of his release," Wener said. Fynan brought with him a no-BS attitude and the respect of the players. The hope was that he could dig them out of the ditch in which they seemed to be stuck.[19]

In the summer of 1929, the Arrows were sold to a local group headed by C.A. Griscom. The group was confident of the Arrows' future success. In their second season, the team saw over 55,000 fans walk through the Arena gates for hockey games—the highest attendance in the CAHL and double the team's inaugural season attendance. Before the start of the 1929–30 campaign, the team made a splash, purchasing Herb Gardiner from the Boston Bruins to replace Fynan as head coach.

Gardiner, at the time, was one of the most well-known members of the hockey world. The now-head coach grew up in Winnipeg, where

The Philadelphia Arrows of the 1929–30 season. Left to right: Standing, Wrigley, trainer; George Nichols; "Dee" Klein; Lloyd Andrews; Moose Cahill; Frank Peters; Arthur Coulter; Herb Gardiner. Seated, Clark Bradley; Vic LaPointe; "Morrie" Roberts, Art Taylor, Roy Lassard (courtesy Bruce "Scoop" Cooper).

he played hockey from a young age and was extraordinarily successful against his peers. Fervently believing he had no future career as a hockey player, he became a civil engineer and worked for the Canadian Pacific Railway in Calgary before enlisting in the Canadian Army and being sent overseas to fight in World War I. During his service, he was hit in the face and chest with shrapnel and suffered a damaged lung. Fortunately, his thick civil engineer book was in his breast pocket, blunting most of the blow and perhaps saving his life.

When he returned home, he was wooed back to hockey, despite not having skated for nearly nine years. He joined the Calgary Tigers of the West Coast Hockey League and immediately was one of their best players. A prolific defenseman, he won the 1924 WCHL championship with the Tigers with future NHLer and President Mervyn "Red" Dutton as his defense partner. In a Stanley Cup final against the Montreal Canadiens, the Tigers were blown out in two consecutive games. But it was Gardiner's play that impressed, including a thunderous body check on Canadiens star Howie Morenz that drew the attention of Canadiens GM Leo Dandurand. The manager offered him a contract to play for the Habs, but Gardiner declined, preferring to stick with his current situation in Calgary. When his league folded in 1926, however, he had no choice and accepted Dandurand's offer to play in the NHL as a 35-year-old rookie.[20]

His opening season in the NHL was legendary. Playing on a

Herb Gardiner as a member of the Calgary Tigers. His intuitive understanding of the game foreshadowed a lengthy coaching career (courtesy Gardiner-Rhodes Family).

Canadiens team that struggled to ice a full team, he played every minute of every game for the Montreal Canadiens in the 1926–27 campaign, earning himself the Hart Trophy as the league's most valuable player. "Gardiner's selection as the winner of the Hart Trophy comes as no surprise," wrote the *Montreal Gazette*. "This veteran from the prairie, who came up to the Canadiens this season from Calgary, has been credited with much of the success that the team attained. He not only has proved a star at left defense, but he has travelled practically 60 minutes in all games; has taken few penalties, but above all, has been the inspiration to the team from the first. He generals them on the ice and when they show signs of crumbling, he always cuts loose with speedy hockey which serves to rally his teammates. His generalship has been the big factor in Canadiens' triumphs and his example as a clean player has been a benefit to the club."[21] (Gardiner would eventually be inducted into the Hockey Hall of Fame in 1958.)

Although mostly known for his playing days, as a coach, Gardiner was highly-respected by everyone in the hockey world, from his players to opposing coaches and players and even the fans. In fact, before joining the Ramblers, he would often dress for a game or practice if one of his players were injured. Even in his past-his-prime age, he was always willing to do whatever it took to help bring his team to the next level, and his players responded in kind.

The Arrows continued to struggle in Gardiner's first year, but the organization was confident in the direction he was headed. The Arrows finished with a 20–18–2 record by the end of the 1930 season and competed in the playoffs for one round before being knocked out by the Boston Tigers in a two-game total goals series. In the 1930–31 season the team started off slowly, but found their groove after a few weeks. At the beginning of January they stood at 8-4-1 and Philadelphia was buzzing over the team's progress. "He has put his team on top of the league," wrote the *Philadelphia Inquirer*. "He has made this city ice-hockey minded. He has stirred enthusiasm to a fever pitch.... Ice hockey is a comparatively new sport to the American sport public, at least in this section, and the sobriquet 'Miracle Man' may seem a bit effusive if applied to Gardiner. However, he may well earn it this season."[22]

Herb Gardiner won the 1927 NHL Hart Trophy as the league's top player after playing every minute of every game for the Canadiens. He was also awarded a medal upon his induction into the Manitoba Hockey Hall of Fame (courtesy Gardiner-Rhodes Family).

Although the team ended up missing the playoffs that year and the following season, Gardiner had progressed his players accordingly and helped grow the young sport of hockey in Philadelphia. Going into the 1932–33 campaign, after bulking up his roster, expectations were suddenly sky-high for the young squad.

For the first time, Gardiner implemented a pre-season training camp. The previous season, he was unhappy with the team's effort and fitness at the start of the season. Rather than have the team arrive just days before the

## 2. The Arrows

season began, he put the team to work over a week ahead of opening night. Included in the roster was Vern Buckles, a forward who, in the same season would go on to play for the Philadelphia Comets of the Tri-State League (see Chapter 4). In addition, the team welcomed a young Wilf Cude to tend their net.

Cude was a Wales native, though his family moved to Toronto when he was just ten months old. After World War I, they moved to Winnipeg, where the youngster began playing youth hockey on the local flyweight team as a forward. In 1919, he made the trek west to Saskatchewan, where he moved into the net to tend

Arrows coach Herb Gardiner, as shown in the team's 1933 game program (courtesy Gardiner-Rhodes Family).

goal for the Melville Millionaires of the Senior League. (The Millionaires were one of the top hockey teams in the world, having won the Allen Cup as the senior league champions just a few years prior. Before the NHL or NHA existed, the Stanley Cup would often be battled for by Senior League teams. In 1915, the year the Millionaires claimed the league title, the Stanley Cup officially became a trophy for the winner of

A ticket stub to a Philadelphia Arrows-New Haven Eagles game in the 1930–31 CAHL season.

The 1931–32 Arrows squad showed the potential the team had to have on-ice success, at one point sitting near the top of the league standings. Here the players and coach Herb Gardiner (second from the right), visit the WIP radio station for a "fireside chat" (courtesy Gardiner-Rhodes Family).

a best-of-five game series between the NHA and Pacific Coast League champions, thereby preventing the Millionaires from playing for the trophy.)

One night in February 1930, Frank Frederickson, who managed the NHL's Pittsburgh Pirates, was out west scouting young talent and became fixated on Cude's in-net abilities. He immediately signed Cude to a contract and flew him to Pittsburgh for a tryout. A few months later, the Pirates closed shop and relocated to Philadelphia to become the Quakers (see Chapter 3). Cude became the starting goalie for Philadelphia's first NHL team and was one of the organization's few bright spots in their futile 1930–31 season.

After the Quakers disbanded, Cude was left without a job. The NHL signed him as the league-wide emergency goalie for any team to use if their starter went down with an injury. Unfortunately for him, he would see just 161 minutes of major league action before being assigned to the Boston Cubs of the CAHL. When he was made available for purchase, Gardiner jumped on the opportunity. (After his single season with the

Extracorporeal membrane oxygenation 127
Extubation 123

**F**

Fatty liver disease, nonalcoholic 70, 72
Fibrinolysis therapy 14
Fibrinolytic agents 12
Forced expiratory volume 63

**G**

Gammaglobulin, intravenous infusion of 87
Gastrointestinal tract 73, 110
Global Registry of Acute Coronary Events 12, 51
Glomerular filtration rate 107
Glucocorticoids 109
  dose, minimizing 107
  supraphysiologic dose of 111
Glucose intolerance 106
Glycoprotein 35, 52

**H**

Heart disease 95, 98
  risk equivalence for 32
  stable 3
Heart failure 99
  congestive 1, 16, 22, 82
Heart valves 55
*Helicobacter pylori* 73
Hematological disorders 81
Hematoma expansion 20
Hemiplegia 2
Hemodialysis 31
Hemolysis, intravascular 85
Hemophilia 83
Hemorrhage 73
  intracerebral 12, 20
  intracranial 19, 20
  retroperitoneal 15, 94
Henoch-Schonlein purpura 112
Heparin 19, 52
  unfractionated 40
Hepatitis
  C virus 71
    infection 71
  viral replication 74
Hodgkin's disease 99
Hodgkin's lymphoma 86, 99

Human immunodeficiency virus 118
  infection 116, 118
Hydroxychloroquine 107
Hydroxyurea 86
Hyperleukocytosis 85
Hypertension 30, 33, 106, 107
  arterial 123
  control of 107
Hypertrophy, myocardial 85
Hypotension 35, 123, 124
  intraoperative 124
Hypothermia 123
Hypovolemia 123

**I**

Immune thrombocytopenic purpura 82
Inflammation, chronic 108
Inspired oxygen, fraction of 126
Insulin resistance 118
Intensive care unit 15, 97
Intravascular thrombi, formation of 85
Intravenous thrombolytic therapy 10
Intubation 123
Ischemia, myocardial 122, 125
Ivabradine 64

**K**

Kawasaki disease 112
Kidney
  disease 35
    chronic 1, 29, 38
  injury, acute 36

**L**

Leflunomide 109
Left bundle branch block 125
Left ventricular
  ejection fraction 22, 96
  mural thrombus 17
Leukemia 2
  acute 85
  chronic lymphocytic 98
Lipid-lowering therapy 118
Lipoproteins
  high-density 118
  low-density 106
Liver
  cirrhosis 1, 4, 69, 72, 74, 76
  disease 2, 75
    chronic 68
    end-stage 72, 74

disorders, common 72
function 74
Low-cholesterol paradox 41
Low-molecular weight heparin 20, 40
Low-platelet count 82
Lung disease, obstructive 59
Lymphoma, malignant 2

## M

Major adverse cardiovascular event 3, 13
Malnutrition, inflammation, atherosclerosis, calcification syndrome 31
Metabolic syndrome 72, 118
Metastatic solid tumor 2
Mitral regurgitation, acute 127
Monckeberg's sclerosis 31
Monoclonal gammapathy 86
Multiple myeloma 86
Muscle 43
Myocardial infarction 1, 9, 16, 22, 29, 59, 62, 106
  coexistence of 76
  perioperative 122, 125
  stroke after 17
Myocardial injury 122
Myocardial Ischemia National Audit Project 60
Myocardial ischemia, intraoperative 124
Myocarditis, inflammatory 113
Myocytolysis 9
Myositis, adult inflammatory 113

## N

N-acetylcysteine 44
National Health Insurance Research Database 76
National Kidney Foundation 30
Nephropathy, contrast-induced 43
Nifedipine 107
Non-Hodgkin's lymphoma 86, 99
Non-nucleoside reverse transcriptase inhibitors 117
Non-ST elevation
  acute coronary syndromes 10
  myocardial infarction 11, 83
Non-ST segment elevation myocardial infarction 60, 61, 122

Nonsteroidal anti-inflammatory drugs 44, 73, 108, 110, 111
Nucleoside reverse transcriptase inhibitors 117

## O

Obesity, central 106
Obstructive coronary artery disease 70
Optical coherence tomography 94
Oral anticoagulant 54, 55
Orthotopic liver transplantation 76
Oxygen saturation 124

## P

Pain, postoperative 97
Paroxysmal nocturnal hemoglobinuria 85
Peptic ulcer disease 2
Percutaneous coronary intervention 10, 13, 19, 22, 30, 54, 72, 73, 82, 93, 119
  stroke after 13
Pericarditis 92
Peritoneal dialysis 31
Pexelizumab, assessment of 16
Platelets
  excessive production of 84
  microparticles, release of 82
Polycythemia vera 84
Polymyositis 113
Prasugrel 95
Proatherogenic lipid profile 112
Protease inhibitors 117
Pulmonary embolism 12
  prophylaxis 20

## R

Radiotherapy 99
Recombinant tissue plasminogen activator 10
Renal disease
  end-stage 30
  reduce progression of 34
Renal dysfunction, chronic 107
Renal failure, acute 36
Renal transplant 42
Reperfusion therapy 4
Respiratory system 86
Resuscitation, cardiopulmonary 126
Reteplase 12
Rheumatoid arthritis 105, 108, 111

## 2. The Arrows 35

Arrows, Cude would go onto an illustrious NHL career. In 1933–34 he led the Detroit Red Wings to the regular season championship, leading the league with a 1.52 goals against average. He led them all the way to the Stanley Cup final before losing to Chicago. His career continued with the Montreal Canadiens, where he became famous for being one of the top goaltenders in the league. In fact, Hall of Fame manager Tommy Gorman of the Montreal Maroons gave him perhaps the ultimate compliment in 1935. "What makes [the] Canadiens great is Cude.... I believe [the] Canadiens have the best goaler in the league.... Cude is the team to beat for the Stanley Cup. He nearly won it last year for Detroit. He may win it this year for [the] Canadiens."[23] Cude's career stat line in the NHL was 282 games played, 100 wins, and a 2.72 goals against average. He retired in 1940 to serve in the Royal Montreal Regiment during World War II.)

The Arrows opened their season on November 9, 1932, against the Boston Cubs. With just 1,500 fans braving the bitter cold and entering the Arena to see their local hockey team, the two squads fought through an extremely rough game to a 2–2 tie. The opening night roster saw Dave Kerr in goal, George Nichols and Frank Peters on defense, and a top line of Eddie Burke, "Yank" Boyd, and Joe McGoldrick. That top line

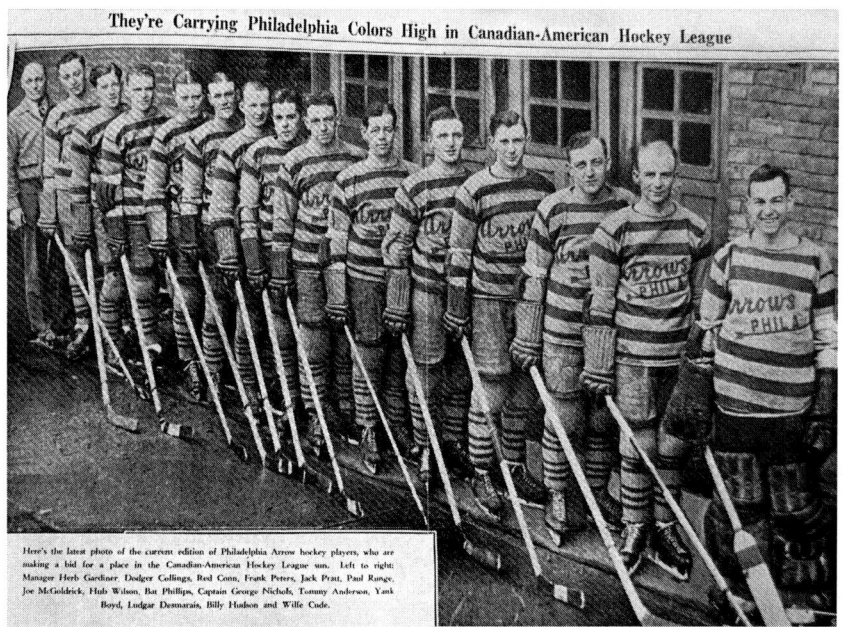

The 1932–33 Arrows team, as featured in the team's 1933 game program (courtesy Gardiner-Rhodes Family).

would change throughout the season until Gardiner believed he had the combination just right.

Just two weeks later, though, Kerr was called up to play with the Montreal Maroons, leaving Cude by himself to tend the crease. The team was mediocre through their first couple months, sitting at .500 as late as January 8, 1933. But with the turn of the calendar also came a turn in the team's fortunes. On January 21, Cude backstopped the team to a 5–1 win over Providence in front of 2,400 Philadelphia fans. Stan Baumgartner of the *Inquirer* praised the "brilliant young goalie, defending the cage mouth valiantly." Center and leading scorer Paul Runge scored four goals in the third period to ice the win.[24]

Two days later, the organization announced that their team president, W. Fred Ford, was resigning from the team because he was unable to devote the time that the Arrows required and deserved. The team named Fitz Eugene Dixon, another member of the ownership group, in his place. Dixon immediately announced that he was hopeful the team would win the championship. His words set the expectations high and pushed the Arrows toward a hot streak that lifted them to the top of the standings. From January 8 to the end of the season, the team went an astounding 23–6–2. That record included a four-game winning streak, a six-game winning streak, and a seven-game winning streak that stretched to the end the regular season. Cude was one of the team's top players. (Tending net wasn't his only talent, either. During a March 28 game against the New Haven Eagles, the *Winnipeg Tribune* reported that in the third period, Cude left his net to kill a mouse with his goal stick after it scampered across the ice. "His 'feat' was applauded boisterously by the women spectators," it was reported.)

Their finish atop the league standings bought them a bye into the league championship round. When the first round ended, the team learned their opponents in the CAHL final would be the Boston Cubs. The teams had fought hard all season, with the Cubs winning the season series, 5–4–3. (On March 23, the Arrows defeated the Cubs, 7–3, in a battle for first place. "When the final bell sounded," wrote the *Inquirer*, "Many of the players showed bad cuts and bruises from the free use of sticks and their opponents' fists.") According to Baumgartner before the best-of-five series started, the two teams hated one another. "Every struggle during the season has been a pitched battle, a free-for-all conflict that aroused the players and fans to a frenzy of excitement," he wrote. "The feud reached its climax a few weeks ago when the referee lost all control of the combat," where the teams took part in a brawl "that might well have been called a riot. If a mere game in mid-season can develop this feeling what will happen with the title and the lion's share of the gate receipts at stake?"[25]

Gardiner started his second line, which at that point consisted of Bill Hudson and Bill "Bat" Phillips at the wings and Jack Pratt at center. The threesome combined for 97 points in the regular season and were described as "an aggregation of speed kings" by the *Inquirer*. The opening game took place on April 6 at the nearly-filled Arena, with about 6,500 fans in attendance. The teams fought hard in what was a surprisingly-clean game, but through two periods no one was able to score. Just four minutes into the third period, Pratt pushed his way into Cubs territory, but was stymied by roughhousing Cubs defense star Joe Jerwa. The two crashed into each other, but Pratt continued fighting for the puck. With the players tied up, Boston goaltender Percy Jackson skated out of his net to knock the puck away. In a final, desperate effort, Pratt lunged toward the puck, sending it slowly spinning past Jackson and across the goal line to give the Arrows a 1–0 lead. The team shut the door the rest of the game, with Cude getting the shutout and giving his team a 1–0 series lead.[26] (The papers led the game recap with a quote that seems to be a perfect summation of 1930s sports journalism. "Jack's wife being home in British Columbia last night and with no platters in sight to lick, Mr. Pratt decided to uphold the family tradition by handing the Boston Cubs a licking.")[27]

Three nights later, 4,500 fans packed the Arena to watch their city's hockey team fight to double their lead in the series. After a scoreless first period, the Arrows ripped through the Cubs defense and scored three. Boston fought valiantly in the third period and scored two goals, but were unable to pot the equalizer before the final buzzer. "They completely disorganized the famous defense of the Bostonians," wrote the *Inquirer*, "Ripped their forwards wide open and even upset the usually staid and reliable goaltender Jackson." With a 2–0 series lead, the Arrows would have two games in Boston and a potential fifth game in Philadelphia with which to clinch the championship.[28]

The first meeting in Boston started strong, with the Arrows scoring the first goal. But Boston was quick to respond with two of their own and Jerwa scored a hat trick in the third period to clinch the 5–1 win for the Cubs in front of 10,000 Boston fans. Two nights later, the Arrows scored first yet again, but could not hold on. Boston scored four straight goals and the Arrows could only put one more past Jackson as the Cubs tied the series with a 4–2 win.

The championship-deciding game would take place in the Arena, in front of 5,000 fans. The Cubs had won just one game in the Arena all season. On top of that, the Arrows had scored first in all four games of the playoff series. All signs pointed to a potential Arrows victory. The game started similarly, with the Arrows scoring two goals in the first period. But amidst a Cubs flurry in the second period, things started to unravel for the Philadelphians. Boston scored three goals in the middle frame and the frustration mounted. "So terrific was the struggle, so fierce the battle of human emotions," wrote Baumgartner, "The rink became a battleground. On four occasions rival stickhandlers were laid unconscious on the ice and in several other instances the rink was dotted with sprawling figures." The war that everyone was waiting for before Game 1 had finally arrived, albeit four games later.[29]

In the middle of the second period, Cude came out of his net to make a save. As he batted the puck away, Boston winger Tommy Filmore hit the goaltender on the back of the head with his stick, causing him to collapse to the ice. Pratt immediately punched Filmore and an on-ice riot ensued. The festivities stretched to the crowd, who began screaming for justice. The referees tried their best to keep control, but Gardiner was just as enraged, demanding something be done. Fans began running toward the ice surface, but not before a group of firemen rushed into the bowl of the building to calm the crowd and quell the disturbance.

Nonetheless, the incident seemed to stifle the Arrows attack. The team tied the game at three before the end of the period, but the third period was controlled completely by Boston. Though they scored just one goal, the Arrows saw almost no chance to tie the game. When the final buzzer sounded, Boston had won, 4–3, and clinched the CAHL championship in a stunning series comeback. The series was immensely close and the loss dealt a heart-wrenching blow to Philadelphia and their hockey fans. "The margin of superiority of the Cubs was infinitesimal," wrote Baumgartner on the final game. "A mere thread that might have snapped either way for 53 of the 60 minutes, the two clubs were as evenly balanced as is possible and it looked as if the battle might go on forever."[30]

The 1933–34 season was moderately successful, with the team finishing in third place with a 17–5–8 record, just one point ahead of the Quebec Beavers and good for a playoff berth. In the first round, however, they would lose two consecutive games to their hated rivals in Boston, eliminating them from the postseason. Nonetheless, the news was bright for the Arrows. The newspapers reported that the team sold enough seats throughout the season to finish the season in the black—an extraordinary achievement for the minor-league hockey team.

The 1934–35 season was largely forgettable, as the team—short on talent after many of their players were signed to other teams or promoted to the NHL—limped through the campaign. However, it did come with some excitement. On January 19, 1935, the Arrows hosted the Quebec Beavers at the Arena. Trailing, 4–3, late in the third period, Quebec coach Leduc replaced his two defensemen with two forwards, leaving five offensive players on the ice in an attempt to win the game. But then, he did something curious that rippled through the hockey world. According to the *Inquirer*. With the Arrows beating Quebec, 4–3, late in the third period, Quebec manager Leduc pulled his goalie and replaced him with a sixth skater—something that was unheard of at the time. "Ice hockey, in its orthodox form, is said to be the fastest and certainly it is one of the most inflaming of body contact sports," wrote the *Inquirer*. "A lively tilt on skates between evenly matched teams will keep a crowd in a frenzy from whistle to whistle. Then you can imagine what happens when the manager of a team that is trailing in the last minute by a single goal, throws defense to the winds and tosses six attacking players into action. That is what happened at the Arena last Saturday night, and, as a result, many of the spectators are still under treatment for palpitation of the heart."[31]

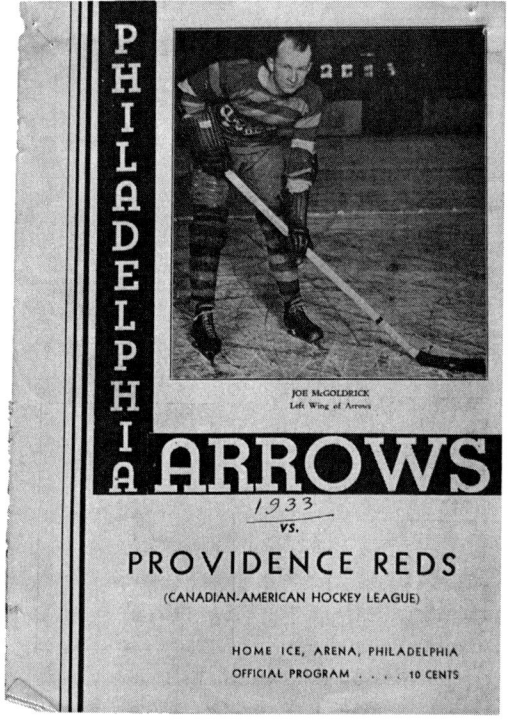

The 1932–33 Arrows were the best version of the CAHL squad, making it all the way to the league championship before falling to Boston (courtesy Gardiner-Rhodes Family).

The stunned crowd leapt to their feet in excitement and discomfort, biting their nails all the while. The Arrows quickly put the puck into the empty Quebec net, icing the game with a 5–3 score. But the press, the public, and the hockey world was stunned. "Whether or not this established a precedent, I do not know," wrote the *Inquirer*, "But it was certainly unorthodox."[32] (Frank Boucher, the Hall of Fame center and coach, is generally credited with being the first NHL coach to regularly pull the goalie in either 1939 or 1940. Art Ross reportedly pulled his goalie once in 1931, but did not make a habit of the practice.)

One of the bright spots was on March 21, 1935, with the team welcoming the Providence Reds to the Arena for an end-of-season tilt. Already well out of the playoff race, the Arrows were simply looking to play spoiler to the Reds' attempts to finish in second place. Providence scored just 18 seconds into the game, but the Arrows suddenly erupted, scoring five in the first period, three in the second, and six more in the third, to ruin the Reds ending to the regular season with a 14–5 victory. Unfortunately, that seemed to be the only good news of the season. As the *Inquirer* wrote, "Too bad the local aggregation couldn't have spread this [sic] 14 goals over a wider area and thus saved them of the humiliation of finishing in last place." The season ended in disgrace, with the team finishing a putrid 15–30–3.

Part of the charm of the Arrows was Gardiner himself. Despite him being behind the bench, he was a much-needed face of hockey in Philadelphia and helped propel the city's history with the sport. Not only that, but he was both a caring and intelligent hockey coach that showed the city the kind of personalities required to gain the admiration of the notoriously-tough Philadelphia sports fans. In one Arrows game in Baltimore, the owner of the rink was being obnoxious and vocal to all of the Arrows players. When one Arrows defenseman got overly-annoyed, he reached over the boards and knocked the owner on his back. The owner, furious, called the cops and demanded the Arrows player be arrested for assault. Gardiner, to protect his player, simply kept him on the ice for the rest of the game, thereby preventing the police from getting to his man. It was instances like this that endeared him to Philadelphians.

Just before the start of the 1935–36 season, it was announced the New York Rangers were taking control of the Philadelphia CAHL club and turning it into their farm team (the American League not having yet been in existence). With that announcement came an overhaul in the team's image, including the roster, management, and the name. Just like that, the Arrows would be written into the history books.

Despite their lack of continued on-ice success and their short life, the Arrows hold a dear place in Philadelphia hockey history as its first ever professional hockey team. The team gave hope to hockey fans throughout the city, while also showing a recipe for success that future Philadelphia hockey organizations could choose to follow or avoid, at their own peril. Strong ownership that was willing to spend to the ceiling to win, combined with a newly-outfitted building, created the foundation for a successful franchise. Most importantly, they proved that an organization could succeed financially, even if the wins were not as plentiful as fans would hope, if it boasted a roster that showed fight game in and game out. If the players and the management showed as much passion for winning as did the fans, a hockey team in Philadelphia could make it.

In the coming years, Philadelphia fans would toss many hockey organizations to the side of the road. The consistent theme of those teams was that they failed to follow the Arrows' successful business formula.

# 3

# The Quakers

*National Hockey League (NHL), 1930–31*

The Philadelphia Quakers didn't start their life in the City of Brotherly Love, but on the other side of Pennsylvania. The Pittsburgh Pirates, as they were known since their founding in 1925, struggled at the box office since their inception. They had strong, passionate ownership that cared deeply for the team, despite their on-ice efforts. Pittsburgh was confident about the long-term viability of its franchise and that they would continue to see major league hockey for many years.

But on January 15, 1927, owner Henry Townsend passed away, leaving the team to his two sons, Horace and Ed. The two were not cut out for the sports world, failing to understand the running of the business and the league rules. When Frank Calder called them out on a rule violation shortly after their father's death, Ed admitted in a written response, "due to the death of my father ... this thing was forced on me so quickly, of handling the Club, and I have never really known the rules of the National Hockey Club." The team continued to have grave financial struggles. At the end of the 1927–28 season, the franchise filed with the league an attendance report that showed just 40,000 fans attended their home games for the entirety of the season, putting them in last place, well behind Ottawa who, at 100,000, was second-worst. The Townsend sons put the team on the market, looking for a viable buyer, while keeping control of Pittsburgh's hockey arena, Duquesne Gardens.[1]

Around that time, Irwin Wener, the Philadelphia entrepreneur who ran the Philadelphia Arena, obtained an option to purchase the Pirates, and made his intention known to move the team to Philadelphia. Wener then attempted to transfer his option to two businessmen who wanted to put NHL hockey in Cleveland. After searching for investors, Wener brought his proposal to the NHL Board of Governors in a March 1928 meeting. The league rejected his attempt and ordered control of the

The Philadelphia Quakers, NHL, 1930–31.

team back to the Townsends. A few months later, they found a new buyer.

Just over 30 years earlier, in 1896, Benjamin Leiner was born in the New York Jewish ghetto, on the Lower East Side of New York City. Fighting the sons of other immigrant parents on the street, Leiner learned the fighting craft, despite his parents' disapproval. By the time he was fifteen, he realized that boxing was what he wanted to do professionally. To prevent his parents from learning of this revelation, he Americanized his name to Benny Leonard and his professional boxing career had begun. As a boxer, Leonard was extraordinarily successful. Between 1917 and 1925, he held the world lightweight championship, losing just six times in 96 career bouts. By the time he retired for the first time in 1925, he was arguably the most successful boxer of his era—and in 2005, he was named the number one lightweight fighter of all-time by the International Boxing Research Organization.

Through his work in boxing (and boxing's connection to the criminal world), Leonard met William Dwyer, the Prohibition bootlegger who owned the NHL's New York Americans. Desiring another piece of the hockey world, Dwyer purchased the Pittsburgh franchise from the Townsends. But the league frowned upon owners having a stake in more than one team, despite there not being a specific rule against it at the time. Dwyer, using his lawyer, Joseph Shalleck, as a middleman, put Leonard in charge of the Pittsburgh franchise, convincing the sports world that the famous athlete was the team's owner.

The underworld criminal believed Leonard's reputation would help to promote the club and ease the financial burden that came with a lack of marketability. However, Leonard also put his own money up to help finance the team out of its struggles. "I think I can make professional hockey pay in Pittsburgh," he said at the announcement of his purchase. "We plan a number of deals to strengthen the outfit."[2]

But the situation in Pittsburgh failed to improve. After the 1929 stock market crash, Pittsburgh's steel industry was badly crippled, leading to even fewer fans attending hockey games. In the spring of 1930, rumors began floating around the league that the Pittsburgh franchise was in trouble and that an ownership change was forthcoming. The team's finances were struggling and it wasn't a secret. On May 12, Pittsburgh coach Frank Frederickson sent a telegram to Calder. (At the time, there was no NHL "front office." The league essentially consisted of the president and, occasionally, an assistant.) He was furious about the rumors and claimed he was owed back pay by Leonard. "Repeated letters and wires ... since end of season have brought no response," he said. Frederickson was naturally concerned about his job and wanted to know his status with the potential new owners, since it was affecting his ability to recruit players to the organization.[3]

The last home game of the season saw the Pittsburgh Pirates play against the Detroit Cougars in Fort Erie, Ontario. (Some Pittsburgh home games were played elsewhere in an attempt to draw larger attendance.) Out of the arena's 3,759-seat capacity, just 739 were filled. The Pirates lost, 4–2, ending their paltry season with just five victories. The team reportedly lost nearly $50,000, double the previous season's loss. "It's a tough racket," said Leonard on March 4, according to the *Pittsburgh Press*. "Enough is plenty." The writer, Ralph Davis, bemoaned the situation, in which the relocation of the team seemed inevitable. Duquesne Gardens was not a suitable arena to house an NHL squad, but Leonard could not find another option in the city.

Davis pinned the blame on Leonard, who he claimed did not do enough to make the team competitive. Despite the owner's claims that the team had loads of new talent ready to join the squad for the upcoming season, it simply wasn't believable to the Pittsburgh fans who had watched the team flounder for so long. "Fans here cannot be fooled about the brand of hockey served up to them," Davis wrote. "They are willing to make all sorts of reasonable allowances, but in the end, they are human, and want a club over which they can enthuse." Leonard also had a building problem and continued to pin his hopes on the city constructing a new home for the team—something that everyone else seemed to know would not happen. "If he is not going to wait," Davis

## 3. The Quakers

said, "There is no good reason why he and his associates should not proceed at once with whatever plans they have. Nothing is to be gained by delay."[4]

On May 10, the NHL Board of Governors met and voted to permit a transfer of the Pittsburgh franchise to Lincoln G. Dickey, who managed the Atlantic City Auditorium, according to the newspapers. (League minutes do not reflect this, though often times in this era the newspaper accounts were more accurate than the league's notes, which were not always all-encompassing.) The league stipulated that the franchise had to operate in Pittsburgh or be relocated to Atlantic City and they believed Dickey and his associates would be the ones to do so. However, it quickly became known that the group was going to attempt to move the team to Cleveland, which angered the league executives. They quickly rescinded the transfer, leaving Leonard again in charge of the team. The Board rushed through the offseason in an attempt to find a suitable location for the team, but time ran short. With just a few months before opening night of the 1930–31 season, they chose Philadelphia as a temporary home for the Pittsburgh franchise. The team would be known as the Quakers, in honor of the city's heritage.

At the time, Philadelphia was the third-largest city in the United States by population (according to the census), with just under two million people. On October 15, 1930, the Associated Press announced the move, with the understanding that Pittsburgh would again be granted the franchise once they had a suitable arena. In the meantime, Philadelphia would temporarily host the team. The NHL would consist of ten squads for the upcoming season: Philadelphia Quakers, Boston Bruins, New York Americans, New York Rangers, Detroit Falcons, Chicago Black Hawks, Montreal Canadiens, Montreal Maroons, Ottawa Senators, and Toronto Maple Leafs.

The only suitable ice hockey venue in Philadelphia was the Arena, where the CAHL's Arrows played. But Leonard was extremely optimistic and more than enthusiastic about sharing his team with the City of Brotherly Love. "We will build a Madison Square Garden–like facility in three years or so," he said to the *Philadelphia Inquirer*. "It will be the kind of place where women can come in evening dress without fear of being hit in the face with a frankfurter."[5]

One of the first moves he made was firing Coach Frederickson. "What my team needed last year was a boss," Leonard said, "And while [Frederickson was] a splendid fellow [he] spent more time teaching the boys how to speak correctly than he did to play hockey and keep training." His new hire would be J. Cooper Smeaton. A decorated World War I veteran, Smeaton was a referee by trade. He had officiated hockey games at all levels since 1913, and while he received offers to play in the NHL in his younger days, he repeatedly turned them down. The Pirates' issue, according to Leonard, was discipline. He believed Smeaton would fix that in a hurry. "Smeaton will rule with an iron fist," Leonard said, "And if necessary we may have a few policemen around to keep order."[6]

Leonard transferred twelve players to Philadelphia from Pittsburgh: Cliff Barton, Harold Darragh, Herb Drury, Gord Fraser, Jim Jarvis, Gerry Lowrey, Ren Manners, John McKinnon, Hib Milks, Joe Miller, Rodger Smith & Tex White. Smeaton would also bring along 35 young hopefuls that he had scouted across Canada. "The entire squad of Quakers is expected to be in this city on Saturday," wrote the *Indiana Gazette* on October 21. "The first few workouts of the squad will consist mainly of running and calisthenics in order to have the players in top physical condition before taking to the ice for their fundamental and technical drills."[7]

The team quickly made a major transaction, purchasing three young, promising players from the Ottawa Senators on November 6 for $35,000: Allan Shields, Wally Kilrea, and future Hall of Famer Syd Howe. "Once you see them in action," Leonard said about his young team, "You will say they have the goods."[8]

Despite Smeaton being the head coach, it was clear that Leonard was in charge and interested in putting himself front and center as the main attraction. If the team was going to linger at the bottom of the standings, as expected, he could at least provide the star power to attract people to games. Leonard put his name all over the team, trying to utilize his celebrity. The official team program and newspaper

Syd Howe would go on to be a member of the Hockey Hall of Fame, but he played his first full NHL season with the lowly Philadelphia Quakers (courtesy Bruce "Scoop" Cooper).

ads referred to the club as "Benny Leonard's Philadelphia Quakers."

He pushed from every angle, trying to reverse the skeptical media and introduce major league hockey to the city. He wanted buzz surrounding the team—he was a showman. He even wrote a letter to Frank Calder requesting he write "a few paragraphs concerning big league hockey, the organization of the league and its improvements and incidentally touching upon the fact that Philadelphia has been fortunate enough to secure the services of so valuable a man as J. Cooper Smeaton."[9] Calder replied, directing Leonard to the league's "weekly publicity sheet," which he was welcome to send out to the local press. Calder also offered to come to Philadelphia himself if Leonard needed him to talk to the press directly, though league records do not indicate that Leonard ever took him up on the offer.[10]

After many years as the league's referee-in-chief, J. Cooper Smeaton would try his hand at coaching behind the Quakers' bench. After arguably the worst season in NHL history, he would return to refereeing (courtesy Bruce "Scoop" Cooper).

The media was pessimistic, to say the least. A scathing editorial told of how, in 1926, the NHL had rejected an expansion application from an ownership group in Philadelphia. (The NHL has no record of this claim. A February 14, 1926, Board of Governors meeting does show a discussion of expansion, but the only cities recorded as being discussed were Detroit, Buffalo, Cleveland, and Chicago. It is possible the editorial was confusing this with Jules Mastbaum's attempt to land a franchise in 1924 or, more likely, that the 1926 application was simply apocryphal.) The author argued that the Arrows were finally turning the corner and becoming successful, and then "the National League heads step in—turn over the big-league franchise to a group of New York capitalists who pilot a last-place club into Philadelphia and tell us to like it."[11]

"Philadelphia is not ready for National League hockey," wrote another, "Not because the fans would not support it, but because we have not a suitable arena in which to stage the games and accommodate the crowds that would want to see it." The rent at the Arena was much more than what Leonard paid at Duquesne Gardens—some reports claimed it was three times.[12]

But on November 11, it appeared Leonard might be right. According to Yong Chae Rhee and John Wong in their research article, "Knocked

### BENNY LEONARD
#### By Lou Jaffe

Leonard is one of the most popular sports figures ever to come into Philadelphia, where he has probably more friends than any other athletic luminary in the world.

Yes, Ben is a New Yorker, but when in the heyday of his boxing career he visited the Quaker City more often than fight fans realized.

By the way, you know, Leonard is the retired undefeated lightweight champion—a man who not only was clean and a good sportsman through his fistic career, but one who kept the game clean and aboveboard.

Now this same young Mr. Leonard is back in Philadelphia in an entirely new role—that of an ice hockey magnate. Benny is owner of the National League team representing the Quaker City in the "fastest game in the world."

Leonard believes in fair play, albeit hard play, and with his manager, J. Cooper Smeaton, former referee-in-chief of the National Hockey League, has inspired the Quakers to give Philadelphia an article of fair and hard play.

With the thousands of friends Leonard already has created for himself in the past fifteen years, there is little question that Benny will have many of his well-wishers rally around for his success in his new field.

Leonard also realizes that he must give Philadelphia a winning combination in order to keep the turnstiles clicking.

"And they're going to click," says Leonard enthusiastically, "because the Quakers are going to be a winning combination."

**BENNY LEONARD**
President and Treasurer of the Philadelphia Quakers.
Retired, undefeated lightweight champion of the world

---

#### A MESSAGE FROM BENNY LEONARD

This season marks the inauguration of National League Hockey in Philadelphia. It is our desire to take every step that will add to your enjoyment and comfort and further your interest in Ice Hockey.

Always remember that this team is YOUR TEAM.

We ask your co-operation and support and will continue to do our utmost to merit them. We welcome your suggestions, will gladly consider your complaints, and invite your constructive criticism.

BENNY LEONARD,
President and Treasurer.

---

**Owner Benny Leonard put himself front and center when marketing the Quakers, such as in this team program during the 1930–31 NHL season.**

## 3. *The Quakers*  49

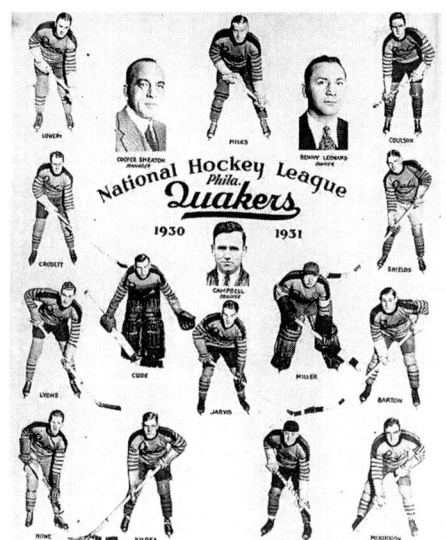

**A spread in the Quakers game program during their 1930–31 NHL season shows the team to the left, and Herb Drury to the right.**

Out! Marketing the Philadelphia Quakers," the ushers were dressed in tuxedos in celebration of opening night. The players donned brand new orange and black jerseys. Leonard had added new lights, speakers, and a new scoreboard to the arena, along with hanging colorful flags from the rafters. It "turned the opening game into a gala event."[13]

The newspaper reporters, despite their skepticism, were intrigued by the possibilities. "The battle cry of the diamond with its battles, its rivalries, and its bitter inter-city rivalry is transplanted tonight when Benny Leonard's Quakers face the New York Rangers in the first major league puck tilt ever staged in Philadelphia," wrote Stan Baumgartner of the *Inquirer*. "Fireworks are promised. A New York and a Philadelphia team never came to grips without producing a battle royal. The Quakers are new to Philadelphia, but in the few short weeks they have been training they have grasped the fighting spirit of an aroused Quaker."[14]

The *Inquirer* reported a crowd of over 3,800 fans in attendance, a respectable start for the small arena (though other sources claimed that number was inflated by a few hundred). But the good news ended there. The New York Rangers completely dominated the game, defeating the Quakers, 3–0. The optimism showed earlier that day was suddenly replaced by the already-heavy pessimism. "From the start it was apparent that the visitors were far superior," wrote Baumgartner in the *Inquirer*. "Once in the lead they coasted and played under wraps. When it was necessary to go, they went, and went fast. At other times they rested." The New York *Times* was equally as rough on the team, saying the Rangers "completely outplayed the home team from the opening bell until the closing gong, and there was never any question as to the outcome after the first goal." The Montreal *Gazette* wrote that the "new Philadelphia team is badly excelled in team play and individual effectiveness." According to Stanley Woodward of the *New York Herald Tribune*, fans began filing out of the arena after the Rangers scored their third goal early in the third period, making "caustic remarks" as they left.[15]

Shortly after opening night, Leonard Cohen of the *New York Post* wrote, "The Philly hosts look like the weakest force in the circuit on paper; they're every bit of that on the ice." The Quakers were shut out again in their second game, this one a 4–0 drubbing at the hands of Toronto. "The Quakers have a whole raft of forwards," wrote Charlie Querrie of the Toronto *Star*, "But outside of Milks and Darragh they are not up to much." The team had no defense. Their goaltender, Joe Miller, had little help and could hardly win a game by himself. Just a week later, the second home game drew about 2,000 patrons. As the team struggled on the ice, so they also did at the gate.[16]

The Quakers game program from the 1930–31 NHL season.

After starting the season 0–4–1, the fans quickly soured on the organization. But a glimmer of hope emerged on November 25 when the undefeated Maple Leafs came to town. Toronto sleep-walked its way through the first two periods, allowing the Quakers to take control of the game. When the Leafs finally kicked

## 3. The Quakers

**The Philadelphia Quakers of the 1930–31 NHL season (courtesy Bruce "Scoop" Cooper).**

it into gear, it was too little, too late. Philadelphia upset the Leafs squad, 2–1, sending the fans into a frenzy. They were, as the *Philadelphia Bulletin* described, "dizzy from excitement."

"It took us some time to get started," Smeaton said to the media, "But I think we are now in proper condition and we can defeat many of the teams in either the Canadian or American divisions." The victory gave the fans a jolt of false optimism, as it would be the last time the Quakers would win a game until after the New Year.[17]

Already struggling financially, Leonard began unloading some of his more expensive players by December, in the hopes he could save the franchise. While the team moved many players to save money, leaving them with a shell of a roster, other teams complained. Chicago Black Hawks owner Frederic McLaughlin even sent a letter to Calder, saying that the franchise was doing "absolutely nothing to strengthen or make interesting its team."[18]

Then, in December, Smeaton received a jolt of shocking news. The three players that Leonard seemingly bought from Ottawa a few months earlier turned out to be simply on loan, and that they would need to be returned at the end of the season. Knowing this would cripple his team even more, Smeaton began negotiating with the Senators in an attempt to keep his young core intact. The Ottawa franchise was unresponsive to his requests, frustrating Smeaton. He wrote a letter to Calder, reminding him that "at all meetings the Governors have always criticized this Club for not trying to help themselves to get a Club and now we are willing to buy these players and it seems that nobody is willing to give us a chance to get anywhere."[19]

Heading into a December 13 matchup against the Detroit Falcons, the local newspapers talked up a blossoming rivalry. Frederickson, who had been fired by Leonard just a few months earlier, was now playing for Detroit and making his first return back to the club whose bench he recently ran. The *Morning Call* told a story, perhaps dubious, of Frederickson's aviation service during World War I. "Speeding across the Mediterranean," it wrote, "He developed motor trouble and came down into the sea. For three days he clung to the wreckage—parched with thirst and starved with hunger. On the final day, just when he was about to give it all up he was rescued. That is the kind of a man Smeaton's warriors will face Saturday." The Quakers showed little fight, losing, 3–2, and leaving Frederickson with the last laugh.[20]

Still amidst a record-breaking losing streak, Leonard came out in the middle of December and announced that he would eat just one meal a day until the Quakers won a game, at which point he would then throw a banquet. "Leonard is rapidly bringing himself down to the lightweight limit," wrote Baumgartner in the *Inquirer*, "And before the hockey season is over he may be eligible for the flyweight division.... It is a cinch that if the Quakers had as much fight as their scrappy president they would not be in the cellar."[21]

A local group even offered a trophy, to be given to the "cleanest" player on the roster. Leonard was appalled, and rejected the offer. "Present it to the man that shows the most fight," he said. "He might be the cleanest player, too. A man who is always in the thick of the battle does not have to waste time playing 'dirty.'" Throughout the season, Baumgartner took a liking to Leonard, even if the Quakers constantly disappointed. He wrote about Leonard's heart, and how passionate he was for the hockey club. He took solace in Leonard's antics and star power, surrounding a team that desperately needed some.[22]

"I played goal once," Leonard jested, "But I will have to admit that I wasn't exactly a success. You see I was so accustomed to dodging in the ring that when I went into the nets I dodged every puck shot at me."[23]

The season's low point was arguably Christmas Day, when the Bruins embarrassed the Quakers, 8–0, in Boston. After Boston defenseman George Owen sent Hib Milks flying with a bruising check, a free-for-all developed, with the benches emptying and all but one player taking part in a brawl. Quakers goaltender Wilf Cude chose to avoid the fireworks, instead lounging nonchalantly on his net. The two officials even took a few hits to the face as they attempted to break it up. When they couldn't

## 3. The Quakers

get control of the situation, the police were called—though only two constables dared jump over the boards and onto the slippery ice, as they nervously looked behind them, begging for help from their colleagues. "The good officers," wrote LeRoy Atkinson in the *Boston Evening Transcript*, "Without skates or [galoshes], were tumbling over the sideboards in all sorts of fantastic attitudes." Up in the rafters, the Boston Garden organist played "Silent Night," hoping it would "bring peace among men," according to Clark Booth and Steve Babineau in their book, *Boston Bruins: Celebrating 75 Years*. After a few minutes, the rest of the police force added their help, breaking up the fight and quelling the situation. The league gave out $15 fines to three players on each team, which Leonard tried to convince to allow them to pay out of the playoff pot to which he tongue-in-cheek claimed they were entitled.[24]

If Leonard hoped the brawl would help boost the Quakers' fortunes, he was sorely mistaken. Although the next home game drew a higher-than-normal 1,645 fans, that number sagged into the triple digits soon thereafter. During a January 1 matchup against the Black Hawks in Chicago, a few fans sitting in the balcony threw eggs at the Quakers players. The Philadelphia skaters lost, 10–3. A few weeks later, the Quakers notched their second win of the season against the Montreal Maroons, an overtime victory, which the *Inquirer* described as "the greatest moment the Quakers and the Arena fans have had in many a day." The win drove attendance up to 1,848 at the next home game, but when the Quakers went back to their losing ways, the fans again stayed home. The final home game of the season saw just 816 show up.[25]

Despite their struggles, Leonard continued to maintain hope throughout the season, at least publicly. "Lose heart because we haven't been winning?" Leonard said to the *Courier-News* in January 1931, "Just watch these kids in a season or two. This team is young and is taking the bumps plenty, but every licking is like going to school. The boys come out of a defeat bruised but with a little more hockey knowledge tucked away."[26]

The team continued to struggle, despite Leonard's high hopes. During the last home game of the season, a March 17 matchup against Chicago, Leonard was, according to Earl Eby of the *Philadelphia Bulletin*, in a "rather cheerful mood.... 'We'll have a winner next year, wait and see!'" Leonard said. The Quakers were shut out, 4–0.[27]

The final game of the season saw the Quakers travel to Montreal to play the Canadiens on March 21, 1931. To add insult to the injury of the embarrassing season, Cude suffered a serious facial laceration late in the second period when Canadiens legend Howie Morenz released a powerful shot that Cude misjudged, hitting him directly in the chin and causing the young goaltender to collapse on the ice. After being carried to the dressing room, the teams agreed to end the period, tied 1–1, and tack on the remaining four minutes to the beginning of the third period.

With no money for a backup goalie and with Cude badly beaten up, the Quakers were unprepared and ready to forfeit the game. However, just as a decision was about to be made, Hugh McCormack, an Ontario sportswriter, volunteered to stretch his minor-league experience and fill in for the Philadelphia squad. Multiple reports cite him even getting fully dressed and preparing to enter the game, before Cude stepped in, his face partially fixed up, demanding to finish the game that he started. "If I don't go out there now," he said, according to the *Montreal Star*, "I will be puck shy for the rest of my life. Give me my stick." He got up off the table, wobbled toward the door, collapsed, and was carried back to the medical table, before trying a second time to return to the game, this one successful.[28]

While one newspaper claims McCormack actually played, historians debate this fact, as nearly every other source cites that Cude played every minute of action. What is agreed upon, though, is that Cude returned to the playing surface to the applause of the Montreal crowd. The teams fought valiantly, trading goals throughout the final 24 minutes. The Canadiens scored one goal in the remaining minutes of the second period, while the Quakers took control of the final frame, even taking the lead with under 15 minutes remaining in the third. Unfortunately for them, the Canadiens tied the game just over one minute later, and both goaltenders shut the door for the remainder of the match, giving the Quakers a 4–4 tie against the eventual Stanley Cup champions to end their horrendous season.

At the end of the season, the Quakers' finances were appalling. According to league documents, the team grossed $40,637.35 for their 22 home games, an average of about $1,847.15 per game. After deducting the 3.5 percent that was required to be given to the visiting teams, it left Leonard with a net revenue of just $39,215.04. Considering that his rent at the Arena was reportedly $38,000 for the season, it was clear that the team was unable to properly operate. Various numbers were reported, but it is fair to suggest that Leonard lost just under $100,000 throughout the season. The team's average crowd of 2,500 was less than that of the Arrows, who continued to draw upwards of 4,000 per game. The Philadelphia fans were simply not willing to pay good money to watch a losing team.[29]

Losing was possibly the only specialty the franchise had. The Quakers won just four of their 44 games, finishing last in the league. Their 15-game losing streak in the middle of the season was an NHL record that stood until the 1974–75 season. Their winning percentage of .136 was a record that stood until 1974–75 as well. And their four wins is still an NHL record to this day for futility. They scored just 76 goals, and surrendered 184, 42 more than the next-closest team.

That September (1931), at the annual Governors' meeting, the league passed a unanimous motion to suspend the Pittsburgh/Philadelphia franchise for the 1931–32 season with four stipulations: (1) the franchise would be paid not more than $20,000 for the rights to a number of players, including Johnny McKinnon, D'Arcy Coulson, Stanley Crossett, Gerry Lowrey, Hib Milks, Bud Jarvis, Cliff Barton, Aubrey Webster, and Wilf Cude. (2) The league could sublease these players to any other team in the league. (3) The league would give the players back to the Pittsburgh/Philadelphia organization at the end of the 1931–32 season. And (4), the organization would be allowed to continue to represent themselves at Board of Governors' meetings. The league continued to suspend the franchise for an additional year at each annual meeting, eventually taking away the team's representative on the Board in 1934.

During this period, Dwyer continued to meet with the Board of Governors quite regularly. In a May 11, 1935, meeting, the Board informed Dwyer that he had to give the league a definitive answer on whether or not he would be operating the Pittsburgh franchise at all. He replied that he would inform the league by August 1 whether he intended to operate the Pirates in any capacity. When the date came with no update, he stated that he had no objection to the International League putting a team in Duquesne Gardens—which they did, placing the Shamrocks in the arena for the 1935–36 season.

The Quakers had failed due to what one writer called a "triple handicap": an underdeveloped fan base, a small building, and a losing squad. While Leonard attempted to make a go of major league hockey in Philadelphia with the right attitude, he based its success on the success of the team. He wanted the team to speak for itself. But when the team could barely compete with opposing clubs, fans tired quickly, preferring to spend their hockey money on the less-expensive and more successful Arrows (tickets to Quakers games ranged from 75 cents to $2.50 per ticket).[30]

While the lack of a suitable arena surely contributed to the Quakers' downfall, a talented team would have been able to kick the can down the road, until a time that the city was willing or able to build a larger home for hockey. Yet, Leonard had neither the resources nor the management in place to ice a competitive hockey team. The Philadelphia fans, who had shown inklings of their future love for hockey through the Quaker City Hockey Club and the Arrows, simply did not want to support a team that seemed unable to fight through each game.

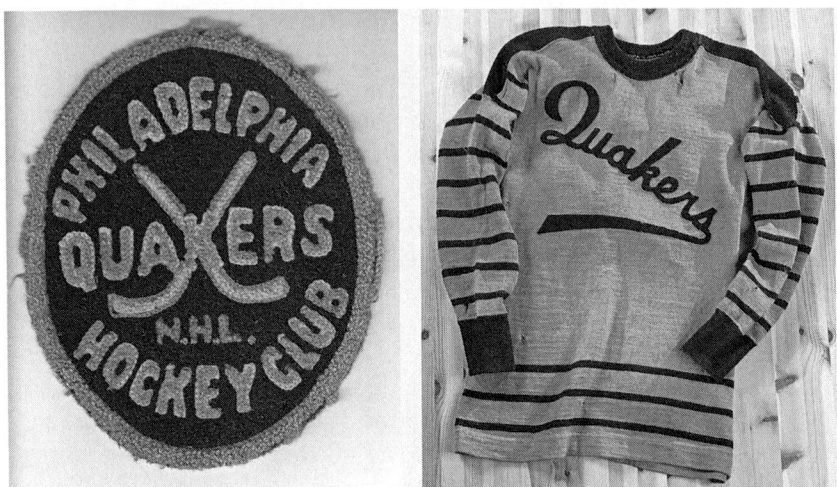

**Two old relics: a Quakers NHL jersey and patch from the 1930–31 season.**

Smeaton returned to Toronto after the season to become the NHL's referee-in-chief, a position for which he was destined after his years of service to the league. Forty-four years later, in a 1975 *Washington Post* interview, Syd Howe reminisced about his short tenure in Philadelphia, a period that coincided with the early stretches of his Hall of Fame career. "We were a rookie bunch, mostly castoffs," he said. "It was a scrappy team, but there wasn't enough talent." He also mentioned that, although Smeaton was a good coach, "he didn't have the material." Howe also discussed Dwyer's role on the team, specifying that the players knew he was the franchise's true owner, that it was no secret.

"The crowds were small," he continued. "People in Philadelphia were not educated to hockey at that time. Those were the depression years and we were making pretty good money, $3,500 to $4,000. We were getting paid pretty regular, too."[31]

Unfortunately, Leonard would not have the opportunity to make his franchise work. And, in fact, the team put him in such a financial hole that he was forced to unretire from boxing and return to the ring in order to secure his own financial future. What started with hope and optimism ended with a bloody goalie fighting to finish the final game, an aging boxer forcing himself back into the ring, and a quiet, dark Quakers locker room as the National Hockey League left town for the foreseeable future. As *Toronto Globe* columnist M.J. Rodden wrote at the end of the fateful season, "No one will miss those hopeless tail-enders."[32]

# 4

# The Comets

*Tri-State Hockey League (T-SHL), 1932–33*

Over a period of just four months in 1932–33, the Philadelphia Comets of the Tri-State League would both appear and disappear, as they became the second short-lived hockey club to share the Philadelphia Arena ice with the Arrows in three seasons. The forerunner to the Eastern Amateur League, the T-SHL operated for just one season, with only four member clubs: the Comets, the Atlantic City Seagulls, the Baltimore Orioles, and the Hershey Chocolate B'ars.

The Orioles had the distinction of being the team of minor leaguer Jack Riley, who would go on to play in the Eastern League, American League, and become the Pittsburgh Penguins' first General Manager. The B'ars were created by Milton Hershey, head of the famous chocolate company, who established the Hershey Hockey Club—the same organization that now operates the AHL's Hershey Bears. While the teams also played some exhibition games against clubs in the New York Amateur League, each team in this tiny circuit was scheduled to play an 18-game league season, consisting of six meetings each against the other three clubs. (The original, full-league schedule was published in the *Baltimore Evening Sun* on October 31, 1932, which showed an 18-game slate. However, the teams ended up playing just 16 games each.)[1]

The season began when the Comets traveled to Baltimore on December 11, 1932, to take on the Orioles, a team that had hefty

**The Philadelphia Comets, T-SHL, 1932–33**

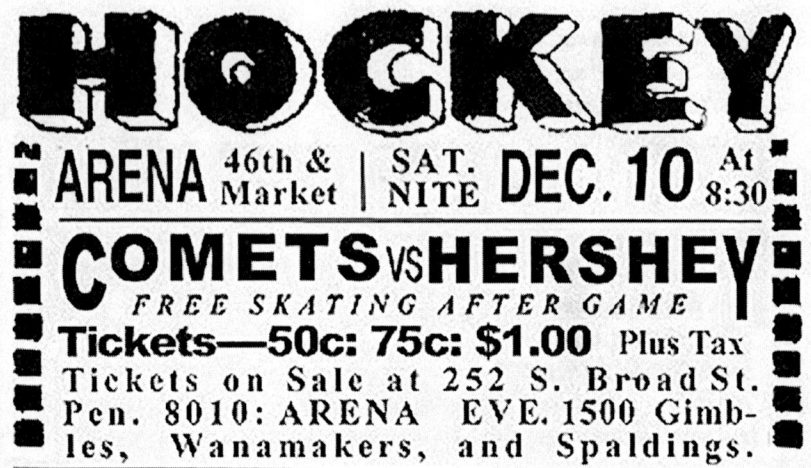

An advertisement in the *Philadelphia Inquirer* for the Comets of the Tri-State League during their single, dismal season.

expectations placed upon them by the Baltimore media. The starting lineup for the Comets saw Bob Van Wickle in goal, Sam Whittingham at left defense, Jim Walsh at right defense, Vern Buckles at center, Gordon Brickman at left wing, and "Frenchy" Mathieu at right wing. Brickman, a speedy forward who had previously been with the Hershey organization, had high expectations, while Van Wickle was supposed to be one of the top goaltenders in the new league.

The Orioles, however, did not disappoint, controlling the entire game and defeating the Comets, 5–0, in front of an opening night crowd of 2,500 fans, including Baltimore Mayor Howard Jackson. Baltimore showed "superior skating, passing, and general teamwork," according to the *Baltimore Sun*, scoring one goal in the first period and two each in the second and third. The Orioles would have had one more, if not for a second period goal disallowed by the officials for being kicked into the net. Despite not being able to put a puck past Baltimore goalie Harwood, the Baltimore media specifically called out Brickman, Mathieu and Buckles for their stellar play, showing potential for a young Comets team. Van Wickle, despite not getting much help on defense, was strong as well, stopping 38 shots.[2]

A few nights later, the Comets travelled to the New Jersey Shore to battle the Atlantic City Sea Gulls, who were already fighting with the Orioles for first place in the new league. With a potential win able to vault them to the top of the young season, the Gulls came out flying at the Atlantic City Auditorium, scoring four goals in the first period

## 4. The Comets

The Philadelphia Comets of the 1932–33 T-SHL season. In the picture are Captain Roger Buntin, Jim Walsh, Bob Van Wickle, Sam Whittingham, Frank Lea, Nate Levine, Frenchie Mathieu, Gordon Brickman, Ed Phillips, George Thornton, Leighton McIllvaine, and Vern Buckles, and Tom Griffiths.

and one in the second en route to a devastating 11–0 victory over the Comets, who still had yet to even score a goal in the three-game season. Van Wickle had one of the worst games that he would have in the campaign, allowing all eleven goals on 34 shots, a .676 save percentage.[3] (The papers refer loosely to the Comets being badly shut out by Hershey in the second game of the season, but the game summary seems to have been lost to history.)

Over the week break between their loss in Atlantic City and their next home contest against Baltimore on December 29, the Comets adjusted their roster and sent word that they were gearing up and improving their weak squad. "It is reported that the 'weak Quaker City sister' has increased its offensive strength," wrote the *Harrisburg Telegraph*, who covered Hershey.[4] The Comets "may turn out to be real, dangerously whizzing Comets after all," wrote the *Lebanon Daily News*, "If reports about the new strength carry any foundation of truth."[5]

Despite a healthier presence on the ice and a bona fide effort, the Comets still came out to a slow start, falling behind, 2–0, to their Maryland rivals. But, with less than one minute remaining in the second period, Jimmy Walsh took a pass from Roger Buntin and fired a puck past Baltimore goaltender Haynes for the franchise's first ever score. And halfway through the third period, Buckles took a pass from Mathieu and tied the game at two, giving hope to the enthusiastic home crowd in Philadelphia. The Comets pressed hard for the remainder of the game, but it was not meant to be. With just under three minutes left, Baltimore put the puck past Van Wickle and held on for a 3–2 win that, despite being another tally in the loss column, was the strongest outing of the season and reason for optimism throughout the city.

"It was by far the most exciting amateur game waged on the West Philadelphia rink this season," wrote the *Philadelphia Inquirer*, "And it was particularly fitting that the largest crowd to turn out for a Tri-State battle in this city was on hand for the activities."[6]

Immediately, the local papers began hyping the upcoming battle between Philadelphia and Hershey, to take place on New Year's Eve in Chocolatetown. "The Hershey club will be more than usually anxious of taking into camp the last-place Philadelphia Comets," wrote the *Lebanon Daily News*. The match was all the more important because both Brickman, the Comets' star, and Whittingham, the Comets' antagonist, were former Hershey stars. "Brickman ... was probably the fastest skater ever seen on the Hershey ice," the paper continued. "Whittingham ... is a big, clever defense who knows the body-checking tricks from Alpha to Omega."[7]

When game time came, it was clear the Comets showed up to play for the second game in a row. The teams battled back and forth, trading goals, leading to a 3–3 tie at the end of regulation. When the game went to an overtime period (which was not sudden death), the Comets ran out of gas, unable to keep up, while Hershey potted two goals for the 5–3 overtime victory.

Heading into the New Year with renewed optimism after two strong games, the Comets firmly believed they were on the rise and ready to challenge the rest of the league. Unfortunately, their three competitors thought otherwise, as the Comets descended even further, losing games by scores that were simply embarrassing. An 8–2 loss to Atlantic City on January 5, 1933, was described by the *Inquirer* as "a terrific battle," until the Sea Gulls spent the last 12 minutes of the game firing pucks past Van Wickle one by one. "With no warning whatsoever, the Comets' defense crumbled before the heavy artillery of the Atlantic City batteries." Fans were hoarse from cheering their team on, hopeful through the first 45 minutes that a tie could be had, before the six third-period goals put the Comets away.[8]

The Comets continued their losing ways, arriving to a January 19 away game against Hershey still having yet to win a game. When the

## 4. The Comets

contest started off as badly as the rest of the season, tensions mounted and Philadelphia's frustrations boiled over. The *Harrisburg Sunday Courier* perhaps said it best: "Reviving memories of the old bar room days, when men were men and frequently carried black eyes, the Hershey B'ars and the Philadelphia Comets forgot about hockey late in their Tri-State League game at the Hershey Ice Palace last night and staged a free-for-all that resulted in the maximum of excitement and considerable blood letting."[9]

With two minutes left in the game and the B'ars up 5–0, Whittingham and Hershey forward Dupuy got into a shoving match in front of the Comets net. Van Wickle then landed a punch on Dupuy's nose, causing the benches to empty.

"Spares from both teams leaped over the barrier and joined the battling contingents," the paper continued, "With sticks drumming rat-a-tat on unprotected skulls and fists and skates flying at a great rate. In the meantime, some thoughtful individual started hunting a bucket in which to gather up the blood as the battle waged hotter and hotter. The referees united in an effort to separate the combatants and Captain Lloyd Blinco of Hershey, the one cool head among the players, and several spectators aided in cooling things, until hostilities ceased. Well, sir, some of the boys were a sight, what with scratched faces, puffed noses and eyes that will not be normal for some days. It was just nice, clean fun."[10]

The loss pushed the Comets into a deeper hole, as by January 25 they sat, still winless, twenty points behind the first-place Sea Gulls. Their troubles got worse as they suffered losses at the hands of the B'ars and the Sea Gulls, heading into February still looking for their first victory of the season. In a February 9 matchup against Baltimore, the Comets disappointed yet again, falling by a 4–1 score, for their twelfth loss in twelve games. "Although the Orioles won by a margin of only three goals," wrote C. Edward Sparrow of the *Baltimore Sun*, "The visitors were so hopelessly outclassed that they made the Orioles look bad. It was one of those athletic contests in which a superior team does not show to advantage because of the poor play of its opponent."[11]

The paper made sure to compliment Van Wickle on his stellar play in goal, along with Brickman for his speed and finesse—though with little support from the rest of the lineup, the two were unable to push the Comets to any sort of advantage. The next night, in a rematch, the Comets looked even worse, giving up 11 goals in perhaps their worst loss of the season.

Heading into a February 16 matchup against their rivals from Hershey, the newspapers again touted what they hoped would be a fierce battle, or at least a continuation of the bench-clearing brawl that had recently transpired. "With Philadelphia anxious to win at least one game and Hershey ready to shift its lineup for its remaining games," wrote the *Harrisburg Telegraph*, "This game should produce the same brilliant hockey which attracted record-breaking crowds to the Palace all season."[12]

But, as one could expect, the Comets failed to produce any semblance of competition, getting routed 15–2 and giving up five goals to Hershey star Sam Foxworthy. A few nights later, the Comets were shut out 2–0 by the Orioles, who picked up their fourth successive shutout in their bid to catch the first place Sea Gulls. "Philadelphia gave the Birds a stiffer fight than expected," wrote the *Inquirer*, but "there was a big let-down by the Quakers in the second session ... due mainly to the fact that the visitors had only four spares on the bench." Van Wickle kept the Comets in the game, making 27 saves and perhaps being the only player on the Philadelphia side to show up.[13]

On February 25, the Comets traveled to Hershey for the final game of the season. With nothing left to gain in an otherwise horrific season, the Comets fell, 9–3, to their upstate rivals, launching Hershey and the remaining two teams into a playoff sponsored by the owners of the Hershey Corporation. The Comets, having gone 0–16, would not be invited to compete.

In their first season, the Comets failed to win a game, scored just 25 goals, and allowed an astounding 119—an average of 7.44 per game. Atlantic City won the league championship with a 15–1–2 record, while Baltimore posted a 12–5–1 record to end up in second place. Hershey had just six wins, putting them in third place. After an 8–2 exhibition game loss to the St. Nicholas hockey club of New York in March, the Comets officially ended their first and only season.

Not surprisingly, the woeful Comets drew scant attention from either the local press or the city's hockey fans who were then quite smitten with the well-established and increasingly-popular first-place CAHL Arrows. Even with bargain basement Depression-era ticket prices of 50 cents to one dollar, the winless Comets could not lure more than a handful of Philadelphia's always-demanding sports fans to see them play. (Arrows tickets at this time went for as low as 55 cents, with some premium seats going for as high as $2.00.) Thus, as did the NHL's Quakers two years earlier, the Comets quietly folded at season's end to become just another obscure footnote in Philadelphia hockey history.

With the Comets gone, the Orioles, B'ars, and Seagulls joined up with four New York senior amateur clubs—the Bronx Tigers, the New York Athletic Club, St. Nicks Hockey Club, and Crescent-Hamilton

Athletic Club—to form the new, seven-team Eastern Amateur League, a league that would operate for four decades.

Some of the Comets' players went on to semi-successful amateur or minor professional hockey careers. Vern Buckles, after being traded to the Orioles midseason, continued through the EAHL until 1939. Doug Bolte, a spare who played a few minutes per night, joined the Metropolitan Amateur League. Van Wickle joined the Penn Athletic Club. However, most of the players were lost to history, with no trace of their future paths.

To this day, little is known about the T-SHL, its formation and its overall operation. Very few newspapers from the era covered their games. Fans, looking for a more competitive pastime, spent their precious, Depression-depleted leisure dollars elsewhere. And while the EAHL, along with the subsequent Eastern League and North American League, would have multiple franchises representing Philadelphia, the Comets and the T-SHL would become just a blip in the hockey world's radar.

# 5

# The Ramblers

*Canadian-American Hockey League (CAHL), 1935–36*
*International-American Hockey League (I-AHL), 1936–40*
*American Hockey League (AHL), 1940–41*

When the New York Rangers announced they were placing their farm team in Philadelphia to replace the Arrows in the CAHL for the 1935–36 season, Philadelphia fans were both sad at losing their inaugural professional team, but simultaneously ecstatic of what the future would bring. The Rangers were successful, just two years removed from a Stanley Cup championship and having made the playoffs every year since their inception in 1926. Philadelphia would become home to some of the best second-tier players in hockey. The new team would immediately become known as the Ramblers and only one player would return from the previous year's Arrows squad (Goaltender Bert Gardiner, who would go on to play 144 games in the NHL). The Rangers kept Herb Gardiner in charge as the head coach, creating expectations that the team would immediately challenge for the league championship. The team wore the same blue, white, and red colors that adorned the Rangers uniforms. (The Rangers, at the time, always named their minor-league franchises with an "R" and dressed them in the same colors as the NHL squad.)

Gardiner was instrumental in putting together

The Philadelphia Ramblers, AHL, 1935–41.

## 5. The Ramblers

the Ramblers roster with Rangers manager Lester Patrick. In building a 12-man roster, Gardiner took eight former amateur stars and four veterans, creating a balance of youth and experience that he hoped would bring the team to immediate glory. The first trio that he brought to Philadelphia was the star line of the previous year's New York Crescents, who won the Eastern United States amateur championship. Mac and Neil Colville, two brothers who played together at nearly every level of hockey until this point, joined Alec Shibicky as the young, speedy first line for the Ramblers. The second line would comprise of 25-year-old Bobby Kirk, 20-year-old speedster Phil Watson and 31-year-old Danny Cox, one of the most respected players in the Rangers organization. The third line would consist of Sammy McManus and Eddie Wares, along with a future player to be named later by the Rangers. On defense, three players would rotate: Walter "Babe" Pratt, a 19-year-old budding superstar; 23-year-old Larry Molyneaux; and 20-year-old Joe Cooper. In goal would be 22-year-old Bert Gardiner, who played for the Arrows the previous season.

Of these exquisite youngsters, Herb Gardiner was most excited about Pratt. In an interview with the *Inquirer*, he called Pratt "the finest defense prospect I have seen in years. He is only 19 years old, just the right age to be taught the finer points of the game. He has height, reach and sufficient weight to carry him through. He is a neat stick handler, can rush and packs a wicked puck." Pratt was still quite young, but Gardiner hoped his raw talent would raise the Ramblers to a level that others would not be able to provide.[1] (Pratt would go on to a Hall of Fame career with the Rangers, Maple Leafs, and Bruins, earning himself the Hart Trophy in 1944, two Stanley Cups, and eventually being named to *The Hockey News'* list of the 100 greatest hockey players of all time. Philadelphia was privy to the earliest part of Pratt's professional career—a gem of the city's hockey history.)

On the other end of the age spectrum, Gardiner named Danny Cox the team's captain. Playing professional hockey since 1926, Cox had a wide-ranging NHL career with the Maple Leafs, Ottawa Senators, Detroit Falcons, Montreal Maroons and New York Rangers. Although Gardiner and Patrick were not certain whether he could continue to contribute to the National League roster, they were certain that he would provide an immense benefit to a young Ramblers team.

Moreover, Gardiner's training schedule kept the players in peak condition year-round. For six weeks before the season started, the coach bunked his 12 players in Winnipeg while they pushed to get in shape for the season. He also scheduled exhibition games against NHL squads to get the highest-end preparation that he could for his roster. In one of these games, the Ramblers defeated the defending Stanley Cup champion Montreal Maroons, 3–1, giving great confidence to Philadelphia that their team was among the best in the CAHL.

As the season neared, the fans were exuberant at the possibility of watching a team specializing in a fast pace of play. "Speed, and plenty of it, will be dished out to the hockey fans," wrote the *Inquirer* a few days before opening night. "This was indicated yesterday when the team went through its practice session at the Arena, the second workout it has had on local ice." The practice was open to the public, and a surprisingly large handful of fans attended to get a glimpse of the new team representing their city. The fans also gawked at the impressive display of talent by the team's first line of Shibicky and the Colville brothers, along with the flexibility and vision of Bert Gardiner in net. Expectations were set even a notch higher, creating a championship-or-bust mentality. "The work of this line will keep the local team in the running for the Canadian-American League championship if the boys function as well in the game as they did during the workout yesterday," wrote the *Inquirer*. "And, there isn't any reason why they shouldn't."[2]

Right out of the gate, the Ramblers did not disappoint. The team instantly rocketed to the top of the league standings. The fans responded accordingly, filling the Arena for most home games. The newspapers constantly describe a Ramblers team that was the fastest and most talented team in the league. "By the very fury of their attack they wear down the opposition," wrote the *Inquirer* in December 1935. "A team may hold them at bay for one period—even two periods, but in that final session sheer power of their offense always cuts through the strongest of defenses."[3]

The expectations might have been sky-high, but the Ramblers met it with a vengeance. The team began the season with a 3–2 win in their home opener in front of 5,500 fans at the Arena. They won seven of their first eight and, by the middle of January 1936, sat atop the league with an 18–5–1 record. However, as the season progressed and the injuries piled up, the team became much more inconsistent and the fan support slowly dwindled. A three-game losing streak in January and another three-game losing streak in March weakened their first-place position. Nonetheless, they were so far ahead in the standings that even a five-game losing streak to end the season kept them above their competition.

By the end of the season, the Ramblers had secured the regular season championship with a 27–18–3 record. The team performed admirably throughout the regular season, both as a team and individually. Cox led the league with 24 regular season goals, while Kirk led the league with 51 points. The two made up a dynamic duo, often propelling the Ramblers to victory. Their spot in the standings secured them a first-round bye and a berth directly into the league final. When the Providence Reds won their first-round series against the Springfield Indians, it renewed a rivalry that had formed in the Arrows' first season, for the first time being a fight for the Henri Fontaine Cup. The series was a best-of-five. (Before the playoffs, the Ramblers played the EAHL All Stars in an exhibition match in front of 10,000 fans at Madison Square Garden. The Blueshirts defeated the All Stars in an overtime thriller by a 4–3 score.)

The first game, played on April 2, 1936, was a tight battle right from the start in front of over 5,000 fans at the Arena. Just over seven minutes into the game, forward Danny Weir scored unassisted to give the Ramblers the early lead. For the next two-and-a-half periods, the fans witnessed a goalie battle of epic proportions, with Providence goaltender Paddy Byrne and Bert Gardiner trading show-stopping saves while each offense continuously put pressure on the opposing goal. With just under two minutes remaining in regulation time, 23-year-old "Toe" Blake (yes, *the* Toe Blake, eventual Montreal Canadiens legend) flashed up the right side and curled behind the Ramblers' net. He poked the puck into the slot, where Reds forwards Jackie Keating and "Red" Conn both swung at and missed the puck. On his second try, Conn ripped a shot past Gardiner, tying the game with 1:38 remaining in the third period.

The teams went to a sudden-death extra period and through the first 20-minute frame, no one was able to solve the riddle of the two goaltenders. But 14 minutes into the second extra session, Joe Cooper, the Ramblers' top defenseman, took a pass on the right side of the Providence zone and ripped a shot past Byrne to clinch the first game of the series for the Ramblers with a 2–1 final score. The fans erupted, creating bedlam in the Arena as they celebrated the team's first of what would hopefully be three wins in the final.

A couple nights later, on April 4, the teams returned to the Arena for the second game of the series. In another close, hard-fought game, the goalies again shined, this time with Providence scoring the opening goal early. With 4,500 rowdy Philadelphia fans cheering on their hockey team, the Ramblers fought back, but were stopped by Byrne every step of the way. "Seldom, if ever," wrote the *Inquirer*, "Has there been a greater exhibition of goaltending at the Arena than the beefy Byrne gave last night." Even a first-period goalmouth scrum in which Byrne suffered a laceration between his eyes could not slow him down. The Reds called a twenty-minute timeout while Byrne was stitched up, and then returned to action as strong as he was before.

The Reds doubled their lead with a late second-period power play goal. Byrne continued to stymie the Ramblers offense, giving up just one third-period goal, to forward Eddie Wares, which brought the Ramblers within one. But Byrne shut the door completely on his opponents for the rest of the game as the Reds took Game 2 by a 2–1 score, tying the series before going back home for the next two contests.

Game 3 took place the following evening and the story didn't change. The teams again fought through one of the closest games of the season, with no team willing to give an inch. The game was much rougher than the previous two, with ten penalties being called by the officials between the two squads. After a scoreless first period, Providence finally opened the scoring halfway through the second period. The goal seemed to spark the Ramblers, because as soon as play resumed they took control of the rest of the game. Just two minutes into the third period, Cox tied the game for Philadelphia and the team continued to threaten on each subsequent shift. They finally connected again when, with just over five minutes remaining in regulation, forward Charlie Mason made a phenomenal individual effort to put the puck past Byrne, giving the Ramblers a 2–1 lead. The team held on and Gardiner stopped every remaining Providence attempt, giving the Ramblers a win with the third consecutive 2–1 game in the series. The Ramblers needed just one more win to clinch the city's first hockey championship.

On Sunday, April 7, the teams met in Rhode Island for Game 4, the Reds needing a win to stay alive. Another rough tilt ensued, with the Ramblers being shorthanded for four minutes at one point in the first period. But Gardiner stood strong and the team played textbook hockey to keep the puck out of their own net. The Reds found themselves down a man quite often in the second period, but similarly, the Ramblers could not get the puck past Byrne. In the third period, with the Ramblers on another power play, Bert Connelly, who scored just three goals the entire season, streaked up the ice toward the net, where he received a pass from Colville. Connelly lifted the puck toward Byrne's glove hand and Byrne, outstretched, couldn't get his hand on it. The puck hit the back of the net and gave the Ramblers a 1–0 lead just four minutes into the final frame.

The remainder of the period consisted of end-to-end rushes and fantastic goaltending on both sides, the hallmark of the series. The Ramblers did everything they could to keep the puck out of their net, including pulling down every player who had a remote chance to score, much to the chagrin of the Reds and their fans. When the final buzzer sounded, the Ramblers were still ahead, 1–0, and had secured

## 5. The Ramblers

themselves the league championship. League president Arthur Ross presented the Fontaine Cup to captain Danny Cox, while Lester Patrick smiled from the stands, thrilled at the success of his new minor-league club in their first season. (When the Rangers won the Stanley Cup in 1940, four members of their team came from this championship Ramblers squad—Shibicky, Pratt, and both Colville brothers. Twelve of the fifteen players on that Rangers roster also played for the Ramblers at some point in their development.)

At the end of the season, the CAHL merged with the International League, leading to the creation of the International American Hockey League—the I-AHL. The league would consist of eight clubs, with the circuit led by the presidents of the now-former CAHL and IHL and overseen by NHL President Frank Calder. With the new league came new faces, as Gardiner worked to put his team in the best position to defend their championship. These new faces included Murray Patrick and Joe Krol from the New York Rovers of the Eastern League, Clint Smith from the Vancouver Lions of the then–North West Hockey

The Philadelphia Ramblers celebrate their 1936 Frank Fontaine Cup championship as a team in the locker room (courtesy Bruce "Scoop" Cooper).

The 1936–37 Ramblers squad was Philadelphia's first entry into the new International-American Hockey League. (Players, L to R) Charlie Mason, Clint Smith, Bryan Hextall, Bobby Kirk, Vernon Ayres, Lloyd Roubell, Bert Gardiner, Joe Krol, Murray "Muzz" Patrick, Cliff Barton, Hugh Gustafson, Eddie Wares, Larry Molyneaux (courtesy Gardiner-Rhodes Family).

League (later called the Pacific Coast Hockey League), and Hugh Gustafson, who caught Patrick's eye at a Winnipeg training school.

One of the biggest acquisitions, however, was Vancouver Lions right-winger Bryan Hextall (the grandfather of future Flyer Ron Hextall). Born in Saskatchewan, Hextall's family moved to Poplar Point, Manitoba when he was six, where he began his young hockey career, leading to his stint in the NWHL. Though not as tall as his hockey-playing colleagues, Hextall made up for it with tenacity and power. A defenseman turned right-winger, he led the Lions to the league championship in the 1934–35 season, before being approached by Lester Patrick to join the Rangers organization. When he agreed, he was assigned to the Ramblers for one season before joining the NHL club full-time.

In his illustrious NHL career, Hextall would go on to score 362 points in 449 games and ultimately be inducted into the Hockey Hall of Fame in 1969. His style of play was revolutionary for a game that had yet to see the likes of Gordie Howe and Maurice Richard. "There wasn't anyone like Bryan," recalled Rangers teammate Max Labovitch. "He was just this strong and amazing hockey player. I consider him to be the Superman of those 1940s Rangers teams."[4] Playing his "off-wing" (a left-handed shot on the right side), which was unusual for the era, Hextall led the NHL in goals in both the 1939–40 and 1940–41 seasons, and led the league in points in 1941–42. But his first tour of duty was with the Ramblers, where he was bound to shine before launching his Hall of Fame career.

Opening night of the Ramblers' 1936–37 season featured a presentation of the Fontaine Cup and a ceremony attended by the higher-ups of the City of Philadelphia. The regular season went just as well as the inaugural campaign, as the Ramblers again finished in first place with 26 wins and 60 points. The team defeated the Springfield Indians in the second round (after receiving a bye in the first round), but were completely outplayed in the final by the Syracuse Stars, losing three out of four games by a combined score of 14–5 and barely missing out on the newly-created Calder Cup.

Just a month into the new league's inaugural campaign, the membership fell by one when the Buffalo Bisons unexpectedly dropped out. The Bisons had lost their home rink, the Peace Bridge Arena in nearby Fort Erie, Ontario, the previous March when the 5,000-seat, eight-year-old structure's state of the art "Lamella Trussless" roof unexpectedly collapsed as the result of a major snow storm. The club started the 1936–37 season playing out of an arena in Niagara Falls, Ontario, but it soon became clear they wouldn't be able to make a financial go of it in the smaller facility. The makeshift league carried on for the rest of that season (and the next) with just seven clubs.

The Ramblers again reigned supreme in the I-AHL's East in 1938–39 with a 32–17–5 record, while the then-first-year Hershey Bears (who were brought in to take Buffalo's spot and bring the league back up to eight teams) took the regular season's Western Division with a 31–18–5 mark making the league's two Pennsylvania-based clubs also the top two in the new circuit. As might be expected, these two rivals also accounted for half of the members of the league's 1938–39 All-Star squads.[5]

The Ramblers contributed four players to the All-Star team, including a pair of first teamers—Bert Gardiner and left winger Kilby MacDonald, the league's third overall scorer. (The next season MacDonald would be named the NHL's top rookie with the New York Rangers.) Ramblers left wing George Allen—who would go on to an eight-year NHL career with the Rangers, Black Hawks and Canadiens—and his linemate, center Billy Carse (the league's number two scorer behind

Pittsburgh's Don Deacon) rounded out Philadelphia's contingent, as both earned second team All-Star berths. The Bears were represented by a pair of All-Stars with defenseman Jeff Kalbfleisch on the First Team and goalie Alfie Moore backing up Philadelphia's Gardiner on the second team.

The story of the Ramblers in their last few years is much more closely identified by the budding Philadelphia-Hershey rivalry that continued for many years. Not surprisingly, that first Philadelphia-Hershey hockey rivalry was no less intense than it was years later (not even counting the few battles between the T-SHL's Comets and B'ars just a few years earlier). It began less than two weeks into the 1938–39 season when the Ramblers and Bears met for the first time ever. In front of a crowd of 5,000 at the Hershey Sports Arena on November 17, 1938, the Bears emerged victorious, 3–1, on goals by Howie Mackie, Red Hamill and Wally Kilrea, against a single Philadelphia marker by Lude Waring. Two weeks later Hershey journeyed to Philadelphia for the first time and the Ramblers were apparently eager for revenge, as the Bears were still the only team to have beaten the powerful Blueshirts when the chocolate and white stepped on the ice at the Arena for the rematch on November 30. The Ramblers' earlier loss in Hershey was the only blemish on their league-leading 8–1–0 record.

While Hershey goalie Alfie Moore held Philadelphia to just one goal in that first match, the Ramblers treated their home ice crowd of 5,500 to six against the veteran Bears netminder to bring the Blueshirts' total to a remarkable 60 goals in just ten games. Unfortunately for the Rambler faithful, however, Hershey's marksmen solved Bert Gardiner an incredible nine times on the evening with Wally Kilrea, Deed Klein, Windy Steele and Jerry Shannon each scoring twice, while Terry Reardon collected a single unassisted marker.

The Bears and Ramblers met again on January 12, 1939, when the Blueshirts invaded Hershey for just the second time. As had been the case with the first two contests, it was again a meeting between two league powerhouses with the Ramblers atop the Eastern Division and the Bears trailing the Cleveland Barons by two points in the Western Division. This time a standing-room only crowd of over 7,500 (including some 600 Rambler faithful who had made the journey in a chartered 12-car Reading Railroad train) saw Alfie Moore shut down the Ramblers by holding the league's highest-scoring team to just a single goal by Babe Tapin while Hershey's Earle Roche, Windy Steele, Deed Klein, Red Hamill and Orville Roulston each put the puck past Bert Gardiner who, in just three games, had already been solved by the Bears an incredible 17 times.[6]

## 5. The Ramblers

**The Hershey Arena was home to many brutal Philadelphia-Hershey hockey games, in a minor-league rivalry that continued through the turn of the century (courtesy Bruce "Scoop" Cooper).**

Hershey's dominance over its neighbor to the east finally ended on February 8, however, when a then-record crowd of 6,620 in the Arena saw them defeat the Bears, 4–1, in a fight-filled contest. "Thus, the battle of the century came to a close after the most brilliant encounter of the year," wrote Stan Baumgartner in the *Inquirer*. "From the opening faceoff to the final gong, it was one of those rough and tumble, stiff body-checking and shoulder smashing struggles that had the largest crowd that ever saw a hockey game in this city continually sitting on the edge of their seats."[7]

The clubs' final two regular season meetings of 1938–39 came in a much-anticipated, late season home-and-home set which opened in Hershey on March 9 and closed in Philadelphia with a return engagement two nights later. While each team would have three regular season games left with other clubs after this final set, for all intents and purposes this home-and-home match-up would determine which of these two powerful clubs would finish with the best overall record in the league and get home ice in the crucial best-of-five playoff series that Hershey and Philadelphia would open against each other less than two weeks later.

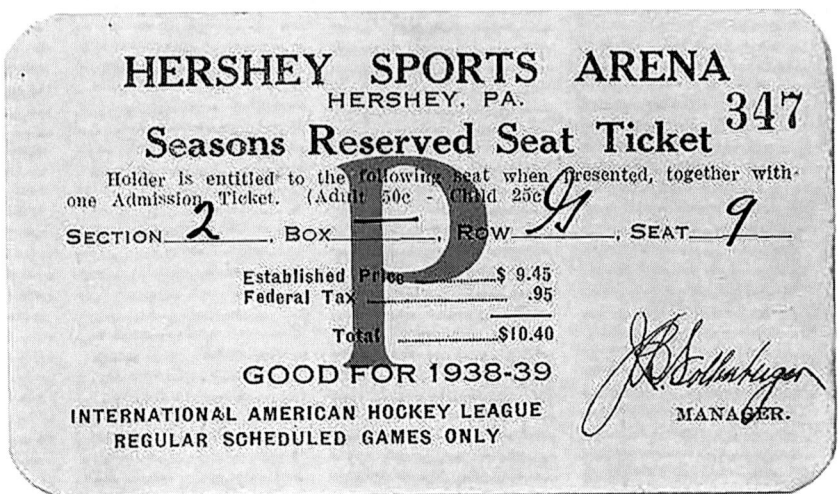

A ticket stub from a Philadelphia Ramblers-Hershey Bears matchup during the 1938–39 I-AHL season.

As in the previous two meetings at Hershey, by game's end the Bears had easily whipped the visiting Blueshirts, 7–3, with the help of a hat trick by Jerry Shannon to pull within two points of the league-leading Ramblers, who had been forced to use former EAHL Hershey Cub netminder Harvey Teno in the contest when Bert Gardiner was felled by the flu. Two nights later, however, Gardiner was back at his post in front of the Rambler twine at the Arena before an emotional, sellout crowd on Saturday night, March 11, for an exhilarating contest won by the Ramblers, 2–1, on a third period goal by Kilby MacDonald. After just six games over five months, an intense rivalry had indeed been born. Over a period of just ten days between March 21 and 30, 1939, however, it would be forged white hot as the two clubs would face each other in the playoffs for the Calder Cup.

Had the Bears not been defeated by the Ramblers, 2–1, in the final meeting of the season on March 11, Hershey would have had home ice for the series with the better overall record. With that close loss just ten days earlier, however, the Bears were forced to play their first ever Calder Cup game in the Ramblers' West Philadelphia lair. The contest belonged to the Ramblers, who were led to victory by rookie Alf Pike, having just been assigned to the team with but two previous games of professional experience to replace veteran George Allen, who had been called up to the Rangers the day before. Pike, who took his spot on Philadelphia's top line next to Billy Carse and Bobby Kirk, responded by netting a hat trick in an impressive 6–3 Ramblers win over the Bears.

The Bears evened the series two nights later at Hershey with a 3–2 victory, defeating substitute goalie Harvey Teno, who had again replaced Bert Gardiner when the Ramblers' All-Star netminder was recalled to the Rangers because of an injury to goaltender Dave Kerr. The largest crowd in Philadelphia hockey history to that date—6,758—packed the Arena for the third game and was treated to a splendid goaltending duel between Gardiner (who was back for just one game) and Alfie Moore, won by the Ramblers, 2–1, on an overtime goal by Cliff Barton 7:14 into sudden death. "In one of the most torrid battles ever witnessed here," wrote the *Harrisburg Sunday Courier*, "Numerous fights broke out between the players, but the officials were lenient and penalties were few and far between."[8]

Bobby Kirk was one of the Ramblers best players, playing parts of four seasons with the team, including the 1935–36 championship campaign (courtesy Gardiner-Rhodes family).

With the Ramblers holding a two-games-to-one edge in the series, the Bears faced elimination, needing a win in Game 4, which would take place back in Hershey on March 28. The Bears were a perfect four-for-four in home meetings against their rivals from Philadelphia and, as in their first playoff meeting at the Arena five days earlier, the Ramblers would have to play without Gardiner—and this time also center Billy Carse as well—who were both back with the New York Rangers to play in their Stanley Cup playoff series against the Boston Bruins.

Thus, for the third time in less than three weeks, the Ramblers took to the ice in Hershey with Harvey Teno in net—and, as was the case five days earlier the spare goaltender played well for the Ramblers, who lost by one goal, 4–3, on a late third period tally by Wally Kilrea (his second of the game) before a sold-out crowd of almost 8,000. With the Bears' fifth victory over the Ramblers in Hershey in five tries, the series was again tied and returned to Philadelphia for a fifth and final game. For the fourth time in three weeks the Ramblers would be facing the Bears without Gardiner. Instead, their fate would be in the hands of the beleaguered Teno, who was 0–3 in his three previous games against Hershey for the Blueshirts.

The rivalry stretched off the ice as well, as the two teams could not agree on when the decisive game should take place. Originally scheduled for Thursday, March 30, the Ramblers wanted it delayed to Sunday, April 2. The dispute required league president Maurice Podoloff to get involved, with each side stating their case. Ultimately, it was decided that the game would take place as originally scheduled.[9]

Teno's fourth try would prove to be the charm, however, as he shut out the Bears, 3–0, in a tight-checking game which, amazingly, had remained a scoreless tie for almost fifty-five minutes. In front of about 6,500 fans at the Arena, Kilby MacDonald finally broke the ice for Philadelphia at 14:40 of the third period, followed by Butch Keeling and Bobby Kirk at 17:02 and 17:32 to earn the Ramblers a berth in the best-of-three Calder Cup final and end Hershey's first I-AHL season on a losing note.

The Ramblers would meet the Cleveland Barons in the final and, despite having lost some players to the Rangers, were considered slight favorites over their Ohio counterparts. The Ramblers would start the series with only 13 players, while Cleveland would have 15, including league-leading scorer Phil Hergesheimer. (Hergesheimer, who was nicknamed "Nip" by his teammates, would eventually play three seasons for the Philadelphia Rockets.) The first two games were in Philadelphia. The Arena crowd of 5,500 were treated to a surprisingly slow affair, but were optimistic that their team would come out on top. Fortune, however, did not seem to go their way. With the Barons up, 1–0, in the middle of the third period, the Ramblers thought they tied the game when center Lloyd Roubell batted the puck into the Cleveland goal. The referee waved the goal off when he said it deflected off MacDonald's skate. When the Barons scored again with under a minute to go, it all but sealed Game 1 for Cleveland. Even a late Ramblers goal with three seconds remaining was all for naught. The fans, unhappy at the Rangers pillaging their players, booed loudly when the public address announcer noted the Rangers win over the Bruins in their playoff game that night.

The Ramblers bounced back in Game 2, putting out a legendary effort in one of the longest hockey games of its era—a 95-minute tilt that only ended when Joe Krol fired a shot into the net in the third extra

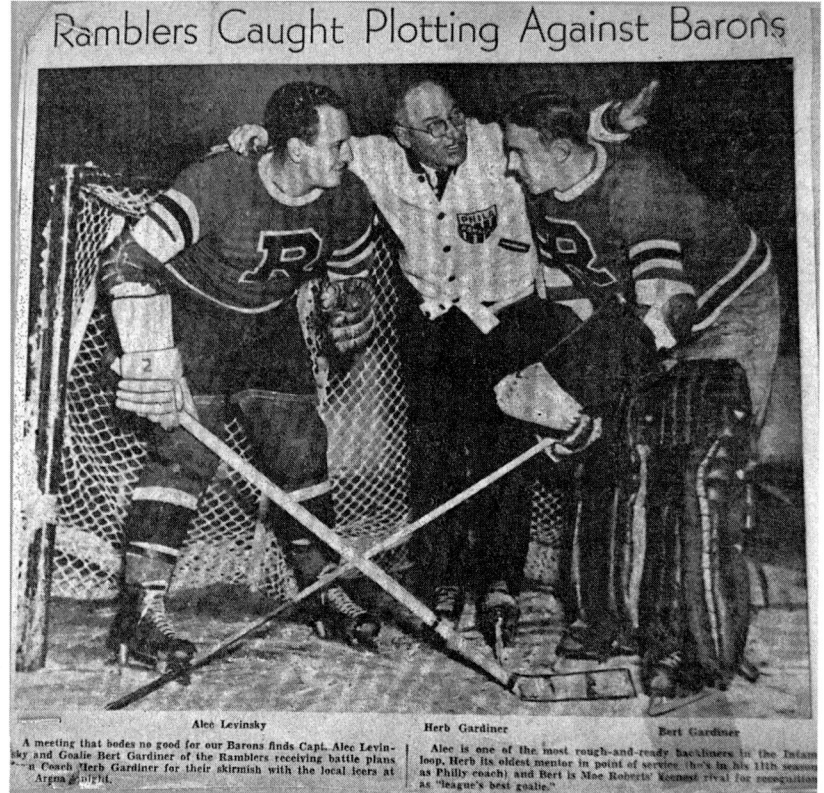

**Coach Herb Gardiner strategizes with forward Alec Levinsky and goaltender Bert Gardiner before their final series against the Cleveland Barons (Special Collections Research Center, Temple University Libraries, Philadelphia, Pennsylvania).**

period to give Philadelphia a 5–4 victory and even the series at one game apiece. A few days later, however, Cleveland played a near-perfect game in front of 11,000 fans, defeating the Blueshirts by a 2–0 score. In the crucial Game 4, with the Ramblers needing a win to send it back to Philadelphia for a decisive final game, the team simply couldn't match Cleveland's speed. In front of 11,421 fans, third-line winger George Patterson ripped a shot past Gardiner (who had returned for the final series) for the only goal of the game. Gardiner stood on his head for nearly the entire game, but the Ramblers could not get a puck into Cleveland's net. The final score was 1–0, winning the championship for Cleveland and ending the Ramblers' season.

In the Fall of 1940, the league changed their name again to one that is much more familiar to the modern fan: the American Hockey

League. In their first AHL season, the Ramblers finished with a mediocre 25–25–6 record, but finished last in the four-team Eastern Division. At that point, the Ramblers roster had already been mostly-swallowed by the Rangers' need for the successful minor-league players, many of whom would go on to have illustrious NHL careers. That was great news for the Rangers organization, but problematic for Philadelphia, who desired to continue seeing a championship-caliber roster.

In the Summer of 1941, with World War II service taking many players from around the hockey world, the Arena management became tired of the constant uncertainty with the roster, knowing they were at the beck and call of the Rangers' major league needs and the war efforts. Their contract with the Arena expiring, the Rangers quickly searched for a new home for their Ramblers, but were unable to find one in a suitable amount of time. So, on September 12, 1941, Lester Patrick announced that the Ramblers would be dismantled and the players sold to other organizations around the league. "As a temporary policy, and during the war years to come," he said in a statement, "the Rangers farm system will embody the New York Rovers, the Regina Rangers and probably one other amateur club in Canada and no further effort will be made to operate a minor league professional club."[10]

Over the course of their six seasons (one in the CAHL, four in the I-AHL and one in the AHL), the Ramblers were a very successful team, winning a championship and finishing as the runner-up two other times, missing the playoffs only in their last two seasons. Many of their players went on to see major league ice time with the Rangers, including Gardiner, who played 202 games for the Ramblers, more than anyone except winger Lude Wareing.[11]

Patrick sold all 14 Ramblers players in less than 72 hours, dispersing them throughout the league to his competitors. In the meantime, the Arena management announced that they would ice their own team in the AHL the following season, owned and crafted by Philadelphia, rather than an NHL squad. And while it sounded great on paper, the Arena seemed unaware of the hefty challenge involved in competing with that level of talent.

# 6

# The Rockets/Falcons

*American Hockey League (AHL), 1941–42*
*Eastern Amateur Hockey League (EAHL), 1942–46*
*American Hockey League, 1946–49*
*Eastern Amateur Hockey League, 1951*

With the Ramblers and the New York Rangers severing their ties, Philadelphia wanted its own entry into the American League. Arena manager Pete Tyrell quickly made the decision in June 1941 to announce the formation of his own franchise in the minor professional league. "It will be necessary for the Arena management to purchase 15 players for the new team," wrote the *Associated Press*. "Work has been started for that purpose."[1]

At the end of July, Tyrell announced that Danny Cox, the popular captain of the Ramblers in the 1930s when they won the championship, would be named head coach of the new team, which had yet to be

The Philadelphia Falcons, EAHL, 1942–46, 1951.

named. Cox had recently coached a Pacific Coast League team in Seattle, but for the first time in his career he would have to start from scratch, the Rangers having taken their farm players and placed them elsewhere. "I believe in attack," Cox said to the media, describing his philosophy in building the roster. "That a strong offense is the best defense—and we must have boys who can carry the disc. The defense will take care of itself."[2]

While Cox worked on picking up players from around the continent, Tyrell hosted a team-naming competition, requisitioning suggestions from the public. After a few weeks, Arena officials agreed on a name sent in by residents Bunny Ramsdell and Bud Burnwood: Rockets. With the identity now in place, Cox continued building up his team. He purchased veteran goalie Alfie Moore from the American Hockey Association, his sixth player pickup (the same Alfie Moore formerly of the AHL's Hershey Bears, who blanked the Ramblers repeatedly throughout the two teams' rivalry). By the time the middle of October arrived, Tyrell had his team's schedule set: 28 games on home ice, along with 28 on the road, stretching from November 1 to March 14, 1942.

But it was clear from the first drop of the puck that the team did not have the manpower to compete without the Rangers farm system. Even luck wasn't on their side. Early in the season, Cox left the team to be beside his sick mother in Canada, missing time before rejoining the young roster at the end of November. By the first week in December, the team held a putrid 4–7 record. At the beginning of December, Tyrell offered the team a $1,000 bonus if they were in first place by the end of the month. The offer, according to the *Courier Post*, "is an attempt to pull the skaters out of a slump which already has cost them four games in a row." The team failed to cash in on the generous offer.[3]

When the team entered February having gone 13 straight games without a win, Cox decided to revise the entire lineup. Already losing some players to the Canadian or American military, Cox shook up the team, benching some regulars and adding in new, younger players in an attempt to give the team a jolt of energy. But when the Rockets finished in last place with a paltry 11–41–4 record (and allowing nearly five goals per game), Tyrell had had enough. Attendance was sluggish and the team showed no prospects of improvement—it was difficult enough to even fill the lineup. The team claimed it only had five players available to return for the 1942–43 season. On September 16, due to the talent level and the fact that, with the war, it was impossible to find replacement players, he announced that the team would fold. "It was a blow to us to have finished in last place," he said, "And we didn't want to struggle through with another cellar club. This city deserves better representation. We can't see how we can ice a strong combination, so we abandoned the idea. There may be hockey players around but we can't locate them."[4]

In the midst of World War II, many leagues struggled and numerous franchises folded. For hockey fans of the late 1930s and 1940s, there were not many options still available to absorb their favorite sport. But one of the leagues that remained respectable throughout the war was the Eastern Amateur Hockey League. Founded in 1933 by Thomas Lockhart, a tenant of Madison Square Garden, the league operated for twenty years before becoming the famous Eastern League that eventually spawned the movie *Slap Shot*.

On October 12, 1942, a quick turnaround after the suspension of the Rockets organization, Pete Tyrell announced that he secured a franchise for Philadelphia in the EAHL: the Falcons. "The Falcons will play at the Arena every Wednesday and Saturday night," said the *Inquirer*.[5]

Just a few days later, the *Associated Press* reported the full story from the league's New York office. With the loss of four teams from the previous year, the Atlantic City franchise, who lost their arena to a new tenant, requested a shift of their operations to Philadelphia. With them came their head coach, Redvers MacKenzie, who would lead the Falcons. After the league agreed to play an interlocking schedule with the New York Metropolitan Amateur Hockey League, the circuit was made up of eight teams: the U.S. Coast Guard Cutters, New York Rovers, Boston Olympics, and Philadelphia Falcons of the EAHL, along with the Brooklyn Arma Torpedos, Sands Point Tigers, Jamaica Hawks, and Manhattan Arrows of the New York League.

With the team getting off to a fast start in their inaugural season, the local residents were high on their new hockey squad. One of the selling points of the roster was their youth. "The pink cheeked youngsters look as though they had just jumped out of the crib," wrote the *Inquirer*'s Stan Baumgartner. "If you are the least bit skeptical, go around to the Arena next Wednesday night and watch the Falcons."

The team was anchored by 17-year-old Saskatoon native Jack O'Hara, a lanky, yet speedy forward who flew around opponents on a nightly basis. "Two years ago if someone had taken O'Hara to Madison Square Garden and introduced him to Art Coulter," Baumgartner wrote, "The big, good natured captain of the Rangers would have reached down, patted O'Hara on the head and asked, 'How old are you little boy?'" O'Hara centered fellow teenagers Johnny Chenier and Andy Theriault, making up a line that was supposed to terrorize opposing defenses. Also a key member of the offense was Tommy Brennan, a Philadelphia native and a player who, 20 years old at the time, would eventually go on to have a cup of coffee in the NHL with the Boston Bruins.⁶

However, the Falcons' success slowed and the team began a steady drop to the bottom of the standings. They finished last of the four EAHL teams, winning 17 of their 46 games and scoring just 167 goals in the process—more than twenty goals fewer than the closest team. Going into their second campaign, the talent did not improve much, but the players understood what Philadelphia wanted in a sports team—grit, passion, and the willingness to sacrifice yourself for the greater good. In a January 1944 game against the Boston Olympics at Boston Arena, the Falcons responded to a 4–1 shellacking with fisticuffs and feistiness.

Freddy Thayer, the big, Boston defenseman, was tripped by Falcons defender Tom Rockey. Thayer, according to the *Boston Globe*, "got up off the ice, chucked his stick halfway down the rink and—fists swinging—almost literally flew at his bigger and heavier opponent." Thayer knocked Rockey to the ice, riding him all the way down, punching repeatedly. The referee and linesman struggled to pull Thayer off of Rockey. "They needed a derrick," wrote the *Globe*, "And none was handy." After a few minutes, Thayer was finally dragged off his victim and escorted to the box. Thayer was given a major penalty for fighting, while Rockey "got two minutes for serving as a human punching bag."⁷

Just the next month, against the same team, MacKenzie pulled his team off the ice for ten minutes in the second period when he felt the Boston timekeeper messed with the clock in order to allow a late

A game program for the Philadelphia Falcons during their tenure in the Eastern Amateur League.

## 6. The Rockets/Falcons

**The Philadelphia Falcons team photograph for the 1942–43 season (courtesy Bruce "Scoop" Cooper).**

goal by the Olympics. Insisting that the clock's hands showed time had expired and that the puck also never crossed the goal line, he refused to allow his team to return to the ice until the issue was fixed. The protest caused timekeeper Anthony Nostargiacomo to barge into the Philadelphia locker room, angry that his integrity was being questioned. Joe Desson, the Falcons tough guy, punched Nostargiacomo in the jaw and was tossed out of the game by the referee. The official threatened MacKenzie with a fine, and even brought in a policeman to settle everyone down. The Olympics won the game, 8–2.[8]

Desson was one of the more intriguing members of the Falcons roster. While a tough guy with notoriety throughout the Eastern League, the man nicknamed "Horse" also had the distinct ability to put points on the board. In March 1944, when he was profiled by the *Inquirer*, he was among the league's scoring leaders with 60 points—albeit while also spending nearly two full games in the penalty box. "There are two schools of thought," wrote the *Inquirer*'s Art Morrow on Desson. "He is a madman with a grudge against all rival ice hockey players, and sane enough, he is nevertheless a wild man who cares more for himself than for his teams." But Morrow, backed up by MacKenzie, claimed that description was erroneous.[9]

"Desson is primarily a team player," the coach said. "It is perhaps true that at times his being in the penalty box has hurt us, but all season he has been in there fighting for the other players—and some of these, just kids, were pretty green at the start. Desson is respected all over the league.... He is a quiet, self-effacing, unusually serious young fellow who just loves to play hockey."

Before the season, Desson had been playing with the highly-talented St. Catherine's Seniors up in his hometown of Ontario, but found himself without a job. After pressing MacKenzie for a job, the coach wanted to understand why he was cut. Desson, very quietly, explained, "They say up here that I'm too rough." The coach hired him in an instant. Desson became a fan favorite and gave the Falcons three full years of service before moving onto the Pacific Coast League (the precursor to the Western League). Over his three seasons, he averaged more than a point per game and found himself with over 300 penalty minutes. Needless to say, he was bound to be loved by Philadelphians.[10] (Desson also played for the Phillies' farm team in Utica, New York, after the 1943–44 hockey season ended.)

Despite the team sitting in the middle of the league standings for most of their second season, Philadelphia was again falling in love with hockey. The team started the season by winning just once in their first eight games, but drew more in attendance than at the same point in their inaugural season. The team showed fight and the game, due to recent rule changes regarding the forward pass, was becoming faster and much more entertaining. The Falcons style of fast hockey, mixed with a punishing, rough style, endeared the team to the fans.

All four EAHL teams were invited to participate in the American Hockey Association (a league that helped arrange amateur playoff tournaments at that time) playoffs, along with the Coast Guard Cutters. (The playoffs were a round robin, not a tournament-style bracket. Teams would play a rotating schedule, and the final standings would determine the winner of the league championship.) The Falcons lost their first three games of the playoff to dive to the bottom of the standings: a 6–1 loss to Baltimore, followed by a 2–1 defeat at the hands of the Boston Olympics, and finally, a 5–3 loss to the New York Rovers on March 18, 1944. But, on March 22, the team turned it around. Scheduled for a double-header against the Brooklyn Crescents, the Falcons came out strong and defeated their opponents in both games by 4–3 and 9–7 scores, in front of 3,500 fans at the Arena. In the second game, the Falcons found themselves trailing, 7–5, before scoring four consecutive goals to clinch their second playoff win.

A few nights later, the Falcons fell to Boston by a 4–2 score, in a contest that required an extra period when the game was still tied at the end of the third period. But the game was noted for its off-ice antics. When a boarding penalty was called against him in the overtime, Desson violently attacked the referee. The police were called to the penalty box to help control him, to little avail. His teammate, Doug Maher, also attacked the same referee after the police held Desson back. The two players tried to climb into the crowd (there was no glass behind the box), but the officers were able to stop them and calm things down, allowing the game to continue.

On March 25, the Falcons secured their third playoff victory by defeating New York, 6–3, in front of 4,000 home fans. A few nights later, against Boston, Falcons winger Armand Lemieux potted the puck into the Boston net with just eleven seconds remaining to break a 2–2 tie and clinch another win for the Falcons. Tied with Boston for second place with one game each remaining, the Falcons needed either two points or a Boston loss in their last matchup—both teams would play the Coast Guard Cutters, who had already clinched the championship. Despite the game being meaningless for the Cutters,

An advertisement in the *Philadelphia Inquirer* for the Falcons of the EAHL in the 1945–46 season.

they completely dominated the Falcons in front of 5,500 fans at the Arena.

The game was rough and tumble from the start, with players trading punches, checks, and insults as well. Desson was given a 10-minute misconduct for roughing the referee, while Frank Brimsek, the future Hall of Fame Bruins goalie, held the Falcons to one goal. (Brimsek played one year in the EAHL, which broke up his service with the NHL's Bruins. Statistics from the era are spotty, but he seems to have played about 27 games with the Coast Guard, winning 19 of them. His nickname was "Mr. Zero," because of the number of shutouts he would regularly post.) After the final buzzer, the score was 7–1 in favor of the Coast Guard Cutters, ending the Falcons' season. But when Baltimore also defeated the Olympics the following night, it clinched a second place finish for the Falcons, a great achievement for a team that fought its way through the season but could never quite reach the peak.

Nonetheless, Philadelphia was buzzing about the Falcons. The team had showed heart and continued to show promise. The fans' confidence was rewarded when the Falcons defeated the Rovers in their 1944–45 home opener by a 7–0 score. "So versatile was the Falcons' attack as it operated with machine-like precision that six of the Birds entered the scoring," wrote Ken Hay in the *Inquirer*. The newspaper also lavished praise on the Falcons' teamwork, claiming they worked together smoothly as a unit. But at the end of the season, the Falcons again finished in third place, unable to make their way to the top of the league standings.

They were again invited to partake in the AHA playoffs. The results were mixed—at one point they came back from a three-goal deficit to tie Washington, 6–6. On March 10, 1945, they beat the Washington Lions, 3–0, in front of nearly 5,500 fans at the Arena. On the 24th, they tied Baltimore, but Boston had already clinched first place in the playoff standings. Second place was still up for grabs, but when the Falcons lost their final game, 5–2, to Boston, in front of a measly 3,500 home fans in Philadelphia, their season ended with them in third place.

Just before the start of the 1945–46 season, the team announced that MacKenzie would no longer continue as the head coach of the team. In his place, the team hired Herb Gardiner, who was familiar to fans as a face of both the Arrows and Ramblers years earlier. The city was fond of him and he was optimistic about his new team's chances. With a superstar in the driver's seat, expectations were sky high for the young Falcons.

With those expectations came passionate, bruising hockey—along with some problematic behavior. In the middle of December 1945, with the team fighting for first place, Desson became involved in a scuffle with Baltimore Clipper Herb Ray as he left the penalty box for a previous five-minute fighting infraction. Ray and Falcon Johnny Chenier, his previous dancing partner, became entrenched in a verbal back and forth, coincidentally in front of where Clippers owner John Carlin was sitting. The owner got involved, forcing Desson to make a beeline, whereupon he punched Carlin in the nose with his left hand. At the next intermission, the police were waiting at the locker room to arrest him. Desson sat in a cell for the remaining two periods, before Gardiner arrived with $101.45 in bail money to bring him home. Desson was also fined $76.45 for his actions.[11]

But, despite the occasional over-the-line behavior of some players like Desson, the Falcons were flying high. The team was winning and fighting with the Boston Olympics for first place in the league. On January 31, 1946, the Arena was filled to its largest crowd of the season, with about 5,500 fans sitting on the edge of their seats to see their hometown team fight the Olympics to a 3–3 tie.[12] And despite the Olympics pulling away in the standings over the last month of the regular season, the Falcons had clinched second place, pushing them into the league's playoffs. On February 21, the league announced the schedule for the upcoming postseason. The Falcons would play 12 games, six at home, in the hopes of winning the EAHL championship. The winner of the playoffs would be invited to the Pacific Coast to play for the national amateur hockey championship. It was fully expected that the Olympics would sweep through the competition after finishing 15 points ahead of the second-place Falcons in the regular season.

The playoffs started ominously for the Falcons, as they fell, 6–3, in their opening matchup with the last-place Washington Lions. After keeping the game scoreless through one period and going up 3–2 after the second period, the Falcons collapsed, allowing four unanswered goals. The following night, the Falcons sleepwalked through an embarrassing, identical 6–3 loss against the Olympics. "Any resemblance between the Philadelphia Falcons and an ice hockey team was purely coincidental," wrote the *Delaware County Daily Times*. The paper called their attack one "that would have had difficulty beating a girls' junior high school team." The loss put the Falcons at the bottom of the playoff standings and in a very deep hole.[13]

But the Falcons suddenly kicked it into gear, defeating the Baltimore Clippers and Olympics in consecutive games before their matchup with the New York Rovers on March 13. Before the game, President Lockhart awarded the team the Hershey Trophy, given to the second-place squad each year. Once the puck dropped, the Falcons came out fast, running up their highest goal-scoring output of the season, putting nine past the Rovers goaltender. The Rovers were up 4–3 at the end of the first period, but the Falcons refused to die, scoring five consecutive goals and holding off the remainder of the New York attack. The 9–4 win put Philadelphia in third place, two points behind first-place Boston.[14]

On March 20, the Falcons dominated the majority of the game against the Lions, winning, 6–2, in front of nearly 5,000 fans at the Arena. The win put them in a tie for second place, still two points behind the Olympics. After falling behind 1–0 in the first period, Philadelphia came back and controlled the rest of the game to hold on for the win. A few nights later, the Falcons again grabbed the bull by the horns, defeating the Baltimore Clippers, 5–1. The following night, in their final home playoff game, they fought to a 2–1 victory over the New York Rovers in front of a record crowd of 6,799 fans at the Arena. But when the Olympics also defeated the Rovers the following night, it left the Falcons two points behind their counterparts in Boston with one game remaining— and it was between the first- and second-place clubs.[15]

The Falcons found themselves in a bit of a bind, though. Because they could only tie the Olympics in the standings at best, the championship, if the Falcons won, would go to the winner of the tiebreaker, which was goals scored. At that point, the Olympics had potted 10 more goals. That meant that to win the league championship, the Falcons would not only have to defeat Boston, but they would need to do so by at least 11 goals.[16]

When the puck dropped, it was clear the Falcons were gunning for their mark. Before a mesmerizing crowd of 9,899 in the famous Boston Garden, the Falcons flew out to an early lead. But each time it appeared the Falcons had a distant shot to do the impossible, the Olympics responded in kind. Boston came back from two separate two-goal deficits, tying the game at 5–5 in the third period on a two-man advantage. Just 22 seconds later, Joe Cuiman stole the puck at center ice, skated in alone on Boston goalie Harvey Bennett, and pushed one past him from ten feet away, giving the Falcons a 6–5 lead.

The last ten minutes of the third period were thrilling, with the Falcons pushing for more goals and the Olympics pushing for a tie. Each time, the defense came out on top. Neither team was able to score again, making the final score 6–5 and leaving the Falcons with a sour taste in their mouths. Each team finished the playoffs with an 8–2–1 record, with Boston besting the Falcons in goals scored 59 to 50. Boston's only two losses were against the Falcons, while the Falcons lost out on the championship due solely to their slow start to the postseason.[17] Nonetheless, Boston was crowned the league champions and left a few days

## 6. The Rockets/Falcons

later for California to meet the champions of the Pacific Coast League. (In a seven-game series against the PCHL's Vancouver Canucks, the Olympics lost in seven games.)

But, with the war ending and players returning from overseas service, Tyrell was optimistic that he could bring his talented Falcons up to the next level and rechristened them the Rockets. On May 6, 1946, he announced that the Arena would host an American League team. In the midst of Leonard Peto's failed attempt to land an NHL squad in Philadelphia (see the introduction to this book and the appendix on the Arena), Tyrell was confident that Philadelphia was ready to support another AHL squad.[18]

However, he was sorely mistaken. Despite player-coach Phil Hergesheimer setting an AHL record for single season goals with 48 and being named a first-team All Star, the team was as hopeless as the NHL's Quakers less than two decades earlier. In 64 games, the team won just five times for a winning percentage of .133—an AHL record that still stands today. The team gave up an astonishing 400 goals to their opponents.

At the end of the season, the Philadelphia Arena announced that it had been sold to Walter H. Annenberg, the publisher of the *Philadelphia Inquirer*. With Tyrell being put in charge yet again to run the day-to-day, Annenberg began work on obtaining approval and funding to build a new arena to house the hockey team and the media conglomerates that he owned. The team also named former Hershey Bears star Wally Kilrea as their new head coach. Ironically enough, Kilrea opened his professional career in 1930 when he suited up for the Philadelphia Quakers in their lone season. Sixteen years later, his career came full circle, as he returned to Philadelphia, this time hoping for better results. Hergesheimer remained on the roster as a player and continued tearing up the league offensively, earning two second-team All Star berths in the 1947–48 and 1948–49 seasons.

While the Rockets improved drastically in their second season, finishing 22–41–5, they still missed the playoffs. The following year the team slumped back toward the bottom of the standings, winning just 15 of their 68 games. With the team struggling to compete, the Arena was forced yet again to shut down their AHL franchise. On March 21, they made the decision official.

"Since our return to the American League for the 1946–47 season, we have been unable to compete on an equal basis with the strong teams now existing in the AHL," Tyrell said. "Therefore, we intend to ask the American Hockey League for a suspension of our franchise until such time as we will be able to complete our planned new building. We hope

PHILADELPHIA ROCKETS 1947—48

**The Philadelphia Rockets of the 1947–48 season.**

to resume our hockey activity as a member of the American Hockey League when we have a seating capacity large enough to enable us to ice a team which will be able to compete on more equal terms with the strong teams now in the league. We have been handicapped for years by limited seating capacity in our present building.... This is a distinct disadvantage to players and makes it difficult for a team to stay in the running."[19]

Tyrell discussed the difficulties of operating a minor league professional team versus an amateur team. The AHL schedule was much less flexible, creating an issue with the Arena's other scheduled events. "At the beginning of the season, when Ice Capades are in the building for two weeks, it is necessary for the hockey team to open its season on the road and play a series of six or seven games before getting acquainted with home ice. In the middle of the season, when Ice Follies are in the Arena for three weeks, the hockey club must again go on the road for a long stretch, playing some 10 or 11 games on the road."[20]

With the Rockets leaving for the second time, Arena manager Pete Tyrell again found himself searching for a hockey team tenant for his building. Over the course of two years, he welcomed the Atlantic City Sea Gulls to the Arena for a few games to showcase their talents in front of the Philadelphia fans. Invigorated by the strong attendance for those games, he decided to apply to a familiar place. In April 1951, the EAHL voted the Philadelphia Falcons and Washington Lions back into the league's membership, bringing EAHL hockey back to Philadelphians. Just a few weeks later, Tyrell announced that Max Kaminsky, former manager of the Rockets, would lead the Falcons from behind the bench. As summer turned to fall, Tyrell announced that the team would train in Niagara Falls, Canada, before opening the season in the States. According to the *Inquirer*, Kaminsky "was enthusiastic about the youngsters already on the Falcons' roster."[21]

As the season started that enthusiasm seemed merited. After winning their home opener a few nights earlier, the Falcons shut out the New York Rovers, 2–0, in their second game, but attendance was weaker than expected, with only 3,000 fans showing up for the matchup. Scoring two power play goals in the first ten minutes of the game, the Falcons played stifling defense for the remaining 50 minutes to hold on for the win. The team was as physical as the fans remembered, with 16 penalties being called throughout the night between the two squads. Twice in the game a team skated with just three men because of an overcrowding of the penalty box.

But it was quickly apparent that the thirst for Falcons hockey had not returned after they left a few years earlier. Fans simply didn't show up to support the team. The low point of the season came on December 16, 1951, when the Johnstown Jets demolished the Falcons, 9–3, in front of a paltry crowd of 1,500 people in Philadelphia. The team was guilty of "poor defense," according to the *Inquirer*, along with "little effective body checking." They were outplayed, outmuscled, and outclassed en route to the loss.[22]

Four days later, on December 20, Tyrell announced that the team would shut down the following weekend, in the middle of the season. "The attendance this season to date has proven that there are not enough Philadelphians interested in hockey to warrant its continuance," said Tyrell, blaming the fans for an issue that was, in essence, caused by the team's lackluster performance.[23] For the second time in four years, a hockey team would be disbanded in Philadelphia.

The Canadian Amateur Hockey Association, which held as members any amateur player hailing from Canada, had a rule that, after December 15, if a player's team disbanded, they were not eligible to return to Canada until the following season. (All but one of the Falcons' players were from Canada. The lone foreigner? Walter Bak of Polish nativity.) With the Falcons having played their last game on December 19, the Association made a ruling that Falcons players would be allowed to return, so long as they did not play another game. With that in mind, to protect his players' interests, the next day Tyrrell announced that the team would shut down immediately, rather than wait until the weekend, as initially planned.[24] The Falcons were in last place when they closed shop, a fitting metaphor for the sad fall of the franchise.

The Falcons ultimately were a successful franchise, at least in their first go-around. Their roster was consistently filled with promising young talent, many of whom saw themselves have successful professional hockey careers. In fact, many players even saw some time in the NHL, including goaltenders Maurice Courteau and Gordie Henry, and forwards Bob Solinger, Tom Brennan, and Hank D'Amore. Nonetheless, the team was the last that would be owned by the Tyrrell-run Arena, as future Philadelphia teams would find other owners and other buildings to house the organizations.

The death of the Falcons ended a hockey monopoly in Philadelphia. The Arena owned numerous hockey teams over the years, but would never again lay claim to their own.* The building was falling apart and it was quickly becoming evident that Philadelphia was lacking a bona fide hockey arena. The era of financial and organizational dominance that the Arena enjoyed would not be seen again until a young group of entrepreneurs applied for an NHL franchise in the 1960s.

---

*Ownership records are quite sparse from the era, but it is believed they owned the Arrows for some time, along with the Rockets and Falcons. It is believed they also owned the Comets, though no ownership records exist from the team.

# 7

# The Ramblers

*Eastern Hockey League (EHL), 1955–64*

With the death of the Rockets and Falcons came a drought of professional hockey in Philadelphia for a few years. The former-Falcons' Eastern Amateur League was struggling and even suspended operations for a year in 1953, hoping to garner more support for their circuit. When they decided to regroup and restart for the 1954–55 season, they rebranded and were reborn as the Eastern Hockey League. At the same time, they began canvassing for new franchises to strengthen the circuit in time for the 1955–56 season. After receiving multiple applications from the region, league president Tom Lockhart announced on September 6 that they had settled on Philadelphia, a city they felt had a rich history of minor-professional hockey.

Announcing the move, the *Associated Press* named George L. Davis, Jr., Don Dragan, Guy Hayden, and Herb Siegel the owners of the franchise, which would be known as the Ramblers. The team would play a schedule of 64 games against the other five teams already in the circuit: Clinton, New York; Johnstown, Pennsylvania; Washington, D.C.; Baltimore, Maryland; and New Haven, Connecticut. The season would open on November 1, giving the organization just under two months to secure their roster. Twenty-eight home games would be played

The Philadelphia Ramblers, EHL, 1955–64.

at The Arena, while the remaining four would be played in Atlantic City's Convention Hall. Ramblers home games, it was announced, would be played on Tuesday and Friday nights at 8:30.[1]

Just a week later, Davis announced that he had picked the man to lead his new club: Edgar "Chirp" Brenchley. He was named coach and general manager and would be in charge of assembling the Ramblers roster. Brenchley had a fascinating hockey history, having been a member of the 1936 British Olympic hockey team that upset Canada and won the country's only gold medal in the sport. Born in Sittingbourne, England, his family moved to Niagara Falls, Ontario when he was quite young, where he learned to play hockey, as most children did at the time. He joined the EAHL in 1934–35 as a member of the Hershey B'ars, before returning to Great Britain the following season to play in the English National League.

The following year, he was one of the lucky young men to be named to Britain's Olympic hockey roster. He played in all seven games of the tournament and scored the game-winning goal against Canada with less than two minutes to go in the game, shocking the hockey world. Just a year later, he would help lead the same team to a silver medal in the World Championships, before returning to North America to again play in the EAHL. By the time he retired from playing in 1954, he was already one of the most well-respected men in the circuit, leading him to become a natural and prime candidate for a head coaching position.

The man was described by one of his teammates as "one of the nicest guys in the world." He wore a full brown suit almost every day and said very little. One *Inquirer* article described him as "a wiry little guy whose vocabulary consists of Hi, Yup, and Nope. You ask Chirp Brenchley the time, and if he replies, 'It's happast six,' you heard a speech."[2]

Brenchley went on a 3,000-mile scouting trip across Canada in search of 20 players to invite to training camp, which would begin in the middle of October. On the 14th, he announced that he had secured the team's first player: goaltender Ivan Walmsley. A veteran of the EAHL and International League, Walmsley was 27 at the time and a highly-sought after goaltender for minor league teams. At 5-foot-10 and 175 pounds, Walmsley had the size (at the time) to anchor a hockey team in goal, and did just that when he led his Johnstown Jets team to the EAHL championship in 1953. Brenchley was quite familiar with Walmsley's work, having been his teammate in the early 1950s in Johnstown before retiring to his newfound coaching career. He told the media that Walmsley would be "the best goaltender in the Eastern League," administering to the young keeper a hefty set of expectations to go along with his new contract.[3]

## 7. The Ramblers 95

Another player recruited to the new Philadelphia club was defenseman Al Fontana, the only American on the opening night roster. Fontana joined the team because, according to him, Brenchley was "the best coach in the league." The final make-up of the first night's lineup was one American and fourteen Canadians. The team opened its schedule at home against the Baltimore Clippers and, despite an inconsistent start to the game, roared through a six-goal third period that led them to a 10–7 victory. Just 3,595 fans showed up to professional hockey's return to Philadelphia, foreshadowing some box office concerns that would stick with the team for its lifetime. But the fans in attendance went wild at the sight of an opening night win, immediately falling for the Ramblers' style of tough, passionate hockey.[4]

Perhaps most importantly, just a few weeks into their inaugural season, the Ramblers picked up center Reggie Meserve from the Washington Lions. Just 21 years old at the time, Meserve had already showed his offensive potential the previous year, his first in the EHL. He would quickly become the face of the Ramblers, averaging over a point per game through his lengthy career with the club. A studious person, he also took night classes at Drexel, on top of holding a full-time job separate from his contract with the team. He even played for a short time with the Toronto Argonauts of the Canadian Football League, showing his all-around athletic capabilities. By the end of his career with the Ramblers, he had played all nine seasons of the club's existence and was the franchise's leader in every major statistical category: 488 games played, 211 goals, 317 assists, 528 points, and 689 penalty minutes.

But the EHL was famously known for much more than its hockey. The league that eventually inspired the movie *Slap Shot* (along with the subsequent North American League), its on-ice brutality and its off-ice antics are what really tell the story of the entire league, let alone the Ramblers. With players making, on average, about $150 per week, they did whatever they could to keep the fans coming back and to keep themselves employed. On November 5, the Ramblers faced the Washington Lions with the Philadelphia squad ultimately coming away with a 6–4 victory. But the story of the game was what happened before and after the whistles. The game was delayed thirty minutes when car troubles forced half of the Ramblers squad to be late to the game. On top of that, referee Frank MacIntosh was forced to hand out a ten-minute misconduct penalty to Washington center Fern Lapointe after he grabbed at the ref in the midst of an argument over a slashing call. Just over ten minutes later, MacIntosh "floored Washington defenseman Rick Albert with a flying tackle" after Albert got into a scrum with the Ramblers' Walt Wingfield.[5]

Later in the season, in a home game against the Clippers, a free-for-all broke out in the midst of the second period. With Rambler Moe Bartoli and Clipper John Brophy in the penalty box for roughing—and most EHL teams at the time sharing a single penalty box—Brophy jumped Bartoli, attempting to choke him with an iron chain that was hanging from the boards. Former NHL executive and Clipper player John Muckler vividly recalled the incident. "I have Broph by one arm trying to drag him out of the box," Muckler said. "The guard has him by the other arm trying to keep him in the box." It took two minutes, eight policemen, all of the on-ice officials and some Ramblers players to pull Brophy off. After being given a game misconduct, Brophy then kicked and pushed one of the policemen, who attempted to arrest him. Team officials eventually talked the policemen into letting Brophy slide, but not before the Ramblers scored multiple goals in the third period and clinched the win by a 7–3 score. "Brophy just went loco that time," said Ramblers center Russ McClenaghan years later.[6]

A few weeks later, Brophy sat at his locker in the Charlotte Coliseum and opened an envelope from Upper Darby, Pennsylvania. "Mr. Brophy," the letter started, "This is to inform you that a group of blood thirsty fans from Philadelphia are planning to mob you this Friday night." Such was the EHL.[7]

The Ramblers first season was mediocre, at best. Finishing in last place with a 23–41–0 record, they showed promise but failed to reach their potential. On top of that, consistently attracting fans to The Arena was an issue. Their largest crowd of the inaugural season was 4,020, at a January 27 match against Washington, in which they lost 4–3. But, unfortunately for the organization, most of the crowds through the season fell well short of that. More often than not, less than 3,000 attended any given Ramblers game.

The bright side of the season was, as expected, Walmsley's play in goal. Playing all 64 games, he single-handedly kept the Ramblers close in most contests. He was one of the best goaltenders in the league and the team was hopeful that he would stick around for a few more seasons—which he did.

On top of that, the team's points lead went to a 21-year-old named Nick "Rocky" Rukavina, who potted 24 goals and 71 points in 63 games, earning him the team's most valuable player award. Rukavina grew up in Kapuskasing, Ontario, a tiny town in Northern Canada of about 5,000 people at the time. After learning to skate on a big trench under the town's railroad tracks, the Canadian of Croatian descent joined the local hockey team and began fine-tuning his craft.

While on holiday to Niagara Falls with two of his friends, their tour guide noticed the hockey jackets that they were wearing. After confirming that they indeed played organized hockey, the guide mentioned he had a friend in town, a hockey coach, who was soon moving to Philadelphia, but in the meantime was looking for players to come to a tryout. Rukavina obliged, whereupon he met Brenchley at the nearby rink. The coach was impressed and had his new player, who was star struck by the idea of playing professional hockey, sign on the spot. Unbeknownst to Rukavina, the signature committed him to play in Philadelphia for the coming year—he immediately went home to quickly pack his bags.

Despite his family not being supportive of his jump to professional hockey, Rukavina moved to Philadelphia, an enormous shift in lifestyle for a man who had never seen a city so large. One of the first things he did upon arrival was have a cheesesteak—"I think I had one every day," he said. Rooming with multiple teammates, Rukavina, standing at 5-foot-4½, needed to get used to the new style of play in the EHL. He wasn't familiar with the overly-rough games, because at home no one was paid to play hockey, so the same passion and aggression didn't exist. But the EHL was filled with players doing anything they could to make a living. He quickly realized that, in order to not be pushed around, he had to play much bigger than his frame. He was described by the *Inquirer* as a player who "tossed his weight around as though he were a giant." After his teammates saw his bulldozer-style of play, running over anything he could, they nicknamed him "Rocky."[8] (No relation to the famed *Rocky* movie, which did not debut until 1976.)

The team's second season was much better on the ice. They finished with a 34–27–3 record, good for second place in the league and the organization's first playoff berth. Attendance improved slightly, but was still a significant issue for the club. Their largest crowd of the 1956–57 season was 4,658 in a February 8 contest against Johnstown, but the average for the season still fell just short of 3,000. Their goal of attracting 100,000 fans to the regular season was left unreached, though they eventually surpassed that number after a few playoff games.[9]

The team made the playoff final and even stretched the Charlotte Clippers to a seventh game. But when the Ramblers took the ice in North Carolina for the deciding game, the Clippers were clearly more prepared, scoring two goals in the first period and five in the third period in front of a raucous crowd of 7,346 fans, clinching the championship with a 7–0 win. The Ramblers were stymied by Charlotte goaltender Les Binkley, a 22-year-old, promising player who went on to become the Pittsburgh Penguins' first ever starting goalie in 1967 (and played five seasons for the young expansion club).

But after the team regressed in the 1957–58 season, finishing

**FREE Half Price TICKETS to the Ramblers ICE HOCKEY Games**

You get one Acme ½ Price ticket with each purchase of $5.00 or more excluding Cigarettes, Milk Products and Fair Trade items. SAVE HALF THE ADMISSION PRICE ON ANY TICKET OF YOUR CHOICE! ACME TICKETS REDEEMABLE TOWARDS THE NEXT 17 RAMBLER HOME GAMES AT THE ARENA BOX OFFICE!

**ALL GAMES PLAYED AT THE ARENA**
46TH & MARKET, PHILA., PA.
PLEASE ASK MANAGER FOR TICKETS

An advertisement in the *Philadelphia Daily News* for the Ramblers of the Eastern League during the 1962–63 season.

30–31–3, in fifth place, and missing the playoffs yet again, Brenchley resigned his position as head coach, allowing Davis to name a replacement. He found it in All-Star right-wing Doug Adam, who was on that championship Charlotte roster in April 1957 and again led the Clippers to a successful 1957–58 campaign. Having negotiated with Davis throughout the 1958 playoffs, the two finally agreed on terms for Adam joining the Ramblers as a player-coach. Adam, who was 34 at the time, immediately left on a scouting trip through Canada, as was the custom at the time, to recruit new talent to the Ramblers' roster.

With the new coach came new off-ice troubles. Rukavina, now a fan favorite and one of the team's top players, went to team management asking for a small raise. When the organization refused, he returned home to Kapuskasing to get a higher-paying job. Rukavina also was not getting along with Adam, who didn't see the star player in quite as positive a light as did Brenchley. Fortunately for the Ramblers, however, Rukavina decided to return after only one season away from Philadelphia.

And although the Ramblers limped their way through the 1958–59 season, finishing in fourth place and losing in the first round to Johnstown, the highlight of their season came in January 1959, when the Soviet Union hockey team came to Philadelphia to play the Ramblers as part of a larger United States tour. The Soviets had played their way through seven previous games, winning five and tying two. Yet, the Ramblers would be the only professional team on the schedule. With international rules in play, preventing the Ramblers from utilizing their overly-rough style to which fans had become accustomed, the team picked a strategy of tight-checking, defensive hockey and stuck with it for the duration of the game.

In front of a crowd of 5,611, one of the largest-ever crowds to see a Ramblers hockey game, the Ramblers pushed the Soviets to a stunning 3–3 tie after a two-goal rally in the last three-and-a-half minutes of the game. The Russians marveled at one player in particular: Walmsley, who stopped an incredible 42 shots, including 32 in the first two frames. "That Walmsley was sensational," said legendary Soviet coach Anatoli Tarasov. "His saves meant the difference in the game." Tarasov also called Walmsley the best goalie they had seen on the tour, and described the game as the roughest of the tour.[10]

But disaster struck for the Ramblers at the end of the 1959–60 season, in which they again failed to progress, losing in the first round of the playoffs for the second consecutive year and failing to attract enough fans to the Arena. On May 27, 1960, the Ramblers filed for bankruptcy in United States District Court. The team listed $29,582 in liabilities against just $6,049 in assets—only five dollars of which, according to Davis, was cash.[11]

Immediately, the owners of the Arena and the owners of the Ice House (in Haddonfield, New Jersey) expressed interests in taking over the team. Haddonfield had been yearning for an EHL franchise since 1956, when the league rebuffed them, claiming it would infringe on the Ramblers' territorial rights.

But this time, with the Ramblers' future unknown, the league agreed to move the struggling Washington Presidents franchise to Haddonfield. Immediately, Pete Tyrrell of the Arena bailed out of the race, announcing he had no interest in competing with a team across the Delaware River.

Enter Ambrose "Bud" Dudley, a known sports businessman in Philadelphia. The athletic director of Villanova in the 1950s, he had just a few months earlier showcased the first ever Liberty Bowl, an annual college football game (which is still played today). He made known his desire to keep the Ramblers in Philadelphia, trekking up to New York to a league meeting to showcase his pitch for taking over the franchise. EHL officials accepted his offer, charging him $7,500 for the pleasure: a $3,500 membership fee to the league and another $4,000 to be held in escrow. Announcing that home games would continue to be played at the Arena, Dudley named Castleman D. Chesley—a TV executive—the team's general manager. Jack Maxwell, the Ice House's publicist, was publicly thrilled at the continuation of the Ramblers franchise. "I'm glad Philadelphia is in," he said. "It will make for a real good competitive setup." (The Jersey Larks, as they would be known, would become defunct after just one EHL season.)[12]

Dudley, despite not being too familiar with the sport, was enthusiastic about his newfangled hockey team. "I am happy to be part of an organization that will keep ice hockey alive in Philadelphia," he said. "We didn't want to see Philadelphia lose a major sport like hockey.... Now all we can hope for is that the fans will come out."[13]

"We hope, at the same time, to make some money," he said the next day. "After all, we're not philanthropists.... We don't profess to know anything about hockey. But we're ready to give this the full promotional treatment."

Dudley was criticized in the press for his previous failed investment in Canadian football. "I've got nothing to say about Canadian football," he said tersely, "Except that I hope to hell hockey comes out better."[14]

The Ramblers had the rights to keep any of the existing players and coaches, but Dudley expressed interest in giving the team roster a facelift. In the end, he kept nine players from the previous year's roster and sent the rest packing. Adam was kept in the player-coach position he previously held, but it was clear the leash would be short.

The 1960–61 season started off terribly, with the team sinking to the bottom of the league standings. But as the calendar turned to 1961, the team went on a hot streak matched just once in its history. "These Ramblers are the best all-around hockey team fielded here in many winters," wrote Ben Callaway in the *Philadelphia Daily News*. "The soft spots have been strengthened, through some smart horse-trading (by Adam) and morale-building which comes from respect of a coach's example on and off the ice." A week later, the team clinched the final playoff berth in the Southern Division and, in the span of just seven days, drew their two largest crowds of the regular season.[15]

Scheduled to match up against the rival Johnstown Jets, their opponents sent some taunts through the press, poking fun at the fact that, other than their second season, the Ramblers had never made it past the first round of the playoffs. As the defending champions, the Jets were keen on keeping that streak alive. Philadelphia fans were nervous, but their nerves were overshadowed by their hatred for their cross-state rivals. The feeling was matched by the players. In fact, Rambler defenseman Gus Gustavsen told the *Inquirer* that if the Ramblers won, "I'm going to buy myself a blazer with a big crest on it that says, 'Philadelphia.' Then I'm going to spend a week in Johnstown, just standing on a street corner where everybody can see me."[16]

The series started ominously, with the Jets routing the Ramblers, 8–0, in the series opener in Johnstown on March 8, in a game that started 42 minutes late due to a snowstorm. Two nights later, at the Arena, the Ramblers offense again sputtered, failing to score a single goal in a 2–0 defeat that left them one game from elimination. Even the papers lost hope, as Bob Fachet of the *Inquirer* showed: "Barring some unexpected sympathy from the Jets, the best-of-five series will come to an end Saturday night."[17] The following night, in Johnstown, the Jets scored the lone goal of the game on a disputed goal that the Ramblers argued only hit the crossbar. After the referee agreed with the goal judge, the goal stood. When the Ramblers failed to score a goal yet again, the Jets ousted them in a three-game sweep in which the Ramblers failed to pot a single goal. After another first-round exit and after failing to agree on terms for a new contract with Dudley, Adam was relieved of his coaching duties shortly after the season ended.

The team again struggled financially, but Dudley blamed that on multiple factors: the winter, which was one of the worst Philadelphia had in many years; the fact that the team was in last place for much of the season, stunting any momentum; and perhaps most important, the ownership group got approved so late, they had no opportunity to do season ticket marketing before the season began. He charged into his second season certain the team would show more success at the box office. He also blamed the now-falling apart Arena. "If we had a decent rink in Philadelphia," he said, "I'd go after a franchise in the American or National Ice Hockey League and give local fans a taste of big-time ice hockey. But we just don't have the facilities."[18]

In October 1961, Obie O'Brien was announced as the team's new head coach. He entered training camp "quite impressed," as he told the *Inquirer*. "They looked eager," he said. "All of them were out on the ice early."[19] But by the end of the regular season, the Ramblers were again just hanging on by a thread, finishing in third place out of four division teams and making the playoffs by just four points (albeit with a 28–38–2 record). Up 2–0 in the first game, in Philadelphia, on March 7, 1962, the Ramblers collapsed, opening the door for their Knoxville

Knights opponents to score the game-winner with just under eight minutes remaining and secure the opening game with a 3–2 win. (The Ramblers were also short Reg Meserve, who was playing for Team USA in the World Championships. He would win a bronze medal.) Two nights later, in Knoxville, the Knights took a 2–0 series lead by outplaying the Ramblers in a 6–1 shellacking.

In the third game of the series, also in Knoxville, the Ramblers held it together and fought hard for most of the game. Yet, they came up just short, losing by a 3–2 score as Knoxville finished the series sweep. The 16-hour bus ride home to Philadelphia gave the team plenty of time to ruminate on another early playoff exit—their second consecutive year in which they were swept in the first round. At the end of the season, O'Brien quit the team after accepting a lucrative offer from Molson's Brewery to work in their Canadian company. "They made me an offer that I couldn't turn down," he said, citing his desire to return to his family, from whom he had been partially away for more than a decade.[20]

In October 1962, one week before the start of training camp, the Ramblers sent McClenaghan to the Long Island Ducks in exchange for the infamous John Brophy. (Brophy famously chased a fan up the concrete steps of the Arena [in full gear], out into the parking lot, and convened a single-man search and destroy mission after the fan poured a beer on his head in the penalty box. After the fan hid quietly underneath a car and Brophy couldn't find him, the defenseman returned to the building and finished the game.) With the team performing adequately and a rush of marketing pushed upon the Philadelphia region, the Ramblers fans responded, filling more seats in the Arena than the previous season. Brophy's on-ice antics likely didn't hurt the effort either. On December 7, when the Ramblers hosted the Ducks in Philadelphia, Brophy and McClenaghan ran into each other and fell to the ice. On his way back to his feet, Brophy gave McClenaghan a heavy shot, pushing his head hard into the ice. The two slashed at each other's legs, before raising their sticks at each other and declaring a stick fight—a regular occurrence in the EHL.

The two traded heavy blows to each other's unprotected heads, much to the horror of the fans in the stands until they were both badly cut and escorted off the ice by a referee making his EHL debut. "I will never forget it for as long as I live," recalled Bob Artese, a Ramblers fan in attendance. "My seats were in Row 3 so you were close to the ice. It was so vicious that nobody wanted to break it up. They must have gotten in five or six shots at each other with the sticks. You could actually hear the sticks hitting each other's heads." Muckler described "blood all over the place," while others mentioned that, by the end of the battle, their sticks were reduced to just shafts—which they also then threw at each other.²¹

After the incident was reported to the league, Lockhart suspended Brophy for between 30 and 60 days and upheld a $50 fine. With the Ramblers down a defenseman and struggling to ice a full team, they pleaded with the league to lift the suspension. A few weeks later, already having missed a good chunk of the season, Brophy wrote a letter to the commissioner, promising good behavior and pleading with the boss to allow him to continue trying to earn a living in the league. After Dudley gave Lockhart a personal guarantee for Brophy's behavior, the defenseman was reinstated on probation. "Any reoccurrence will meet with serious consequences," Lockhart said. In his first game back, Brophy travelled with the team to Long Island to play the same Ducks squad that aided in his suspension. The fans hung a silver halo from the rafters with a sign that said, "Brophy to try for halo. He promises to be a good boy."²²

A few weeks later, on January 25, the Ramblers gave the city of Philadelphia a show. With WFIL-TV in house to broadcast the third period of the game, the team went on a record-shattering tear, scoring 10 goals in the final frame en route to a 14–3 victory over the Johnstown Jets. The team broke many EHL records that night, including: most goals in a game, most goals in a period, largest margin of victory, most assists in one game, most points in one game, fastest two goals in one game (seven seconds), fastest three goals in one game (thirty seconds), most hat tricks in one season, and more. Every Rambler registered at least one point. "I have never seen a team so fired up," Muckler said. "They came out on the ice like they wanted to knock Johnstown right out of the rink."²³

But Philadelphia's patience with Brophy ran out quickly. In the playoffs, Brophy got angry at a referee and shot a puck at him. Just a few weeks into the next season, he speared Clinton player Art Rose and was ejected from the game. The referee described the incident to the *Inquirer*: "Brophy got off his knees, took one step, and rammed the blade into his chest." The next day, Doug Adam called Brophy into his office and informed him that he was being traded to Long Island for cash. The team just wanted him gone.

The 1962–63 season saw similar troubles, as the Ramblers finished again with a losing record, but in a newly-designed Northern division in which four of five teams made the playoffs, the 29–36–3 Philadelphia squad qualified for the postseason. The Ramblers fought hard in the opening game against the Clinton Comets, but the team couldn't push the envelope, losing Game 1 by a 4–3 score. In the series' second game, a home matchup, the Ramblers grossed their highest gate receipt in team playoff history, but still could not rise to the task, losing by a 4–2 score. When the Ramblers lost on March 9 by a 5–2 score in Clinton, New York, it marked the third consecutive year that the team was swept in the first round and their tenth consecutive playoff loss.

After the 1963–64 season, in which the team finished as the league's worst team and missed the playoffs, Dudley told the media that the team turned a profit for the first time since he took over the squad (though a separate media report claimed the team lost $20,000).[24] The team also, in a game against the Knoxville Knights, enjoyed one of the largest crowds in Ramblers history, attracting over 5,000 fans. "The Ramblers," wrote the *Intelligencer Journal* in 1963, "re-established the sport as a prime favorite in the Quaker City after long years of nothing very much."[25] Optimism was high for the Ramblers and EHL hockey, and the city's hockey fans were hopeful that it would create a new golden age for Ramblers hockey.

But in August 1964, out of nowhere, the league announced that they were suspending the Ramblers franchise after the organization failed to place their required money into escrow for the league. "There will be no hockey in Philadelphia this season," said Doug Adam, who had returned before the 1963–64 season as the head coach. The media reported that Dudley had lost $80,000 over the course of his ownership, contributing to the team's inability to meet their financial obligations.[26]

With no other professional organization in the city, Philadelphia again faced the prospect of having no hockey team, something that had only happened for one small period since the early days of the Arrows. Arena president Pete Tyrrell announced that he would make a bid to keep the Ramblers in town. He even went so far as to sign Adam as the coach and general

The Philadelphia Ramblers had a cult following for their decade-long stint at the Philadelphia Arena (courtesy Gardiner-Rhodes Family).

manager of a team that, as of that moment, did not exist.[27] The playing roster was again frozen by the league, as had been done a few years earlier when Dudley took over the team. Immediately, a group from Haddonfield made a bid to bring back their defunct franchise as well. On August 20, Tyrrell announced that he was out of the running for the franchise. "We could have obtained membership if we had been willing to take one or two players from each team and start from scratch," he said, "But I wouldn't take 20 discards because I wouldn't want another Mets in Philadelphia." (The New York Mets famously finished their first Major League Baseball season with a horrific 40–120 record.) Dudley joined the New Jersey group, which was awarded the franchise just three days later (and would be known as the Jersey Devils).[28]

The blame for the Ramblers' death was ultimately placed on attorney Louis Lasch, one of the team's stockholders, by the media. "If Philadelphia doesn't have a hockey team this year," said Leonard Tose, a trucking executive who also served as a team shareholder (and would also go on to own the Philadelphia Eagles from 1969 to 1985), "They can blame it solely on one man."

"He agreed to sell one day, then disagreed the next," said Joe Selm, minority shareholder of the team. "He was the little man who liked to see his name in the paper. The club still owes me $5,000."[29]

The disappearance of the Ramblers was a shame for the fans who fervently supported the league and the team, and for the players who became like a family off the ice. Players still reminisce about old stories and the hijinks in which the team would partake, including the time the players received a tour of actress Grace Kelly's house. (Kelly's sister was married to Ramblers executive George L. Davis and Kelly herself attended many Ramblers games.) When Rukavina took a pillow as a memento and put it in his home, the players perpetually teased him that the pillow was not actually Kelly's, but her dog's.[30]

The true story of the downfall of the Ramblers may never be known, since all who were involved at the executive level are now gone. But what is certain is that the organization holds a dear spot in Philadelphia hockey history. As the last professional hockey team in the city before the birth of the Flyers, the end of the Ramblers signified the end of an era in Philadelphia, the last time professional hockey as a whole would struggle within the city. Just a few years later, hockey would become arguably the preeminent sport in the City of Brotherly Love.

# 8

# The Flyers

*National Hockey League (NHL), 1967–Present*

Expansion was not something that the National Hockey League was wont to accept in the 1960s. Even discussing it seemed absurd to many of the league's owners. "Expansion of the National Hockey League is a distant project, if it ever happens," said NHL President Clarence Campbell on February 17, 1965, just two weeks after multiple media outlets reported that the league was holding a special owners' meeting in which they would determine a plan to double the size of the league. At the time, the NHL consisted of the Original Six: the Chicago Black Hawks, Detroit Red Wings, New York Rangers, Boston Bruins, Toronto Maple Leafs, and Montreal Canadiens. These six had comprised the entire league since 1942, when the Brooklyn Americans closed up shop.

The league had been resistant to expansion, due to an "if it ain't broke, don't fix it" view. Teams were selling to about 95 percent capacity, the league was profitable, and the owners were happy. The problem was that the owners had hit the ceiling of their potential revenue by selling nearly every available ticket. Short of raising prices above what was affordable at the time, there was only one other way to garner revenue: a television contract. But the league lived solely in the Northeast United States and Canada. National networks in the United States were not interested in broadcasting a *Regional* Hockey

The Philadelphia Flyers, NHL, 1967–present.

## 8. The Flyers

League. They wanted a National Hockey League. The media faulted the NHL as well for confining themselves to only certain markets.[1] (As the Flyers began building their organization a few years later, one of the team executives approached Black Hawks owner Bill Wirtz and asked how they handled press releases. "We don't send out releases," Wirtz responded. "We sell out every game, why should we send out releases?" Thus was the general position of the NHL in the 1960s.)

"The National Hockey League makes a mockery of its title by restricting its franchises to six teams, waging a kind of private little tournament of 70 games just to eliminate two teams," wrote columnist Jim Murray of the *Los Angeles Times* at the time, referring to the four-team playoff. "Other big money sports are expanding, but hockey likes it there in the back of the cave. Any businessman will tell you that in a dynamic economy you either grow or perish. Baseball had to be dragged kicking and screaming out of its rut. Football groped its way on the end of a short rope. Hockey just can't sit there in the dark forever, braiding buggy whips."[2]

But the owners were not interested and Campbell pushed back. "The league ... is not actively promoting or encouraging expansion of the number of its members at this time," he said, "But it is prepared to consider each individual application on its own merits."

"Right now, we're a pretty successful operation," he said another time. "When you come right down to it, nobody can match it. We'd only be buying a headache and what for?"

"Increasing the league doesn't increase your revenue five cents per club," he told the press during a news conference in the '60s. "You'd simply have more hockey and all diluted. If you expanded by only two clubs, each NHL team would have to provide six players. You just tell me what the result would be if you took six players off any team in the NHL. Any team! And what the hell do you think it's gonna do to the spectacle? It has to dilute it. These six players at the bottom echelon couldn't sell tickets, they couldn't sell a show, you couldn't put them on the ice by themselves. They are the fillers. You can't schedule Montreal or Toronto at home on Saturday and then on the Coast on Sunday. Who the hell would run the risk? You could get snowed in ... and in order to go to the Coast, Toronto would have to give up three or four of its Canadian television dates and *that's* revenue."[3]

But the NHL had a knight in shining armor: Rangers president Bill Jennings. He was a staunch advocate of expansion, knowing it would, in the long-term, grow the league's footprint, thereby putting more revenue in each owner's pocket. According to David Cruise and Alison Griffiths in *Net Worth: Exploding the Myths of NHL Hockey,* Jennings tried at least seven times between 1962 and 1964 to convince his colleagues of its merits, but each time was knocked down. Traditionalists such as the Maple Leafs' Harold Ballard and Stafford Smythe were vehemently opposed. "Great idea," suggested Smythe sarcastically. "You figure out a way to put the franchise fee in my pocket and I'll go along. But a bunch of guys in San Francisco who have never seen hockey aren't getting any of my players."[4]

The league had numerous reasons why it did not make sense to expand at that time. For one, expansion would cause the league's expenses to drastically increase, but it did not guarantee that revenues would increase the same amount. Travel was one of the biggest expenses at that time and adding teams would further increase this number.

In Major League Baseball, a visiting team travels to one city and stays there for three or four days to play a full series. In the NHL, teams travel for one game at a time—and that does not include any playoff games.

New teams being brought into the league would also suffer from a lack of talent. With dominant players on NHL rosters in the '60s, such as Bobby Hull, Frank Mahovlich and Jean Beliveau, new teams would simply not be able to match up. If six new teams began their NHL lives, they would be starting with players of minor league caliber. This would cause a drastic imbalance of competition in the league that could last more than a decade. Despite that, cities around the country were clamoring for the opportunity to obtain a franchise, knowing the diehard tendencies of hockey fans.

"Hockey never has pretended to be the national sport, except in Canada," said Shirley Povice of the *St. Petersburg Times* in 1966, "But its major league franchises are dearly coveted. There is no fan more incorrigible than the hockey buff. It is in Boston that best proof of this is offered, in the complaints of the Boston Celtics basketball owners. The Celtics have won the last seven NBA pennants yet are consistently out-drawn in their own home town by the Boston Bruins hockey team that hasn't won the NHL title in 25 years."

Even the Celtics' legendary coach, Red Auerbach, could see the difference in popularity between the sports. "The Bruins open the door and the Boston Garden fills up every night they play," said Auerbach. "We keep winning titles and have to hustle and scratch to draw a sellout crowd."[5]

The league turned to television since revenues plateaued. Television had become a huge moneymaker in professional sports by this time. In the sixties, ABC paid Major League Baseball $12.35 million for the rights to broadcast games of the week on Saturday afternoons. CBS paid the National Football League $28 million for the broadcast rights for the 1964 and 1965 seasons—seasons filled with just 14 teams at the time. Even more outrageous was that NBC paid the American Football League—the NFL's biggest competitor—$35 million to broadcast the eight-team league's games for five years.[6]

Bruce Norris, then president of the Detroit Red Wings, agreed. "[Red Wings] games should be shown over one of the big U.S. networks," he said. "The chief obstacle in the way is that down there [the TV networks are] inclined to think of hockey as strictly a Canadian game. We've got to get them thinking differently about it. We've got to change the game's image."[7]

Some NHL owners even held a meeting with numerous television executives and showed them tapes filled with highlights of NHL games. The executives watched the video politely, then advised to call them when the league decided to expand. One TV executive even mentioned that the lesser-known Western League had just as good a shot of getting a national TV deal as the NHL. The NHL owners were crushed. They believed their product was the best in the world, but some television executives didn't even believe they were the best at their own sport. Until that time, Original Six teams were small businesses. The owners were making a nice profit and they didn't want to gamble. They were big fish in a small pond and a lot of them were afraid that by bringing in new people, by expanding, that they would become smaller fish in a larger pond. But if they wanted to grow financially, they had to grow physically.

"The way the by-laws were structured, each team could keep their local television revenues," said former NHL President John Ziegler. "The Canadian teams, along with CBC, had developed a substantial revenue source from their 'local television,' which was basically national—Hockey Night in Canada. That revenue stayed with them. The U.S. teams decided that they should pursue a liked effort in developing a national broadcast—a television presence. In order to do that, it turned out, they needed to expand in the United States. The arrangement became that the Canadian teams would vote for expansion, but they would keep exclusivity for Canada's television; and the American teams could have exclusivity for the television rights for the United States."[8]

On February 14, 1965, Campbell called expansion "a distant project." Just four days later, however, newspapers reported that expansion had been confirmed, and that St. Louis would be granted a franchise, despite no potential owner in sight. (Chicago Black Hawks owners James Norris and William Wirtz owned the St. Louis Arena and wanted to get it off their hands. They traded their votes for expansion in exchange for a franchise in St. Louis, where a potential owner would have to buy the arena from them.) And just three weeks after that, on March 12, 1965, the league announced in a press release that they would add six teams to their circuit. On the original list of cities interested in a franchise, Philadelphia was nowhere to be found. Philadelphia's name did not even arise until June, when they were listed as a city being considered, next to Oakland, Minneapolis, Baltimore, Pittsburgh, Vancouver, Washington, and Houston (Los Angeles and St. Louis having already been approved).

But less than a year later, NHL hockey was again returning to Philadelphia, as the fans soon found out. On February 16, 1966, the Philadelphia *Daily News* posted an announcement in their classifieds section: "Notice is hereby given that Articles of Incorporation have been filed with the Department of State of the Commonwealth of Pennsylvania at Harrisburg, PA," it said. "The name of the corporation is Philadelphia Hockey Club, Inc."[9]

With these words, the Philadelphia Flyers organization was, legally speaking, born. Filed by the law firm Shapiro, Stalberg, Cook, Murphy, and Kalodner, the announcement had been rumored since the previous week. But the Philadelphia group had a long road ahead of them, even though the NHL had just recently made known its intention to expand. It quickly became clear who the big names would be—which bids were in the market to land an NHL squad for their cities.

Just a week earlier, the Associated Press reported on the three-day expansion meetings that were being held by the NHL, to determine which cities would be awarded. Attending these meetings were Art Rooney, the founder of the National Football League's Pittsburgh Steelers and an influential voice in the professional sports world, representing Pittsburgh; Ralph Wilson, the Buffalo Bills' owner, speaking on behalf of Buffalo's expansion bid; Dan Reeves, owner of the Los Angeles Rams, pitching for a team in Los Angeles; Jack Kent Cooke, the Washington Redskins' owner, also pitching to be Los Angeles' representative; and Jerry Wolman, the owner of the Philadelphia Eagles, hoping to squeeze Philadelphia in under the wire. Wolman, as the AP reported, was the minority shareholder of the Philadelphia group applying for a franchise—the newspapers, at this early stage, seemed only aware of Wolman as a member of the bidding group.

The meetings, which took place over three days, consisted of 13 groups from eight cities making bids for the six franchises that were to be awarded by the NHL. The requirements? An arena that could seat a minimum of 12,500 for hockey, $2 million cash (to be paid directly to an Original Six franchise), and the ability to start operations by the Fall of 1967. Teams that felt they could meet these challenges were invited to apply to the league, along with a $10,000 application fee, to convince the Board of Governors that their city should be chosen.¹⁰

In the week leading up to this news, Wolman was his usual, eccentric self. A man who gave a 15-year contract to a losing coach, then doubled down on his staunch belief that it was the correct decision after public outcry, can't be bothered to ponder any sort of negativity or regret. "We need 12,500 seats?" he asked, referring to the NHL's arena requirements, "I'll put up 15,000. Maybe 18." The man who bought the Eagles in 1963 and became the youngest owner in the NFL never answered to anyone but his own ambitions. (Perhaps the best illustration of Wolman's personality is his response to a reporter's question as to why he overpaid for the Eagles franchise: "Because I fucking wanted it," Wolman replied.) That was just his personality. And the hard-nosed Philadelphians loved his tenacity, even if they often disagreed with his on-field decisions.¹¹

The ambitious executive grew up in Shenandoah, Pennsylvania, attending J.W. Cooper High School. He left home in 1951 as a used-car salesman, taking with him his wife, Anne, and a few dollars in his pocket. They made a pact that they would drive until they found a hitchhiker. Wherever he was going, that's where they would move. The first person they came across was going to Washington, D.C. The Wolmans followed suit.

The two lived a frugal life, to say the least, while he tried to make ends meet. Anne would cook meals on a hot plate in a room that cost them six dollars per week. Wolman got a job as a paint store salesman. As he gained experience, he met more and more builders and was enamored with the profession. He figured it was something he could do and eventually decided to enter the real estate development world. "There's nothing like it," Wolman said in a *Philadelphia Inquirer* feature written at the time. "You start with vacant land; you put in the foundations, watch the steel go up. And one night you pass by and see lights in the windows and you know you've created something."¹²

The Jerry Wolman Construction Co. was founded in Silver Spring, Maryland, and it quickly became one of the most successful development companies in the region. Just a few decades later, the man was worth over $35 million. His company had created 25,000 housing units and 4,000,000 square feet of office space, motels, and shopping centers. He built in Washington, D.C., Chicago, and the entire Delaware Valley.

"Nobody makes it by himself," Wolman said. "In my case, the main thing was the help I got from people around me—laborers, foremen, my brother [Manny], bankers, and mortgage companies. Otherwise, the secret is hard work, having God look after you, and a certain amount of luck."[13]

Wolman's work ethic was legendary. He would routinely wake up at five o'clock after not getting to bed before one o'clock in the morning. "Sometimes I work through the night," he explained. "I'm lucky to have plenty of energy. I don't see as much of my family as I'd like, but my wife is tolerant of my hours."

His business acumen was praised by many who worked with him, especially his brother, Manny. "He's got a photographic memory in business," Manny said. "We're always getting into arguments: how many acres at a site, how much steel in a building, how many units in a project. I'll swear he's wrong; then we get out the papers and he's right."[14]

One of his dreams, though, was to own the Eagles. As a young boy, he would hitchhike down from Shenandoah to Philadelphia to see games, and even was a team water boy at one point. As his success with the Eagles grew later in life, he was introduced to a pet project: obtaining and building a major-league hockey team for Philadelphia. He admittedly knew nothing about hockey, claiming he had maybe seen one or two games in his life. But his specialty was construction, and to even merit consideration from the NHL, Philadelphia needed a brand-new arena developed from scratch. Fortunately, that was Wolman's strong suit. And if Wolman knew anyone to get the hockey team established and off the ground running, it was his right-hand man at the Eagles, Ed Snider. (This chapter does not cover anything on-ice, nor does it cover in detail anything past 1967, so as not to infringe on the many publications already available. For more in-depth reading of the Flyers' on-ice history, I recommend *Full Spectrum* and *The Philadelphia Flyers at 50*, both written by Jay Greenberg.)

Ed Snider's parents owned a grocery-store chain that had great success in Washington, D.C. After he graduated from the University of Maryland, Snider became a partner with Edge Ltd, a record company, where he worked for some time. Then Snider, along with brother-in-law Earl Foreman and Wolman, joined the Eagles—Snider acted as the organization's treasurer and vice president and owned a minority stake in the club, running the day-to-day operations so that Wolman could focus on his development company. To do so, Snider moved from Washington to the City of Brotherly Love.

One night, while having a cocktail with a sales manager for Carlton Records in Al and Dick's Bar in New York City, Snider's colleague relayed some information that confused Snider a bit. "Look, I've got an extra ticket to the Garden tonight, the Rangers are playing Montreal," he explained.

"What's that all about?" replied Snider.

"It's a National Hockey League game," his friend said. "Would you like to go with me?"

Snider fell in love with the game immediately. It was the play of Rangers goaltender Gump Worsley that caught Snider's attention. "Maybe it was the fact that he didn't look like an athlete or that he wasn't wearing a mask, I'm not sure," Snider explained. "But I know I was fascinated.... It was, without question, the greatest spectator sport I had ever seen."[15]

But Snider had no idea that the NHL was planning to add six teams to their league or he would have acted immediately. "There was nothing in the Philadelphia papers about the NHL's plans for expansion," said Snider. "As far as the papers here, the NHL didn't even exist."[16]

Ed Snider and Earl Foreman on the Philadelphia Eagles sideline in the 1960s.

Later that year, Snider was in Boston watching the Celtics play the Philadelphia 76ers in an NBA game. When he exited the arena after the game's completion, he saw hundreds of people lined up at the box office. When he asked his friend what the people were waiting for, the friend responded that they were trying to buy tickets for the Boston Bruins. "Are they in the playoffs or something?" Snider asked his friend. "Oh, no, they're in last place," the friend responded. "They put 1,000 tickets on sale on game day. Those are the only tickets you can get."

"The game in New York and that Boston ticket line left an indelible impression," Snider said years later.[17]

In March 1965, when the NHL was preparing to accept applications from around the continent for six additions to the league, Snider's old banking buddy, Bill Putnam, was helping Jack Kent Cooke develop a bid for an NHL squad in Los Angeles to appear by 1967. (Cooke was easily the most eccentric of the new NHL owners. A man who built a brand new, multi-million-dollar arena simply because he didn't like dealing with the Los Angeles Coliseum Commission, he designed his L.A. Forum with ancient Greece and Rome in mind. "People will say that the Forum was one of the finest buildings erected during the twentieth century," he said at the time. "It's man's greatest tribute to athlete's foot.") Putnam became friends with Cooke while working at JP Morgan. Cooke came to Putnam to work on buying out his partner at the Washington Redskins in an attempt to become the majority owner. When that plan failed to come to fruition, Putnam helped Cooke purchase the Los Angeles Lakers. After Cooke informed him of the attempt to land an NHL team, Putnam was intrigued. "I decided sports was more fun than banking," Putnam said.

Putnam informed Snider of his move and the fact that numerous professional hockey teams were for sale to be added to the NHL. Snider, learning this information for the first time, ruminated for a bit and approached Wolman, his partner at the Eagles, asking whether they should apply for an NHL squad and build an arena. When Wolman agreed with the idea, Snider was ecstatic. "With his reputation as a developer and entrepreneur and my ideas, we went forward," Snider remembered. "It became my project."[18]

Snider immediately got in contact with Bill Jennings, who headed the expansion committee. After asking what Philadelphia's chances would be if they applied for a team, Jennings acknowledged that they were one of the largest markets in the United States. However, he could not get over the fact that Philadelphia's history of hockey was, in his opinion, extremely weak. Snider insisted that Philadelphia would be a great town for the sport and that the fans would never turn their back on a major league team once it was placed in the proper building. (Perhaps a reference to the failed Quakers, whose arguably biggest issue was the lack of a sizable and modern hockey arena.) After a lengthy conversation, Snider agreed to apply for the team, along with the $10,000 application fee, on the condition that the bid would remain a secret. (Years later, Snider would marvel at how little research they did before bidding for an NHL team. He once told a friend that, if it would have been in present day, with all the market and economic research and focus groups that now go into major business decisions, he would never have had the courage to take the financial risk. But, fortunately for Philadelphia, Snider and Wolman were young and a bit reckless—often a great combination for entrepreneurial success.)[19]

"We didn't want competition," Snider explained. "There must have been ten groups that had expressed interest in the Eagles when Wolman bought them, driving up the price. I knew Cooke ... already had competition for the L.A. franchise.... Nobody else in Philadelphia seemed to be aware that the NHL was even expanding. That's the way I wanted to keep it."

They went to various banks to secure the funds necessary to buy a new franchise. No one was interested. "What is it, soccer?" one bank executive asked. When they were informed it would be a hockey team, they responded, "Hockey will never go over in Philadelphia." But the group finally found a bank willing to help—the last one they visited. The bank's vice president had played hockey when he was younger and decided to support the ownership group in their bid to land a major league franchise in the City of Brotherly Love.

"I went to [the head of city council] Paul Dortona and he loved the idea. He took me right in to see Mayor Tate," said Snider. "Mayor Tate loved the idea, and he called the city solicitor and the city finance director and right on the spot, he said, 'Let's get the legal work done and figure out the finance work.'" (Wolman had previously had fierce and public legal battles with Tate. In 1965, *Daily News* reporter Lou Scheinfeld broke the story that Tate was negotiating to bring an American Football League team to the city, despite Philadelphia having an exclusive football agreement with the Eagles. In a messy battle with the city's power brokers, Wolman eventually got Tate to back down—a very important public win for him that perhaps gave him the audacity to request strong city support for the hockey team.)[20]

After discussing the idea with the Mayor and the other heads of the city, Snider requested that the mayor call and send a letter to both Clarence Campbell and Bill Jennings to explain what Snider had done and to ensure that Philadelphia was a viable city for expansion. "He did that while I was sitting there," Snider said.

The ownership group was a long shot among every other city applying for a team. In addition, Philadelphia was hardly on the NHL's radar after what happened last time the city was granted entrance into the prestigious league. (See Chapter 3 for more about the Philadelphia Quakers.) The group was adamant, though, and they continued to work towards securing the league's choice. Snider, realizing the amount of work he had with the potential hockey team and that which he currently had with the Eagles, called on Bill Putnam to come back to Philadelphia to work with the hockey team. "He told me that the job with Cooke was not working out the way he thought it would," said Snider. "I told him I had the perfect opportunity for him."[21]

He was named the president of the Philadelphia hockey team. Putnam, together with Jerry Schiff (Snider's brother-in-law), Wolman and

Snider, owned 91 percent of the team (Putnam owned 25 percent, while Schiff, Wolman and Snider each owned 22 percent) and numerous other investors had the other 9 percent. "Snider said neither he nor Wolman will participate actively in the management of the hockey team," said the *United Press International*.[22]

The story of the Flyers' creation is much less about business, finance, or even hockey and more about partners joining up to create a force stopped only by their own relationship. Wolman and Snider were, in the words of the team's first Vice President, Lou Scheinfeld, "fascinating to be around." (Scheinfeld, whose *Daily News* reporting endeared him to Wolman, was hired after the city was awarded the franchise. He became very close with both Snider and Wolman and is still involved in the Philadelphia sports scene to this day.) They balanced each other perfectly. Snider had the wild ideas, while Wolman had the financial backing to make them work. Scheinfeld referred to them as Damon and Pythias, the two characters in the famous Greek legend about friendship. "They were such can-do guys," Scheinfeld said years later, reminiscing about his two late friends. "I mean, Philadelphia had never seen anything like this." Wolman and Snider were a team that took the city by storm. Together, they believed they would create a monopoly in the Philadelphia sports scene.[23]

The job duties were divided as such: Wolman would be in charge of financing and constructing the new sports arena. Snider would make sure the project continued progressing through the city's higher-ups. Putnam would follow up on the team's application and kept in contact with the men atop the National Hockey League.

The group sent a brochure to the NHL advertising Philadelphia as a potential hockey town, according to Jay Greenberg in *Full Spectrum*. "On the cover was a picture of a hockey player in a red and grey uniform, with a yellow Liberty Bell in a circle on the front of the jersey," Greenberg writes. "Entitled 'The NHL in Philadelphia,' it blamed the city's past hockey failures on the poor facilities. The brochure emphasized the area's 5.5 million population and the base of established spectator support for the other major league teams."[24]

But after Wolman and Putnam presented their bid to the league, including the blueprints for their planned arena, Putnam recalls a less-than-excited reaction from the NHL Board of Governors. "I remember Norris pounding his fist on the table and saying, 'Philadelphia is a lousy sports town,'" Putnam said. "But they did seem impressed with the arena proposal. I was hopeful, but I wouldn't say I was optimistic."

Putnam was so sure the bid would fail, he remembers telling his wife on February 9 that when Bill Jennings called, he would once again

## 8. The Flyers

be out of business. But when the phone rang, the voice on the other line simply said, "You're in."[25] Despite the misgivings of the NHL owners, Philadelphia was chosen over Baltimore because the size of their arena was to be larger. Baltimore was named the first alternate, in case one of the six new teams didn't have the $2 million franchise fee. Vancouver was named the second alternate.

Snider believed Philadelphia would love hockey as much as he did. "I just had this belief that if you're a regular guy and know what regular guys like, you can't be wrong," he explained. Within an hour of the announcement that Philadelphia was getting a franchise, the Eagles' receptionist began getting calls from fans interested in buying season tickets for the new hockey team.

As Putnam put together the hockey operations department of Keith Allen as coach and Bud Poile as general manager, Snider assisted on the business side of the organization. (Putnam, having worked on the West Coast and been familiar with the Western Hockey League, knew Poile from his work with the San Francisco Seals and Allen from his work with the Seattle Totems.) In April 1967, after an immense amount of marketing and a media push, it was reported that the team, which had been named the Flyers, had already sold 1,000 season tickets, garnering over $200,000 in revenue.[26] Interestingly enough, the Flyers, knowing the history of the sport in their city, offered the first set of season tickets to Herb Gardiner, the famous coach who had led the Arrows, Ramblers, and Falcons years earlier. As the most well-known hockey man in Philadelphia, Gardiner was honored to accept. "I think this is just great," Gardiner said. "I tried to get a few people to build a rink and bring a team here ... but the deal fell through. I've been hoping somebody could do the job ever since."[27]

After being granted the franchise, the next step was to present the expansion fee of $2 million in cash to the league. It was to be done on one day in June, by every new franchise as their ticket into the NHL. Wolman and Schiff had both withdrawn from the team's bid (more on this later), which left Snider with a 60 percent share of the team and beer executive Joe Scott (who bought into the team) with 15 percent. Putnam, still serving as the team's president, retained his 25 percent share of the team. This left Snider mostly on his own to get the money, which wasn't as simple as he thought.

Snider already had remortgaged his house and borrowed $75,000 from two banks in order to pay Wolman and Schiff for their shares of the team, so he did not have many options remaining to raise the extra money needed for the expansion fee. Half of the $2 million fee was coming from a loan from Fidelity Bank, while Wolman promised to give the other half. When Wolman began having financial problems and backed out, the group found themselves in trouble. "It was seven to ten days before the money was due that Jerry told me he didn't have it," Snider recalled.[28]

Together, Snider and Putnam sold three years of broadcast rights for $350,000 and borrowed $150,000 from friends. They still were $500,000 short and their luck was running out. Banks were rejecting their loan requests and they had already borrowed from all the friends they could find. Saturday, June 3 came, with the money still missing. The check was due in Montreal on Monday. Snider had a call in to Bill Fishman, president of ARA Services. Fishman needed to use his personal stock in the company as collateral for a loan and needed to wait until Monday to get a response from Provident Bank, from whom he requested the money. "I didn't wait," Snider said. "I called [Provident executive] Roger Hillas at home. I got him off his lawn mower. He came to the phone and said he would do it."[29]

(Lou Scheinfeld recalled a story that illustrates Snider's tenacity, his passion, and his desire to always get what he wanted in a 2016 interview with Zach Gelb and Mike Zahn on WHIP radio. When driving down the Schuykill to work one day, Scheinfeld was passed by a speeding Ed Snider in his bright orange Corvette, with license plate "FL1." The two began racing each other to the Spectrum. When they got to the red light at Broad Street and Pattison, Snider floored his car straight, while Scheinfeld turned left, drove over the curb behind the Spectrum, across the pavement, and into his parking spot just seconds before Snider arrived. Flabbergasted, Snider accused him of cheating. "Did you go

The most famous name in Philadelphia hockey, Herb Gardiner was granted the first set of Flyers season tickets by team president Bill Putnam ahead of their opening season (Salvatore C. DiMarco, Special Collections Research Center, Temple University Libraries, Philadelphia, Pennsylvania).

## 8. The Flyers

up on the pavement? You can't do that!" The two got into an argument and didn't speak for two days. Five years later, Scheinfeld was in a pool in Acapulco with Snider, his wife Myrna, and Myrna's sister in a heated football game. "Next touchdown wins," Snider said. Myrna flipped the ball to Ed and swam by Scheinfeld. Snider launched the ball way over everyone's head and right to Myrna, who was standing outside the pool on the opposite side. "We win, game over," Snider said. "Wait a minute, you can't do that, she can't run down the pavement," Scheinfeld says. "Oh, it was okay for you?" Snider replied. The two didn't talk for two weeks.)

The money was set and the due date was upon them. Snider was at the bank, ready to wire the money to Montreal, when the lights in the bank went out. The power was out in a 15,000-square-mile area stretching from New Jersey to Maryland and as far west as Harrisburg, Pennsylvania. Snider was completely stunned and unable to get the money to Clarence Campbell and the NHL owners. The group had all of the major players—save for Snider—in Montreal for the event: Putnam, Scheinfeld, Poile, Allen, and PR man Joe Kadlec.

"Putnam was up there in his hotel room dying," Snider recalled. "He can't get in touch with me or anybody.... I was thinking that after all we'd been through, they were going to give the franchise to somebody else."[30]

Somehow, word got to Bill Jennings about the power outage, so the owners waited, albeit impatiently, for a check from Philadelphia to appear before them. When the power was restored near midday, Snider wired the money through New York and to the Royal Bank of Canada to Scheinfeld and Putnam. As the two began walking across the street with the check, Putnam looked down and dropped his head in fear. The check was made out to the "National Hockey League," which was incorrect— the group was supposed to write the check directly to one of the existing teams. (Newspapers at the time reported the Flyers wrote their check to the Toronto Maple Leafs, but the principals involved all recall writing the check to the New York Rangers.) They went back to their room and called Snider, who responded with a simple, "Oh my God, I'm going to have a heart attack." The bank re-wrote the check, trashed the original, and sent Scheinfeld and Putnam racing across the street into the hotel's conference room. As they walked up to the meeting room, they passed by the smirking team representing the Baltimore bid, who were waiting with their $2 million check, with the full expectation that Philadelphia would not be able to pay up. The duo went into the meeting room where Campbell was waiting with Bill Jennings, expecting an ecstatic, smiling president. "I still remember Clarence Campbell sitting there with this dour look on his face saying, 'Do you have the check?'" Scheinfeld remembers. Putnam handed it over. Campbell looked at it, handed it to Jennings, who looked at it, and then returned it to Campbell. "That will be all," he said, emotionless.[31]

Scheinfeld waited in silence for a moment, before asking, "Do we have the franchise?" Campbell replied, "If the check clears, which we doubt." (It was a cashier's check, guaranteed by the bank—which simply illustrates the lack of confidence the league and the public had in the group's ability to come up with the $2 million in time.) Scheinfeld asked for a receipt or something that confirmed they paid the fee. "That will be all," Campbell repeated. The two turned and exited the room nervously—but not before walking by the Baltimore group and cracking, "Oh, I guess you guys are fucked."

They returned to the hotel room and called Snider. "How did it go?" he asked. "I think okay," Scheinfeld responded.

"What do you mean you think? Did we get the franchise?"

"I think. He didn't say yes, he didn't say no. He said, 'If the check clears.'"

"Did they give you any certificate or anything?"

"They gave us nothing."

"Oh God," Snider concluded, half-joking, "I shouldn't have sent you up there."

When the group returned to the lobby, though, they knew they were in. A group of reporters convened upon them to find out who they were and to get more information about the new NHL franchise that would soon arrive in Philadelphia.[32] (Coincidentally, the Six-Day War in Israel began that day, which pushed the hockey news from the expected page one of the next morning's *Inquirer* to page 38.)

But with all the various balls up in the air, a dark storm was brewing behind the scenes. Starting in 1964, Wolman's construction company began working on a 99-story building in Chicago, the John Hancock Center. The modern structure was to be outfitted with 750 apartments, offices, stores, and restaurants: "a community under one roof," as the *Inquirer* described. The most ambitious project of his career, Wolman was forced to temporarily stop construction in 1966, when a flaw was discovered in the engineering method used to pour the concrete. At that point, the building was over 20 stories high, but the structure was already settling as if it were at full height. While examining the issue, Wolman stopped taking in any revenue, causing a massive credit crunch. (John Hancock Financial had also, at that point, pulled their support, which all but ensured Wolman's financial ruin.) Unable to resolve the problem with his own finances, he was forced into

## 8. The Flyers

bankruptcy and out of the project. Suddenly, his fortune had vaporized. Reports indicated his losses were between $6 million and $11 million on the project, though Wolman later claimed it was closer to $20 million.[33]

Struggling to come up with the cash needed to satisfy his creditors, Wolman sold his shares of the Flyers to Snider, who paid $880,000 to each of Wolman and Schiff for their interests, growing his own share to 60 percent—a majority that would remain for decades. In exchange, Wolman purchased Snider's interest in the Spectrum, leaving Wolman in charge of the building he constructed—essentially, it was a trade of shares.

Despite his financial hardship, all parties continued to deny that it played a factor in the decision. "Jerry Wolman is rearranging his holdings with all of his partners" Snider announced to the press, "And this is just one facet of the arrangement. He intends to stabilize his finances and stop the rumors which are floating around the city. This transaction does not mean Wolman has lost faith in the Flyers or Philadelphia as a hockey city. Jerry just thought it in his best interest to sell his 22 percent, which was really meaningless. His main concern is football." As part of the arrangement, Snider gave Putnam a long-term contract to continue running the organization, so that Snider could focus on his duties with the Eagles and keep an eye on the Flyers in the background.[34]

Wolman and his allies continued to circulate stories to combat rumors of his financial downfall, including that NFL Commissioner Pete Rozelle frowned upon his owners having financial interest in another sport (which was never supported by any evidence). But the larger problem was the public's reaction to the deal. Philadelphia knew very little about this Ed Snider guy and they seemed to have an issue with Wolman, their beloved sports owner, stepping aside. Everyone naturally assumed that Snider was simply a front man for the Flyers, while Wolman pulled the strings from behind. Naturally, this angered the prideful Snider. He insisted publicly that Wolman no longer had any connection with the Flyers, "except as our landlord when we sign a long-term lease to play in his Spectrum."[35]

Nonetheless, Snider spent the summer before the Flyers' opening game on the defense from Wolman, constantly battling media reports and public perception of their roles in the hockey club. There were accusations of cost-cutting in the construction of the arena, which Snider denied. Spectrum president Hal Freeman came out and said that "if we wanted to save money, we could have easily purchased a scoreboard for $20,000. Instead, we'll have an electronic computer which costs a quarter of a million dollars. This should give you some idea if we're pinching."[36] (Ironically, the scoreboard was not actually ready in time for the home opener. Photos of the game show a shell of a scoreboard, which was not yet completed.)

"I've got no worries, none whatsoever, about the Spectrum and the great place it's going to be," Snider said to the *Philadelphia Daily News* on August 29, 1967. "Believe me, if I wasn't so certain of its success, I wouldn't be so completely confident of the success of our hockey team that will be playing there." But, despite his confidence and bravado, Snider failed to convince the newspaper of his argument.

"If he wasn't so darn sure it'll make money," the piece concluded pointedly, "He'd gladly let someone else—like Wolman—pay the bills."[37]

But as opening night neared, rumors again began to fly about Wolman's financial issues. Though Snider forever denied the story, multiple reports suggested that, in order to bail himself out of bankruptcy, Wolman requested control of the Flyers so the team could be handed over to his potential lenders. Snider controlled the hockey club, forcing Wolman into a corner. Wolman pleaded with Snider to relinquish his

The Spectrum began construction 15 months before the Flyers opening night game in October 1967 and was completed just in time (Special Collections Research Center, Temple University Libraries, Philadelphia, Pennsylvania).

## 8. The Flyers

shares so that Wolman would be spared financial ruin. Snider refused. (Wolman, in an autobiography published before his death, claimed that Snider agreed to do so, then reneged at the last minute. This accusation has never been supported by any evidence.) Snider instead offered to get Wolman cash by purchasing his shares of the Eagles for an exorbitantly low price, which infuriated the also-prideful Wolman. The two men, who had been best friends for years (they had, just a few months earlier, opened three new cocktail lounges in Philadelphia in yet another business venture), were suddenly enemies. Snider refused to off-load his hockey team, while Wolman thought he was entitled to Snider's help after so many years of the two supporting each other.

Scheinfeld vividly remembers that timespan and the claim Wolman brought to them that he had an eight-figure loan lined up from a group of Kuwaiti oil tycoons. "Snider and I became worried that this project was going to fail because he was running around the world trying to get money," he recalled. There even was a rumor that the businessmen were planning to flip the Flyers organization to the previously-denied Baltimore group for a quick profit. Snider sat down for a lengthy discussion to see how they could help their friend, but concluded that, not only did they not want to give up the franchise, which they had grown to love, but that they weren't convinced there was even a legitimate loan offer.[38]

The infighting came to a head on October 19, 1967, the day of the Flyers home opener. Enraged that his partner was not doing as he asked, Wolman fired Snider from his position at the Eagles. The move created a brief but ugly legal battle, because since he had a contract, Snider's allies claimed Wolman did not have the legal ability to remove Snider from the organization. Earl Foreman, the executive vice president of the Eagles and Snider's brother-in-law, told the media that Snider's alleged firing did not happen—though Wolman rebutted this with his own calls to the newspapers.

"I intend to call a meeting of the board of directors," Foreman said in a statement, "At which time this matter will be discussed and thoroughly reviewed. There has been no discussion by the board of directors in the past. Mr. Snider will be at his office performing his duties." On October 20, the Eagles three-man board of directors—Wolman, Foreman, and Snider—would meet at the club's office on 30th and Market Street to determine Snider's fate with the football team. Although there were three members of the board, Wolman owned 52 percent of the team, allowing him to have the final say. Even though Foreman believed each board member received one vote, Wolman legally had the right to dissolve the board as the majority shareholder and appoint a new board that would side with him. Despite his objections, there was no use for Foreman to fight.[39] Nonetheless, his perceived betrayal by Wolman created a chasm between the two shareholders, leaving a mess in their wake. That night, Snider walked into the Spectrum distraught. "He was visibly shaken," Scheinfeld remembered. He was "very, very upset about it." The unbreakable bond between two dear friends who had a dream to increase the city's sports presence was coming crashing down.[40]

Despite what was happening behind the scenes regarding Wolman's struggling finances, the public perception was that the feud between Snider and Wolman boiled down to Snider's objection to Eagles GM-Coach Joe Kuharich, who did not get along with the Flyers owner. At a news conference on October 20, Snider, Wolman, Foreman, and Kuharich sat around a room sniping at each other while the media lavished in the drama.

"I'm enjoying this," Kuharich said from his position.

"Maybe next time it will be your party Joe," Snider retorted.

"It happens every day," the GM-coach replied.

Kuharich was basking in the glory of seeing his foe pushed out of a team that was now clearly his. But he also was angered by the media interest in a person that he deemed to be irrelevant. "I've never seen anything so ludicrous," he snapped. "You're here for nothing. If I got fired there'd be two people here." He continued on his rampage against Snider. "Why is everyone so surprised? The guy Snider spends 60 percent of his time with the hockey team ... what's he doing for the Eagles? You only get a couple of hours work out of him a day. He comes in at 12 o'clock. What's the big deal? What's the surprise?"

"He's unbelievable," Snider said, shaking his head and staring down his rival. "I've never bad mouthed him. I won't start now. He's just following the party line." Meanwhile, Wolman sat a few feet away, dressed in a black, pin-striped suit, looking despondent. When reporters asked Wolman who was going to run the day-to-day of the team and fill in for Snider's duties, he stared at the ground and didn't respond.[41]

According to the *Philadelphia Inquirer*, as Snider left the office for the last time, the entire building seemed to be in mourning. A cleaning lady approached him, saying, "Sorry to see you're leaving, Mr. Snider."

"I don't tread where I'm not wanted," he said with a smile, stepping into his limousine.[42]

Weeks later, as Wolman began leaking false information to the press that he had financed the Flyers and provided the ownership group with the funding needed to pay for the franchise, Snider could not hold his tongue any longer. With rumors circulated by Wolman, on top of a report that Snider had reneged on an agreement to transfer his Flyers shares to Wolman to help him secure the supposed eight-figure loan from the group of Kuwaiti oilmen, he called Fred Byrod of the *Philadelphia Inquirer* and provided documentation to refute all of Wolman's unsupported claims—claims the developer continued to make until his death in 2013.

"I'm not going to start throwing brickbats at Jerry over our other differences," Snider started. "That's past and that's where I want to leave it. But I just couldn't remain silent about the Flyers when I read the untruths and misrepresentations printed about them." He continued to lay out the documents supporting his claims. "To get the NHL franchise, we had to pay the league $2 million at a meeting at Montreal, Monday, June 5," Snider told the *Inquirer*. "The previous Saturday, we still lacked $500,000 of that and Bill Putnam and I were getting desperate. We had a promissory note for $1 million from a Philadelphia bank.... We had two other loans, totaling $500,000. Finally, a friend agreed to borrow $500,000 and turn it over to us on a short-term loan Monday morning.... If it had not [worked out], we would have lost the franchise and everything we had spent on it up to that time."[43]

Regarding Wolman's claim that Snider agreed, then reneged, on helping him obtain a loan from the Kuwaitis, Snider said simply, "I did refuse to go along with Jerry on that. I did not think it wise to let foreign money get control of the hockey team. But more important, there was that final $500,000 we had borrowed, for which I had a personal responsibility, and I was afraid I could not guarantee repayment in time if I yielded my stock."

Snider went on, describing the financial game of Twister that he and his partners were forced to play, and providing an evidence-backed rebuttal to Wolman's claim that Snider hung him out to dry.

"During the summer, New York interests made a bid of $3½ million for the team. Putnam and I wanted to keep the club. But I wanted to help Jerry in another way if I could." Eventually worked out was the exchange, reported in the Philadelphia press August 26, by which Snider gave Wolman his 40 percent of the Spectrum, 14 percent of Connie Mack Stadium and 10 percent of an Allentown garden apartment project headed by Wolman. "We re-structured the whole deal financially after that to get better terms. We arranged a new bank loan for $1.5 million, retained a loan of $375,000, and got $250,000 from stock sale. I wasn't worrying about [the stock exchange], because I was eager to help Jerry, and I felt if I did, the score would come out even sometime. But figured on a conservative cost basis, I gave up my equity in the Spectrum, worth about $4 million, and in Connie Mack, worth about $50,000, for additional Flyers' stock worth about $400,000. Forget about the Allentown thing. Would you say that was running out on Jerry?" After the ordeal, the two never spoke again.[44] Jerry Wolman passed away in 2013 at the age of 86. Ed Snider passed away in 2016 at the age of 83.

The storm continued to gather in February 1968, as the roof of the Spectrum partially blew off in the midst of an Ice Capades performance. What could have been a quick repair of major structural damage became a political football, with each party pointing fingers at the other, preventing the arena from getting fixed in a timely manner. After another section of the roof blew off a few weeks later, Mayor Tate shut down the arena, refusing to allow it to operate until it was fixed to the city's satisfaction.

Upon further investigation by district attorney Arlen Specter, he alleged there was foul play between Wolman and the Philadelphia politicians, as both Wolman and Matthew McCloskey, the Spectrum's builder, had contributed handsomely to Tate's mayoral campaign. As Specter kept digging, he discovered that the Spectrum did not have the proper building permits while it was being constructed, and even more shocking, still did not have a certificate of occupancy, despite having been in operation since the previous October. After months of messy political games, the Spectrum was finally repaired in time for the team's first playoff game.

The Flyers, of course, became a rousing success in Philadelphia quickly after their rocky first season. With Snider in full control of the organization and a strong team of executives around him, the team became a back-to-back Stanley Cup champion in the 1970s and launched themselves into the financial success that is now Comcast-Spectacor, the Flyers parent company who took control of the organization in the 1990s. Through over 50 years of history, the team has churned out dozens of characters, both on and off the ice, and is still arguably the most popular sports team in Philadelphia, along with one of the most successful franchises in NHL history. *Forbes* regularly ranks the Flyers in the top ten of their annual NHL franchise valuations. And the Flyers rank second in all-time points percentage, just behind the Montreal Canadiens as of the start of the 2019–20 season. (Not counting the Vegas Golden Knights, whose sample size is too small.)

The story of the beginnings of the Flyers is one of drama, but more importantly, one of triumph. What started with two men, like family, attempting to build something extraordinary, could have ended in disaster, as business and politics tore them apart. Instead, what Philadelphia

# 8. The Flyers

It was the gumption and persistence of Ed Snider and Jerry Wolman that got the Spectrum built in the first place, seen here at the end of its life in 2009 (courtesy Bruce "Scoop" Cooper).

saw was a partnership evaporating and turning into one of the most unfortunate rivalries in the city's modern history. For years, Snider would often give people his famous glare if they brought up Wolman's name—until the day he passed, he still was pained by the break in their relationship. The two could move mountains together and very nearly did.

"I loved Jerry Wolman," Scheinfeld said. "And Ed knew it. But look, I was a reporter, I'm trained to be objective, to get both sides of the story. Ed was tough. Either you were 1,000 percent with him or you were the enemy. And I didn't feel that way." Scheinfeld felt he could be business partners with Snider, while still having the love for Wolman that he always did. He was possibly the only person in the Flyers organization that was able to continue a relationship with Wolman and remain as close to Snider as he did.[45]

Ultimately, the story of the Flyers comes down to these two men and the partners who surrounded them. When Wolman released his autobiography, Snider was furious at the perceived lies that were published. He wanted to start a media war. He wanted to sue for defamation. But he was talked off the ledge and instead issued a fairly mundane statement: "Jerry Wolman and I worked very closely together many years ago, and at one time enjoyed a good relationship.

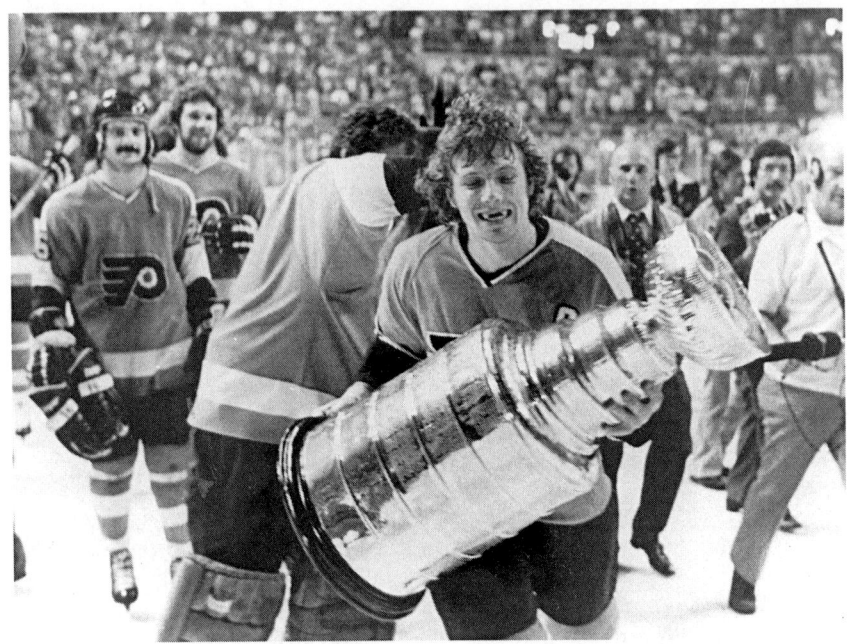

In 1975, Bob Clarke and his Flyers won their second consecutive Stanley Cup, an extraordinary achievement for a fledgling NHL organization (Salvatore C. DiMarco, Special Collections Research Center, Temple University Libraries, Philadelphia, Pennsylvania).

Unfortunately, in many partnerships, things don't always work out and people move on."

"It was too bad," Scheinfeld said. "They went from Damon and Pythias to Cain and Abel. It went from love to hate. But watching them together in the good days, man, they were some team. They were just so good together. But you know, a lot of marriages break up."

The creation of the Flyers boils down to a few men taking a huge financial risk to put a major league hockey franchise in Philadelphia. Regardless of who said or did what, who was right or who was wrong, what is inarguable is the effect Snider's ownership had on the Flyers organization and in Philadelphia.

"We wouldn't have had the Flyers, we wouldn't have had the Spectrum," Scheinfeld said. "We wouldn't have had Comcast-Spectacor or any of the other businesses Snider built. Or [the Ed Snider Youth Hockey Foundation]. What Ed did, what was dumped on him—and I worked with him every day—the guy rolled up his sleeves, he was a hard worker, a bright guy, and he did some great things for Philadelphia."[46]

Despite dangling by a thread multiple times in the club's first few years, the group's risk turned into one of the most beloved pieces of Philadelphia and one of the most valuable members of the National Hockey League. And though Snider is no longer around to see the progression of his cherished franchise, the organization continues to operate based on the business pillars that were put in place and the foundation that was set over half a century ago.

# 9

# The Blazers

*World Hockey Association (WHA), 1972–73*

Major league hockey in the early 1970s was exclusive to the National Hockey League. If players wanted to play the game they loved at the highest level, they were generally at the mercy of NHL owners and their demands. Even the creation of the NHL Players Association in the 1960s did little to help the players' plight. The stars of the league still had almost no say in the trajectory of their careers. Salaries were capped at low levels and if an owner did not want you, they were free to stash you in the minors, preventing you from ever playing NHL hockey again without their permission.

As the calendar turned to 1971, two chronic "disrupters" decided it was time to do something about it. Gary Davidson and Dennis Murphy had previously disrupted professional basketball with the creation of the American Basketball Association, before venturing out looking for their next challenge. They found it in the world of ice hockey.

On June 26, 1971, the two announced that they

The Philadelphia Blazers, WHA, 1972–73.

would form a new, 14-team major hockey league to compete with the NHL. At the time of the announcement, the two businessmen had already granted conditional franchises to Los Angeles, New York, Miami, Honolulu, and Milwaukee. Other franchises were going to be awarded based on applicants posting a $25,000 franchise fee, a $200,000 bond, along with providing evidence of $2 million additional to invest in their teams.[1]

"The National Hockey League has been very restrictive in its expansion and there are several major cities without hockey," Davidson said. Although he declined to elaborate on the specifics at the time, he confirmed that Miami had plans to put a franchise in place. Local businessman Herb Martin had a grand idea to construct an office-sports arena complex in South Beach, bringing with it a WHA franchise. He even signed goaltender Bernie Parent to a five-year, $750,000 contract—money unheard of at the time for a hockey player.

"I got a telephone call from someone in the World Hockey Association, asking if I'd like to join them," Parent wrote in his autobiography, *Bernie Parent: Unmasked*. Desiring to stay in Toronto, Parent informed his boss, the notoriously-stingy Harold Ballard, of his contract offer and asked for a small, $5,000 raise in order to stay. When Ballard tossed him out of his office, Parent hopped a plane to Miami to sign the deal. Coincidentally, he ran into Toronto coach John McLellan on the plane, who asked Parent why he was going to Miami. After informing his now-former coach of his decision to jump to the WHA, McLellan went pale.[2]

But when, in the spring of 1972, Martin could not come through with his arena plans and failed to make the franchise fee payment to the WHA, the league had to quickly look elsewhere. Enter two ambitious, young Delaware Valley residents.

Jim Cooper and Bernie Brown knew each other through previous business dealings. Cooper was a known attorney in Atlantic City, while Brown was a trucking magnate, the owner of NFI Industries in Vineland, New Jersey. Cooper, desiring to dabble in the world of sports business, approached his friend and told him of a crazy idea he had. Brown, having never seen a hockey game, deferred to his teenage children, who were big sports fans. The family—sans Brown's wife—thought it was a wonderful opportunity to bring a second hockey team to Philadelphia and they pounced on the idea. The two became 50–50 partners and canvassed the WHA for ownership of the Miami franchise. At the start, Cooper ran the team, while Brown solely provided financial assistance from afar, so that he could continue running his business. With little time to spare, the league had no option but to approve the deal. In an

The Brown family stands behind Bernie and Carol Parent as the Blazers sign the goaltender to a stint in the WHA. Back, L to R: Anne Koons (née Brown), Sidney Brown, Jeff Brown, Ike Brown, Shirley Brown, Bernie Brown (courtesy Brown family).

ironic chain of events, Parent would be returning to Philadelphia to play hockey—just not for the Flyers.[3]

"I firmly believe that hockey is just in its infancy [in Philadelphia]," Cooper said at the introductory press conference. "It's the most exciting sport there is, typifying the tempo of life as it is today.... And I feel there are enough potential fans in the metropolitan Philadelphia area to support two teams. I don't think it'll hurt the Flyers, either. Actually, this type of competition, which creates real fan interest, has to be good for both teams."[4]

While the Flyers vehemently disagreed with Cooper's assessment, the ball was rolling for the new Philadelphia club, which was initially known as the "Phantoms." Nonetheless, they had a daunting task in front of them. In just under four months, the duo had to put into place a general manager, head coach, full front office staff, and a full roster that could compete with the other franchises, which had been building for the previous year.

At the time, Philadelphia sports was a joke. There had been no recent track record of success, and both fans and the media were getting restless with the perpetual futility. "This is the town with a baseball team that blew a six-and-a-half game lead with 12 games to go," wrote

## 9. The Blazers

Frank Dolson in the *Philadelphia Inquirer*, "A football team that has had one winning season in the last 10, a National Hockey League team that blew a playoff berth in the last four seconds of the season, a coachless pro basketball team whose star might spend more time in court than on court next season."[5] (76ers star Billy Cunningham attempted to jump to the rival American Basketball Association and fought the NBA in court for the right to do so.)

The new team, which was officially christened as the Blazers, were sure they would put an end to the string of bad luck, immediately putting in place Murray Williamson as general manager. Williamson recently coached the United States Olympic team to a silver medal in the 1972 Sapporo Olympics, a stupefying feat for a country that was still in its hockey infancy, from a developmental perspective. Cooper believed that Williamson was the guy to accelerate a roster build and ice a competitive team by opening night.

But, with the press conference scheduled the next morning to announce the signing to the media, Williamson dropped a bombshell to Cooper at 11:35 the night before: he was leaving. In four hours of work, Williamson had made immense strides. He added eight players to the Blazers' list, negotiated with three other league managers on trades, discussed terms with three lawyers on which NHLers would be available to him, and interviewed two head coaches for the open position. But it was at that point that he realized the job in front of him was simply too daunting. He didn't believe he could put a team together from scratch in just four months. So, he handed in his resignation, perhaps the quickest in major league hockey history.

"I give him credit for telling me," Cooper said at the press conference the next day, "But I wish he had told me 10 hours before. It would have saved us a lot of aggravation and embarrassment."

"I'm a winner," Williamson told the press. "I go into something to command the No. 1 spot. You go for first; you don't go for anything else.... I want to build a No. 1. You have to figure out what the chance is, how long it will take. You have to ask yourself, 'is it worth the sacrifice?' You've got to evaluate things.... You can move mountains if you have enough dynamite ... as long as you have enough time to plant the sticks and light the fuses." Just like that, the Blazers were both back to square one, and given a public stamp of disapproval by one of the most respected hockey minds in the United States.

"Already," wrote Dolson with a great deal of snark, "They have added an unforgettable chapter to a Philadelphia story most of the natives wish they could forget.... Let the record show that Philadelphia has finally found a smart general manager."[6]

In the meantime, Cooper, understanding that he did not have the luxury of waiting for his perfect general manager to arrive on a noble steed, began signing players on his own—a spending spree not seen to that point in hockey history. The first to jump ship was former Flyer-favorite Andre Lacroix, the now-Black Hawks forward. Signing a five-year contract worth between $300,000 and $500,000, Lacroix, who still made a home in the region, was thrilled to be back in town. "I think Philadelphia will be happy with the Blazers," he said. "Bernie and I would not have signed if we didn't think so." Lacroix also gave a grave warning to the NHL establishment. "I think you will find many NHL players, established players, who will jump to the World Hockey Association."[7]

Next, Cooper signed Bruins great John McKenzie to be player-coach of the Blazers, a three-year contract worth $100,000 per year. At 34, McKenzie still had a bit of jump left in him, but wanted to use his leadership more efficiently to help what would be a young Blazers team. Frankly, McKenzie was peeved that the Bruins no longer saw value in him. "If the Bruins had protected me in the [expansion] draft, I would not have considered talking with the World Hockey Association," he said. "Because they didn't, I thought my time in Boston would be a little shaky.... I got security and I'm going to learn the coaching and business end of hockey."[8]

At the end of June, Cooper finally found his lead man. Dave Creighton, the 42-year-old general manager of the AHL's Providence Reds, was hired to run the Blazers. "We're not going to be the Montreal Canadiens or the Boston Bruins the first year," Cooper admitted, "But I don't think we'd have trouble beating any expansion club in the NHL." When asked to clarify, Cooper smiled and assured that yes, the Flyers would indeed be categorized as such. "We will be pleased to play them in a city series," he said surreptitiously, lobbing a challenge to the other side of the city that would ultimately go unanswered.[9]

Compounding their early and plentiful problems, the Blazers still needed to find a place to play. The Spectrum was an option, but the Flyers seemed to be toying with them, rather than seriously negotiating, and Cooper knew it. He gave them a hard deadline to decide, and when the Flyers failed to meet it, Cooper went straight to the higher-ups at City Hall. Philadelphia made available to the team the Civic Center Convention Hall, which had never before been used for ice hockey. In a deal quite favorable to the Blazers, the team signed an eight-month lease while the city agreed to install $359,000 worth of improvements, including installing an ice rink. The Blazers agreed to pay a flat $7,000 fee per game to the city. Philadelphia would also take a percentage of the concessions from each Blazers game. Cooper reassured the skeptics that

## 9. The Blazers

the team had taken out a surety bond to protect the city, in case the team folded in under three years. Home games were scheduled for Wednesdays, Fridays, and on weekends. And the ticket office would open immediately at their brand-new office downtown. Cooper didn't miss out on another chance to needle the Flyers: "Anyone who has stood in the wind and rain at the Spectrum waiting to buy a ticket should appreciate our indoor windows," he said with a smirk.[10]

Cooper and his front office staff continued to sign players, slowly filling out the roster that would take the ice on opening night. At the end of July, they introduced defenseman Dave Hutchinson, who they appointed the team's "policeman." At 6-foot-4, 200 pounds, Hutchinson was known for banging bodies around in the Canadian Junior League, where he posted two consecutive seasons with at least 150 penalty minutes. Hutchinson was so rough that he was, at the time, still facing assault charges from an on-ice brawl that took place in Ottawa a few months earlier. Amidst a bench-clearing brawl, when seeing one of his teammates being held down and pummeled by two opposing players, he launched himself into the back of the offender and knocked him down hard to the ice. "After I hit the guy, everybody cleared out," Hutchinson explained at his introductory press conference. "It was a bad brawl and the fans came after our bus afterwards."[11]

The Blazers played their home games at the Civic Center, seen here in the 1990s before its demolition (courtesy Bob Busser).

"He's got a lot of zip," said Blazers head scout Phil Watson. "He's always hollering on the bench. Some guys go through the motions. Not him." With Hutchinson, the Blazers were making a statement: no one was going to push them around.[12]

But the biggest news was when Cooper announced the team was negotiating with Bruins pest Derek Sanderson, a talented forward who was famous for getting under the skin of opponents, as well as his off-ice personality that endeared him to the notoriously-tough Boston fans. In Sanderson's autobiography, *Crossing the Line*, he describes in detail the process of being courted by the Blazers.

Bringing his business partners and lawyer with him to a meeting, Cooper entered and introduced himself. "Derek," Cooper explained up front, "We don't know a lot about hockey, but this was a chance for us to own a sports franchise and have some fun, so let's do it." Off the bat, Cooper offered Sanderson $2,300,000 over ten years—money that most professional athletes could only dream about at that time. Stunned, Sanderson began pressing them with questions about the quality of the new league, its chances of staying afloat, and the team's prospects for success. Deep down, Sanderson truly wanted to stay in Boston, he had no intention of signing with the Blazers.

Amidst his hesitance, Cooper immediately upped the offer to $2,600,000. Sanderson, knowing he was in the position of power, began asking for specific favors. He wanted Cooper to promise that the franchise would never move under his ownership without Sanderson's permission. Done. He wanted assurances that the team would not be sold without his permission either. Done. He wanted to be named captain. Done. He wanted to be on the power play. "With the money you'll be making," Cooper responded, "You'll barely be off the ice." Sanderson wanted two drivers, one for himself and one for his girlfriend. Done. He wanted a two-bedroom suite for road games. Done. He wanted a job for his dad. Cooper immediately made him a scout at $50,000 per year. He wanted his dad to be able to scout without having to leave his hometown. Done. Sanderson mentioned his fear of flying. Cooper assured him that he could simply go to as many road games as he could. Then, as the contract was being written up, Sanderson realized that Pele, the famous soccer player, was making $2,600,000 as well. "Put another $50,000 in there and I'll be the highest-paid athlete in the world," he said. Without batting an eye, Cooper agreed enthusiastically. "That'll get us headlines in magazines and newspapers!" he said.

The final contract terms were $2.65 million over ten years. Sanderson would get $300,000 for each of the first two years, $200,000 for each of the next five years, $250,000 for each of the last three seasons,

## 9. The Blazers

$25,000 per year for doing public relations work for the team, and a $50,000 cash bonus. The contract also allowed him to retire after five years if he wanted, whereupon he would become a scout at $100,000 per year for the rest of the contract.

Sanderson asked for a few days to think it over, still with no intention of taking the offer. In the meantime, the news leaked to the national media, who were stunned at the notion of an athlete making that much money. But the Blazers were getting antsy. On July 28, they gave Sanderson a deadline of one week or the offer would be pulled. "Derek knows how badly we want him," Cooper said, "But I also told him that if we can't get him, there are some others we might be able to sign with the money." Those close to him, even McKenzie, his former teammate, couldn't imagine him not taking the money.

But Sanderson's heart was in Boston. He went to meet with Bruins owner Weston Adams, Sr., to whom Sanderson felt loyalty. He showed his former boss the contract and asked for his advice. "Mr. Adams," Sanderson said, "I will do whatever you advise me to do." Adams told him that if it were him, he would take the money. But the owner also advised him to demand guarantees on it: the money should be in escrow, so that it was impossible for him to not be paid. Adams also told him to continue living at the previous level he was used to, so that he saved for his future. Even with all that, Sanderson insisted he wanted to stay with the Bruins.

"Under the circumstances," Adams responded, "I think we can give you the $80,000 you are looking for." Sanderson agreed, but said his only stipulation was that Bruins legal counsel Charlie Mulcahy, with whom Sanderson often battled, would not be present when the contract was signed. Adams agreed and sent Sanderson to see his son, who ran the team. When Sanderson sat down to sign his $80,000 contract, Mulcahy stuck his head in the door. "I still think you're only worth 75," he said. Immediately, Sanderson stood up and left. He returned to Cooper and, on August 1, the Blazers made the biggest WHA splash up to that point, securing the services of a superstar NHLer.[13]

Sanderson was famous for his off-ice antics, nearly as much as his on-ice talent. "I met him for lunch in Center City before a road trip," *Daily News* beat writer Bill Fleischman reminisced years later. "Accompanying him was a flight attendant, a major babe. Near the end of the lunch, he asked if he could borrow some money for the trip. I probably had $40 or $50 with me. I think I loaned him $20. Can't recall if he paid me back."[14]

As the season neared, the fans and the media were curiously and cautiously excited about their new hockey team. The Flyers, at the time, still were not too successful—they had made the playoffs three times in five seasons, but had never moved past the first round. And while they had the potential to take the next step, fans agreed they were still a few years and a few pieces away. The Blazers, on the other hand, offered something new and exciting. On September 13, 1972, the *Philadelphia Daily News* published their Blazers season preview, hyping the team and the league for the city. Amidst their multi-page spread was a player-by-player preview, introducing the city to the men who would represent the city in the new league. The paper described the Blazers as "potentially, the league's most explosive team, but far from set."[15]

Before the season could start, the WHA and the Blazers were caught in courts, fighting the NHL on the rights to their players. The Flyers were suing the Blazers for the rights to McKenzie, who they claimed they acquired from the Bruins before McKenzie jumped to the rival league. The NHL simultaneously was attempting to use their reserve clause, which gave teams full rights to a player for life, even if their contract expired. The WHA claimed this was a violation of anti-trust laws, to which the NHL attempted to argue that they were not subject. From September through November, the leagues continued to battle each other, until the WHA eventually won multiple decisions, including an all-encompassing one in U.S. District Court on November 9, 1972, in which the NHL was ordered to not sue players jumping to the WHA, on the basis of anti-trust law that prevented the reserve clause from continuing to be used. The decision was a boon for professional hockey players that would eventually see their salaries skyrocket toward the current levels.

But even amidst legal battles, the WHA season was ready to begin, and that included a Blazers team that was still struggling to get itself together. A nervous McKenzie attempted to get used to coaching a team, rather than simply playing on it—yet a court injunction prevented him from playing until after his NHL contract expired on October 1. And fans could not agree on whether the Blazers presence was good or bad for the city.

"I'm a 'Blazer Gazer' because I can't bear the thought of watching the dull, uninspiring Flyers waging their annual battle for fourth place again," wrote one fan in the *Philadelphia Daily News*. "The Flyers have perpetuated a time-honored tradition in this city—that losing, not winning, is the name of the game."

"Why should I have to pay extra money to see the Blazers when I can watch one of the best players in the world (Bobby Clarke) for less in the Spectrum's new seats?" wrote another.

"The Blazers are something new, something exciting, something for which Philadelphia has waited a long time," wrote a third.

"You can't beat an NHL team for superb professional hockey. The Blazers lack the necessary talent to be a hard-hitting hockey club," wrote another.[16]

With opening night a couple days away, Bill Fleischman of the *Daily News* gave his final preview of the new team. "The Blazers have enough solid players to challenge for the East Division title presuming the courts don't sidetrack Sanderson and other NHL jumpers," he wrote. "What we won't know until later is how much the supporting cast will help." Although many experts disagreed on how the new team and the new league would fare, most everyone acknowledged that the league would be an offensive juggernaut. Teams had focused on attracting the offensive stars from the NHL, with very little attention paid to defense. "The WHA," said Sanderson, "Will be a demolition derby."[17]

An advertisement in the Philadelphia Daily News for the Blazers of the WHA in the 1972–73 season.

When the home opener arrived on October 13, the Blazers hoped to demolish their first opponent in the New England Whalers. But there was a major problem with the ice that made the players uncomfortable. "The Civic Center was a joke," wrote Sanderson in his autobiography. "The refrigeration piping ended about four inches away from the boards, and so there was this black slush all around the edge of the rink. We were losing pucks in warmup. Not only that, but they had built the ice over sawdust. It created a crust, because when the wet sawdust slipped below the pipes, the top was a frozen shell with a hollow gap underneath. You can hear the echo when you skate over it."[18]

When Sanderson expressed his concern to the referee, the official nervously responded that they couldn't cancel the game, that thousands of fans had paid to see the first game. Instead, they brought out watering cans and fire extinguishers in an attempt to make the ice playable. When they brought the Zamboni out to resurface the ice, it broke through the hollow ice, getting stuck halfway through and spinning its wheels hopelessly. At that point, everyone knew the game had to be cancelled, but no one wanted to be the one to pull the trigger. When the decision finally was made, the fans were understandably unhappy. As Sanderson went out to announce the decision to the fans, they began tossing the bright orange souvenir pucks that were handed out at the entrances in celebration of opening night. Sanderson continued speaking until the barrage of pucks was too much to handle. As he left, he said, "Don't give up on us because of this! We need your support after they get this ice fixed. I hope you can get out of the building—the parking situation isn't great. Remember that there was only one entrance to the parking lot when you came in? Well, there's only one exit going out."[19]

With that, he quickly ducked out of the rink, with a trail of fighting fans behind him. Cooper, needing to quell an angry rush of paid spectators, issued an apologetic statement that did little to calm everyone's nerves. "Maybe this is what we get for trying to open on Friday the 13th," he joked separately from the statement.[20] In what some called a gesture of good faith (but what others called an ulterior motive), the Flyers offered the Blazers the use of the Spectrum until the Civic Center ice was repaired. Nonetheless, Cooper refused, insisting the team would make do.

But once the season officially started, things just got worse for the Blazers. They lost their first seven games, sinking to the bottom of the league standings. On November 2, the team got its worst news of the young season: while stepping out of the penalty box, with fans throwing various items at him, Sanderson

Fans attending the home opener of the Philadelphia Blazers were given this souvenir puck when they entered the building. When the game was cancelled because of ice conditions, most of them ended up on the ice.

## 9. *The Blazers*

slipped on a piece of debris on the ice. His left leg went one way while the rest of his body went the other. The fall tweaked his back quite seriously. He was deemed out of commission for at least 10 days—though those close to the team knew it would be much longer. He had resigned the captaincy of the team, while McKenzie surrendered his role as head coach, deciding to focus solely on playing. Bernie Parent had broken his foot. Around the same time, GM Dave Creighton resigned, leaving Phil Watson in charge, to the dismay of many players. Watson was known to be a screamer—he liked to rant and rave at the players, which did not sit well with many of the team's stars.

To top it off, Sanderson began being harassed by the frustrated Philadelphia fans, who weren't happy about the team's success, his injury, and more importantly, his inflated salary. "The fans had started telling me I was a bum," Sanderson said, "But I would turn around and say, 'At least I'm a rich bum!'" A few days later, at a press conference to discuss his injury, Sanderson couldn't hold his tongue. "This is a town where, as far as the fans are concerned, everyone is a bum or a loser," he said. "The biggest reason the fans in this town are sour is the press. You guys never say anything complimentary. No athlete enjoys playing in Philadelphia. I know a couple Eagles who'd be overjoyed if they could play a 14-game schedule entirely on the road."[21] (Sanderson's comments to me regarding Philadelphia and its fans, spoken in retrospect, rather than with the emotion of the time, were nothing but positive. "The fans were good," he said. "The people of Philadelphia are good people.")

The situation came to a head when, in November, the Blazers ran out of money. Cooper approached Brown to ask him to contribute more. When Brown attempted to confirm that Cooper would also be contributing the same amount, the lawyer demurred. The two argued, and ultimately Brown put his foot down, insisting that either they shut the team down, or that Brown would take over complete control.[22] On November 18, Jim Cooper resigned from his post as team president. "A disagreement over management policies apparently has caused an irreconcilable split between James Cooper ... and Bernard Brown," wrote the *Inquirer*.[23] Brown bought out Cooper's shares for $125,000, leaving him as sole owner of the team. The issue was that Cooper had been running the team completely on his own, while Brown admittedly knew nothing about the sports business world. Now, Brown was running the entire show by himself, and many, including Sanderson, did not believe he knew the economics of running a professional hockey team.

"I talked to Brown and said, 'Take a look around, Bernie,'" Sanderson said. "'You've only got 10,000 seats in here. I'm no businessman, but if you add up the top six players' contracts, I don't think the economics make sense.'"[24] And Sanderson was right. Attendance was suffering greatly. On December 9, the *Inquirer* reported that just 750 fans showed up to see the Blazers, despite the 3,391 announced attendance.[25] At that point, the team was 7–18 and still looking up quite a way from the league cellar. Brown and Sanderson were publicly fighting, with Brown looking for a way out of the star's contract. The aura around the team was toxic and Philadelphia fans were staying away. In actuality, the team needed to sell an estimated 8,000 tickets per game to break even. They weren't even halfway there.

At the beginning of January, with the team reeling, Brown resigned his position as team president and instead hired businessman Dick Olson to run the team. (Olson was in the food and transportation industry in Minnesota and knew Brown through business dealings. Brown knew that Olson happened to be a hockey enthusiast—though not necessarily familiar with the business itself.) Brown remained the owner, but allowed the business decisions to be made by someone else. The hiring was a sign of good news for a team that struggled to get going, but now had high expectations for themselves. "We got off to a terrible start," Brown said. "We've had to regroup from that. We feel we're at a stage where we can overcome that." In the middle of January, the team finally saw some light. Sanderson and his attorney settled with the Blazers with his full contract being bought out for $1,000,000. In a press conference, his attorney acknowledged that Derek did not necessarily act properly, but at the same time he faulted the Blazers for how they handled the situation on their end. "Whenever someone starts a new franchise, there are miscalculations," he said. "They did not sell tickets as anticipated. They felt Sanderson wasn't needed."[26]

With the ugliness behind them, the Blazers suddenly seemed to turn a corner. Sitting at 18–27 on January 19, the team rattled off three

A ticket stub to a Philadelphia Blazers game at the Civic Center versus the Winnipeg Jets in the 1972–73 season.

## 9. The Blazers

**Blazers forward Andre Lacroix battles with Jets superstar Bobby Hull in a December matchup between the two squads (Special Collections Research Center, Temple University Libraries, Philadelphia, Pennsylvania).**

consecutive wins, followed by a five-game winning streak in February. In the midst of that streak, after scoring a hat trick in a 9–2 victory (in front of nearly 5,000 fans at the Civic Center), McKenzie came out and made a bold statement, claiming that the Blazers were better than the Flyers in certain areas. "We weren't playing together earlier in the season," he explained. "Too many of our guys were thinking individually. You do that and you're bound to be in trouble. Now we're thinking as a team and playing as a unit.... The only glaring difference between us and the Flyers, I'd say, is that they're getting the crowds and we're not."[27]

At the same time, Andre Lacroix was tearing up the league, putting up points in nearly every game he played and challenging for the scoring crown. The team continued compiling a winning record in the short-term, culminating in a 5–1 win on March 31 against Chicago, their penultimate game of the season, clinching a playoff spot. Right winger Danny Lawson recorded a hat trick to hit 60 goals for the season—only the third major league player to ever hit that mark at that point. Lacroix, the other member of the now-famous "Fire Line," made up of Lawson, Lacroix, and Don Herriman, recorded four points, giving him 121 for the season, three more than the player chasing him, who had just completed the final game of his team's campaign—thereby clinching the scoring championship for the young forward. Lacroix, surprisingly, credited his hot-headed coach with his season's success.

"He made us practice, practice for an hour and a half," he said. "He just kicked the bleep out of us. We used to swear at him in French and he knew it. But we weren't in shape. He put us in shape."[28]

With a season-ending win against first-place Winnipeg in front of 6,000 home fans, the Blazers clinched third place with a 38–40 record, an outstanding accomplishment considering their start to the season. "I really had no dreams of anything like this early in the season," McKenzie said at the conclusion of the calendar. "Things started getting better around Christmas, but even then, making the playoffs seemed out of the question. But we just got better and better. I think right now we've

**Blazers goaltender Bernie Parent and defenseman Ron Plumb keep the puck out of the Philadelphia net in a February 1973 home game (Salvatore C. DiMarco, Special Collections Research Center, Temple University Libraries, Philadelphia, Pennsylvania).**

peaked in just about every department. Even the defense has been good the last month and that was the biggest problem early."[29]

The Blazers were optimistic heading into their playoff series against the second-place Cleveland Crusaders. In the opening game on the road, the two teams battled, before Cleveland pulled out a 3–2 win in overtime. But after the game, another disaster struck. Claiming he hadn't been paid and that the money guaranteeing his contract was no longer in escrow, Parent walked out on the team, refusing to return to the locker room until the contract dispute was solved. When Brown held firm, the Blazers were stuck with their backup goalie, a 20-year-old named Yves Archambault who was picked up earlier in the season from the Eastern League. The story, according to the Brown family, was that Parent's agent approached Brown and demanded he guarantee the following year's salary. When Brown requested they wait until the playoffs were done to discuss the next season, the agent stormed out and advised Parent not to play. Supposedly, Parent later regretted following his agent's advice.[30] Parent, to this day, refuses to talk publicly about his time with the Blazers.

Blazers forward Andre Lacroix tries to get a puck past a sprawling Gerry Cheevers, goaltender for the Cleveland Crusaders (Joshua Bernstein, Special Collections Research Center, Temple University Libraries, Philadelphia, Pennsylvania).

A seventh-round draft pick of the Canadiens the previous summer, Archambault showed promise but, untested and just recovering from a bout with mononucleosis, was unable to come through in his short major league audition. The next three games the Blazers lost by a combined score of 16–4, as Cleveland completed the sweep and knocked Philadelphia out of the playoffs before they could even get their feet set. Nonetheless, optimism reigned as players immediately looked toward the start of the next season.

"We'll be back, that's for sure," said McKenzie. "We have good material, a lot of younger players matured since the start of the schedule and they will improve. We are looking for some new material, especially defensemen. We'll be in it right from the start next season."[31]

The next day, Brown and Dick Olson held a press conference confirming that the Blazers would operate again the following season. Acknowledging that the team was in talks with the Flyers to play in the Spectrum, they again expressed their confidence that Philadelphia could support two major league hockey teams. They also combated the rumors that Parent and his lawyer were peddling, claiming that Parent had been paid according to a payment plan he had himself set up at the beginning of the season, and that the team held a letter of credit for the amount of Parent's salary, as he had requested. They claimed Parent was forced into a corner by his attorney.[32]

The fiasco left a sour taste in the mouth of Philadelphia fans, who worshipped the young goalie and still believed that he would be the Flyers' ticket to Stanley Cup success one day. "Every time he went to work," wrote John Plaisant of the *Delaware County Daily Times*, "Parent saw more rubber than a Goodyear inspector. He didn't need a mask for protection. He needed a German Shepherd." No one knew who to believe. Did the Blazers shirk their fiduciary obligation to the star goalie? Or was Parent's lawyer bluffing? Further, was it even acceptable to walk out on your team in the midst of a playoff run, regardless of the circumstances? It was messy, there were no confirmed facts, and the fans simply wanted to see the city ice a competitive hockey team.[33]

On top of that, rumors began to circulate that Brown was preparing to sell the team to someone who would relocate it to Vancouver. On May 9, 1973, Brown vehemently denied the claim. "I haven't put it on the market. So how can I have any offers for it?" he told the *Inquirer*.

When told he didn't directly answer the question, he snapped back. "I've heard all kinds of things," he said. "It ain't going anywhere at the present time…. Everybody's talking and I'm sitting back and doing nothing. Guarantee they'll be here? I couldn't guarantee I'll be here alive next year." As the media continued pressing him, he pivoted, focusing the conversation on the problem players that the team housed in their inaugural season. "A lot of these players got too much money," he said, "And they didn't want to play.... Very truthfully, this Parent thing, he did a terrible thing to us and the team. He broke the contract, I didn't. But if I had broken it, everybody would be on my neck. He could do it and walk away and everything's fine—which isn't fine."[34]

In reality, Brown was indeed in talks with Jim Pattison, a Vancouver businessman and owner of two local radio stations and General Motors franchises. The two quickly agreed on a price of around $2 million. However, when the lawyers drew up the papers, the two businessmen realized that they never specified whether the amount was in U.S. or Canadian dollars—a distinction that could cost either of them hundreds of thousands of dollars. After intense discussions, they agreed the price would be in American Dollars. Then, Pattison requested that the amount be paid over time—Brown insisted on cash at the time of the sale.[35]

Three days later, the rumor became a reality. Pattison announced that he had purchased the Blazers from Brown for $1.9 million cash. "I called Mr. Brown and initiated the discussions about 10 days ago," Pattison said, directly rebuking Brown's denials from a few days earlier. "After a series of amiable discussions, we worked things out." The deal gave Pattison the right to the team, which he would indeed relocate to British Columbia, included 28 contracted players and the rights to 60 protected players.[36]

The Blazers employees were stunned, not having been told directly that the team had been sold. "The owner isn't here, the president isn't here," said executive vice president Hal Freeman, who ran the Spectrum until he was fired in October 1972. He was hired a week later by the Blazers.

"I'm next in charge but I don't know a thing."

"We have no word here of the deal," said director of public relations Kevin Johnson. "Mr. Olson has not been in town the past three days and we haven't had the opportunity to talk with him."[37]

In the Civic Center offices, secretaries were still answering the phones as if the team still existed. On May 14, Olson returned to the office and confirmed with his employees that the team had indeed been sold. "Maybe the Blazers had been a joke to some people," wrote Frank Dolson in the *Inquirer*, "But not to those who worked for them and, excluding Derek What's-His-Name and perhaps one or two others, those who played for them."

"I don't think they gave Philadelphia a chance," said Lacroix sadly. "I really believe if we played in the right building people would come. I don't think they gave it a good try. It was too quick for me. They didn't do it the right way. They had a press conference in Vancouver before they advised the players here."[38]

The silver lining? A month later, Parent signed a contract with the Flyers, facilitating his return to the NHL while remaining in the city he loved. And of course, fans know how that relationship turned out.

Nonetheless, the Blazers hold an interesting piece of Philadelphia hockey history as the only other major league team to call the city home in the modern era. Many Philadelphia hockey fans were ecstatic at the thought of another professional team in the city, and thousands continued to support them even as they struggled out of the gate. Even as the team was packing its bags to move across the continent, fans were less angry and more disappointed. "Maybe this town just can't support two hockey teams," one fan told the *Inquirer*.

Others were simply not shocked, considering the way the team was run. "They didn't treat their fans like they said they would," said another. "I got season tickets because I thought they would be a contender.... Would I have bought season tickets for next year? Why should I?"[39]

Many accused Brown of not understanding how a professional sports organization operated, including some of the players. "The first time Brown met with our general manager," recalled Lacroix a few years after the fact, "He said he wanted all of the players to report for work at nine in the morning and stay until five each night. He expected us to practice for a while, work around the building for a bit, then practice some more. All he knew was that his truck drivers worked from nine to five, and he couldn't understand why he was paying us all that money to work for two or three hours a day."[40] (Years later, as players looked back on their time with the Blazers, each one spoke about how well they were treated by Brown and Cooper and how much they respected them as people.)

One of the biggest issues the Blazers had was self-inflicted: ticket prices. With an arena that wasn't quite up to par with the Spectrum and a roster that could only compete with the Flyers a small percent of the time, the team charged an exorbitant fee for seats. They matched the Flyers price point of $3.50 per ticket in the cheap seats, but their most expensive seats were $8.50, a full dollar higher than their NHL relatives down the street. And nearly half the seats at the Civic Center would cost that higher amount, relative to 16 percent of the Spectrum's seats. Even at those prices, with a stadium that only sat 9,000 people, the team would have to nearly sell out every game in order to combat the inflated salaries they were paying.[41]

Midway through the season, with the city begging and the team struggling, the Blazers finally caved to pressure and lowered their prices a bit. But at that point, it was too late. Brown had invested close to $4 million and the damage was done.

"Pretty soon the well runs dry," said a foreshadowing Ed Snider before the Blazers even played a game. "When all their bills start coming in, then we'll see. If they can do it, fine. But I know what it costs to run a team. If they want to be competitive, they'll have to get in the same price bracket. They're the ones boosting costs."[42]

"Candidly, no athlete was worth it," Sanderson said. "You could take Muhammad Ali, put him on a football field in the morning, a basketball court in the afternoon, a baseball field in the evening, and a ring at night, let him win all four and he still wouldn't be worth it."

"The Blazers expected me to waltz in and be the savior for the franchise," Sanderson said, "But if Jesus Christ himself had strapped on some skates and pulled on that... Blazers sweater, they still weren't going to fill the rink with fans. The Flyers were Philadelphia's team. They were the Broad Street Bullies, and as much as I hated them, they were still an exciting team to watch."[43]

# 10

# The Firebirds

*North American Hockey League (NAHL), 1974–77*
*American Hockey League (AHL), 1977–79*

The brisk fall of the Blazers left Philadelphia again with just the Flyers. While this was not a problem in and of itself, the issue was that the Flyers were becoming exponentially popular. They were becoming a perennial playoff team and challenging for a championship each year, making a ticket to the Spectrum either too expensive or simply impossible to obtain. That left many diehard hockey fans empty-handed at a point when many wanted to express their fanhood for the sport. The Blazers gloriously failed to fill that void. Philadelphia was clamoring for another professional hockey team to play understudy to the Flyers major league entertainment.

At the end of the 1972–73 season (and just a week-and-a-half before the Blazers picked up and moved to Vancouver), the four-decade old Eastern League held a closed-door meeting at the Barbizon Hotel in New York City with team owners and league officials. The southern teams were having an expense issue related to traveling to the northeast, while some of the teams up north were near-bankruptcy. The Jersey Devils were paying their players in cash, because they couldn't guarantee that, if a check were written, there would be enough money in the bank for it to clear by the time they cashed it. The team

The Philadelphia Firebirds, NAHL/AHL, 1974–79.

also could no longer afford their team bus, instead getting to away games via friends of the owner driving players around the region.

After realizing there was no solution that could keep the EHL intact, it was announced that the league would formally dissolve and form two new leagues: the Southern Hockey League and the North American Hockey League. The NAHL began play that Fall with seven teams. In May 1974, the Flyers won their first Stanley Cup, sending jolts throughout the hockey world and the passionate fans of Philadelphia. With the city high on hockey, the media began reporting rumors that the region would become home to a new franchise in the NAHL. The whispers were that the team would be placed in the Cherry Hill Arena in New Jersey, but the owners of the building claimed they had no knowledge of any such plan.

At the end of June, the true announcement was made official: Philadelphia would have a new minor league hockey franchise, their first since the demise of the Ramblers. Like the Blazers, the new team would call the Civic Center home. The owner was announced as Ed Piszek, head of the Mrs. Paul's frozen food company, who would run the team with his son, George. But more exciting for the fans, the face of the ownership would be former Phillies pitcher Robin Roberts, who would own a small piece of the organization.

Roberts was a fan-favorite in the city. A true man of the people, Roberts travelled to work by taking a Reading commuter train from suburban Rydal Station to North Broad Street Station and walking seven blocks to Connie Mack Stadium at 21st and Lehigh. Over a phenomenal 14-year career with the basement-dwelling Phillies, he compiled a 234–199 record, along with 1,871 strikeouts—numbers that would eventually garner him an induction into Cooperstown, the Baseball Hall of Fame. One of the few major league baseball players at the time with a college degree, Roberts was a quiet, intelligent athlete who didn't make a fuss and was far from colorful. Rather, he dug in each day, worked hard at his job, and endeared himself to the Philadelphia sports fans, famous for demanding nothing but a 100 percent effort each game.

"Despite the fact that Roberts was a pitcher," wrote teammate Richie Ashburn, tongue-in-cheek, "He has some good qualities. He is a good family man, he goes to church regularly. He's honest. He pays his bills."

"He was a man without guile," said another teammate. "A big handsome lunk. Nothing ever fazed him."

"For two generations of fans, he symbolized the best in athletic competition," wrote James A. Michener in the *Sunday News*. "When he won, he was gracious. When he lost, so often in extra innings with his teammates giving him no runs, he did not pout. Day after day he went out there and threw that high, hard on down the middle, a marvelously coordinated man doing his job." Roberts sat on various non-profit boards, mentored young people in the region, and helped broadcast Phillies games. But as head of the new hockey team, he hoped to stretch his star power into other parts of the Philadelphia sports scene. The organization hoped he would bring attention and gravitas to their efforts. Roberts informed the media that the ownership group paid nearly $100,000 in league fees to get started.[1]

Roberts announced in August a "Name the Team" contest, similar to others that had been held by previous Philadelphia hockey teams. At the same time, he was looking for someone to lead the team. A friend of his from the Phillies, traveling secretary Eddie Ferenze, grew up in Lethbridge, Alberta. When Roberts mentioned to him that he was struggling to find a head coach, Ferenze recommended a childhood friend who had made waves coaching minor league hockey: Gregg Pilling, who had won the Southern League's championship the previous year as the head coach of the Roanoke Valley Rebels. (The 1974 Cup-winning goal for Pilling's Rebels was scored by a 24-year-old right winger named Mike Keenan, who, a decade later, would go on to coach the Flyers, as well as seven other NHL teams. He would coach teams to championships in the Ontario Hockey Association with the Peterborough Petes, the AHL with the Rochester Americans, the NHL with the New York Rangers, and Russia's Kontinental League with Metallurg Magnitogorsk.) He also had a Philadelphia connection, having played under Flyers coach Fred Shero with the AHL's Buffalo Bisons.[2]

Pilling was called into the new hockey team's office to interview with the Piszeks, Roberts, and legal advisor Jerry Lieberman. After a few minutes, Roberts informed Pilling that the head coaching job was his. To his surprise, Pilling turned it down. "What do you mean, you decline?" Roberts asked, dumbfounded. "Why did you come up here for the interview?" Pilling said that he wanted to be both general manager and head coach—complete control of the team's hockey operations. Roberts retreated into Piszek's office to discuss. A few minutes later, he returned, saying, "Congratulations again, you're the general manager and coach of the new Philadelphia North American League hockey team."

"We didn't have a name, we had a temporary office, we didn't have team colors. We had nothing," Pilling said, reminiscing about his time in Philadelphia. "That's really why I wanted to come to Philly. What a glorious opportunity to be on the ground floor of starting up a brand-new franchise." Pilling went home to Roanoke, packed up his apartment, rented a U-Haul trailer, and came right back to Philadelphia, eager to

## 10. The Firebirds

start building his roster. He stayed with Flyers enforcer Dave Schultz for two weeks while looking for a permanent home.³

One week later, the winning entry was announced in the team's naming contest. Out of thousands of names submitted, including 716 by one fan eager to win the prize of four season tickets, the organization agreed: the new team would be called the Firebirds. They also announced a partnership with the Flyers and Washington Capitals, in which each team would utilize the Firebirds as a farm team for some of their players. "We don't want to compete with the Flyers," Roberts said at a press conference. "We hope to get the young fans and the families who can't get into the Flyers' games since they have a sold-out situation."⁴

"The Flyers only have so many seats," he said another time. "We are not in competition with them. The Flyers have awakened this town and we hope there will be a spinoff of their spirit in our operation."⁵

"Fans can identify with a minor-league player sometimes, where an NHL player seems too far off," added NAHL Commissioner Bob Dextraze. "Kids can see the minor leaguer and realize they can be a pro, too."⁶

Training camp would open on October 7 at the University of Pennsylvania's Class of '23 rink. A few weeks later, the Firebirds were offered an expansion draft. However, because the franchise was granted after the schedule was already released, the other teams demanded more money per player. The Firebirds rejected the offer, figuring they would find better players elsewhere anyway.

"Drafts are a joke," Pilling said. "I've scouted juniors and the minors and I've already contacted 19 players. They'll come here if they don't make some club in a higher classification." Asked about the comparisons to the Blazers and the Jersey Devils, the EHL team which played in the Cherry Hill Arena for nine seasons, both of which failed in a short period of time, Pilling was quick with his reply. "The Blazers were in direct competition with the Flyers," he said. "We're not, obviously. We're an alternative. And, we'll be competitive. People also try to draw comparisons between us and the Jersey Devils. Again, there's no comparison. We're not in the Cherry Hill Arena."⁷

The Firebirds' first year roster would include seven players of Pilling's championship Rebels squad: Rychard Campeau, Pierre Henry, Nick Haramis, Jack Chipchase, Michel Plante, Dale MacLeish (the brother of the Flyers' Rick MacLeish), and goalie Danny Sullivan. Also following Pilling to Philadelphia was the Rebels' trainer and emergency goalie, North Carolina native Dave "Sudsy" Settlemyre, who later went on to fulfill the same roles with the budding AHL Maine Mariners in 1977. (Settlemyre was later the long-time equipment manager for the NHL

Flyers, a position also held by his son, Derek.) On defense it would also feature tough as nails Ray Schultz, the brother of the Flyers' own enforcer, Dave "The Hammer" Schultz. In goal, the team would be backstopped by recent Flyers draft pick Rejean "Reggie" Lemelin. After taking part in Flyers training camp earlier in the Fall, the team didn't believe he was even ready for AHL hockey, so they assigned him to the Firebirds, allowing him to remain in the region while developing his game. Lemelin, having played in the Quebec Major Junior League, was highly regarded. He was drafted into both the NHL and the WHA, before deciding to pursue his goal of becoming an NHL player. Expectations were high for the young, Quebec native.

With training camp behind them, the Firebirds opened their season with three straight overtime games, coming out the other side with a win, a loss, and a tie. They spent the next half-month struggling to get their legs and attempting to gel as a team—by November 8 they were 5–6–1 and sat toward the bottom of the league standings. But as they returned home from a road game in Mohawk Valley to play the Maine Nordiques at the Civic Center, a spark seemed to ignite something in the locker room. The team demolished their northern rivals 9–4, setting them off on a six-game winning streak that propelled them upward.

But, just as quickly as they turned it around, lady luck seemed to walk out on the Firebirds. A November 20 loss to Syracuse started a five-game losing streak that returned the team to below .500. The streak included a famous walkout by Pilling in which he pulled his team off the ice in protest. At an away game against Maine, Lemelin was injured on the play that resulted in Maine's fifth goal. When Pilling pulled Lemelin to replace him with backup Dan Sullivan, the referee refused to give him a two-minute warmup period to which Pilling felt he was entitled, based on WHA rules (under which the NAHL operated). Pilling brought his players to the locker room, refusing to return to the ice until Sullivan was given the opportunity to warm up. The referee refused, demanding the Firebirds return to the ice. When Pilling ignored the warnings, the referee forced the Firebirds to forfeit the game.

Roberts was furious at his coach, who was fined $1,000 and suspended five games for the act. He described the decision as "fair because of the consequences of such an act when you're dealing with paying customers…. This won't be a reflection on the Firebirds, but on Gregg." The incident created a rift between the two that only widened as the season progressed.[8]

The streaky Firebirds continued their roller coaster inaugural season, embarking on a seven-game winning streak in December that pushed them far into first place, a shocking development for an expansion franchise. Included in that streak was a December 17 win against the Long Island Cougars in which Pierre Henry scored a hat trick and forward Bobby Collyard added a goal and two assists of his own to push himself into a tie for the league points lead with 44.

The next night, the Firebirds clinched the seventh win of the streak in a nasty battle against the Johnstown Jets in front of 1,039 fans at the Civic Center. Tied early in the second period, a brawl broke out when the Firebirds' Les Crozier and the Jets' Jack Perpich began tussling. Others added to the fun, culminating in the Carlson brothers (Steve and Jeff, who would go on to play two of the Hanson brothers in *Slap Shot*) dropping the gloves with just about everyone on the ice. The referee handed out 130 penalty minutes, including two match penalties, while the Firebirds squeaked away with a 6–5 victory.

As their first regular season began to dwindle, though, the Firebirds again began to slump. Sitting in first place on March 8, the team dropped its last five games to fall into second place just before the playoffs, finishing behind the Syracuse Blazers. The frustration was evident in a March 16 game at Cape Cod in which the Firebirds started a bench-clearing brawl, resulting in five major penalties, four misconduct penalties and a double-minor. The fight yielded nothing, as the team lost 5–4 and were mathematically eliminated from the regular season title.

Nonetheless, Philadelphia fans responded to their new hockey franchise. In their final home game of the regular season, against Cape Cod on March 7, an NAHL-record crowd of 9,184 showed up to watch Lemelin backstop the Firebirds to a 5–0 shutout win, according to a March press release from the league office. "I think we have proven that there is room for the Firebirds in Philadelphia," said Roberts excitedly after the game. Dextraze concurred, stating that "it's a fine tribute to the owners, players, and staff of the Firebirds. The fans have treated the Firebirds well and the entire league is pleased with their progress."[9]

Matched up against the Long Island Cougars in the first round of the playoffs, the Firebirds came out strong, battling their way to a 4–2 victory in front of a Philadelphia crowd of 4,316 to take a lead in the best-of-five opening series. "All year we haven't been going to the body at all," said Mike Clarke after the win. "About five games ago we figured we'd have to get something going or forget it for the playoffs."[10]

After falling in their second game by a 3–2 score, the Firebirds went to Long Island for the next two games. The Cougars took Game 3 with a dominating 5–2 win, despite the Firebirds' protests. The night got off to a fiery start when Pilling arrived with a fake newspaper, which was created on his behalf by George Piszek. The paper's top headline stated that the Chicago Cougars, who owned the Long Island squad, was out of money and would be unable to pay any of the players in their employ. "We were just trying to get them unsettled and not thinking about the hockey game," Pilling said years later, laughing at the memory.

As the night progressed closer to puck drop, the players noticed that the new ice surface, which had been put down earlier in the day to replace the recent circus, was soft, chipped, and covered with holes behind the nets. The game was delayed a half-hour while the officials attempted to fix the poor conditions. When they couldn't, Pilling took his team to the locker room and refused to go out. The referee agreed, sending both teams to the locker room in an effort to cancel the match. But, with the Firebirds on the team bus ready to pull away and the players already having enjoyed a few drinks, a call came from Commissioner Bob Dextraze that the game had to be played. An hour later, after more repair work was futilely attempted, the game commenced and the teams cautiously played through an ugly contest, with the game-winning goal coming when Pierre Henry tripped over a divot in the ice and lost control of the puck.

The final game of the Firebirds inaugural season took place—eventually—on April 4. While the game was scheduled to start at 8:00 p.m., the Firebirds were nowhere to be found. Their bus had yet to arrive at Long Island Arena, angering both the Cougars and the commissioner, who said, "We're going to play the game, no matter what time they arrive. We'll talk about disciplinary measures later." As the clock turned to 8:15, then 8:20, the team still was missing in action.

"He's pulled this before," said Cougar center Howie Colborne, referring to Pilling, under whom he played for part of the season before being loaned to Long Island.

"I'm sure he'll come up with some fantastic story," said Cougar goalie Chris Grigg.[11]

While the story being circulated was that the Firebirds' bus was stuck on the Verrazano Bridge because of heavy winds, the hometown team and fans were buying none of it. As the clock hit 8:25, the bus finally pulled into the parking lot. Pilling exited the bus with a "wry smile," according to the *Inquirer*. "Couldn't get the damn bus over 45 miles an hour," he said. "The wind was blowing the bus all over the place." Despite his attempt at gamesmanship, the Firebirds were unprepared for the game, taking an 8–2 defeat to clinch the series for the Cougars and end Philadelphia's first NAHL campaign with disappointment.[12]

The Firebirds' first season was marginally successful on the ice. Although the team couldn't push the limits in the postseason, their second-place finish was quite respectable for a brand-new team. Lemelin was awarded rookie of the year, posting a 3.37 goals against average (an incredible feat in a league year in which the average team scored upwards of four goals per game). Collyard finished fourth in the league with 42 goals and tied for third in the league with 103 points. The Firebirds more than showed potential—they were pretty talented.

But off the ice the team was hampered. The Piszeks reportedly lost close to $400,000 in just the one season. The team reported about 100,000 fans attended their games, but only 74,000 of those were paid. With an average admission price of $3.65, that left the revenue looking pretty slim. On top of that, the team paid the city a minimum of $1,350 per home game, plus an additional 12 percent of any gate revenue over $7,500. The financial picture was clearly grim, once you accounted for player salaries, league fees, and other operating costs.[13] (Not to mention the night in February 1975 when a burglar broke into the Civic Center locker room and stole $20,000 worth of hockey equipment from the team. Soon after that, the rink's sprinklers malfunctioned, drenching the team's equipment and requiring them to replace most of it a second time.)

One issue was that the public knew very little about the Firebirds. There was almost no marketing done by the team and the press was fairly stingy with their coverage. After the season, Pilling told a story of the return from the team's first road trip. The bus pulled into the Civic Center parking lot and the security guard stopped them.

"Who are you?" the guard said.

"We're the Firebirds."

"What are you, a band?"

"No, a hockey club."

The guard yelled to his colleague, "Hey, you know anything about a hockey club?"[14]

Getting the fans involved proved similarly challenging. "Last year," said Firebirds executive vice president Frank Keenan, "We were waiting for the crowds to knock our doors down. The Flyers had won the Stanley Cup and there were 17,000 each night at the Spectrum. We figured there were 50,000 people who wanted to see hockey and that they'd come to us. Well, it wasn't that easy. Now, we're out knocking on their doors."

Perhaps it was naïve to expect fans to come rushing to the gates of a brand-new minor league hockey team without much public relations push from the front office. But at the same time, the front office was having power struggles, so much so that at the end of the first season, Robin Roberts pulled out from the team. George Piszek, Ed's son and the team's president, described Roberts to the press as "a little boy who sees something in the store and wants it and can't have it." The Piszeks put a lot of money into the team and were willing to continue doing so.

The Firebirds team bus was recognizable almost everywhere they went—except sometimes their own arena's parking lot (courtesy Bruce "Scoop" Cooper).

Roberts, on the other hand, did not have quite as deep pockets as his colleagues and was uncomfortable continuing to finance a money-losing operation.[15]

On top of the financial issues, Roberts apparently was unhappy with the way Pilling handled his team, specifically when he pulled the squad off the ice in Maine. The *Inquirer* reported that instance was a "pivotal factor." On top of that, Pilling felt he didn't get the support he needed from Roberts. Nonetheless, the organization parted amicably with the Phillies legend and moved forward, looking toward their second season.[16]

At 1975 training camp, Pilling was optimistic about the upcoming season. There were still many holes to fill, including one left by Collyard signing with the WHA's Cincinnati Stingers (he would quickly return to the Firebirds after being cut by Cincinnati shortly thereafter). The team included 15 players from the previous year's roster, while also adding some players that could help them be more physical on the ice, such as Bill Evo, Dean Boylan, Denis Patry, Gord Brooks, and more. "I want a bigger hockey team this year," Pilling said. "We've got enough small players now."[17]

## 10. The Firebirds

Brooks had a different story than most of the Firebirds, in that his NHL career had already happened, relative to most Firebirds players, who were still chasing their shot at the major league. Having played for the St. Louis Blues and Washington Capitals, he had the talent to compete with the best. Before the 1975–76 season, however, he received a letter from the Capitals that he would be assigned to the Firebirds minor league team. Having only been to Philadelphia when he was traveling to play the Flyers, he was unsure of what to expect. Fortunately, he had an old friend already on the roster.

Collyard, who had been with the Firebirds since their inaugural season, had played with Brooks since 1970 for parts of five seasons, through the Central League, the Western League, and the NHL. When Brooks landed at the Philadelphia airport, Pilling and Collyard were waiting to welcome him to the city. The astute coach immediately paired the two old linemates together again, adding forward Randy Osburn to the left side. Osburn, who Brooks later called the best around the net player he had ever seen, was a master at distracting the opposing goalie, redirecting pucks into the net, and finding a way to get the puck on goal through traffic. Together, the three made up perhaps the most dynamic line in the NAHL's short history. (Some even compared their offensive production to that of the Flyers famous LCB line [Reggie Leach, Bob Clarke, and Bill Barber]. In the 1975–76 season, the Firebirds top line combined for 113 goals, 177 assists, and 290 points. The LCB line combined for 322 points the same season, albeit at the NHL level.)

The Firebirds' second campaign was seemingly opposite to their first. While their inaugural campaign saw a strong team fall in the standings as the year progressed, the 1975–76 campaign began with the team dropping to the cellar and needing to claw its way back. A six-game losing streak that started on October 18 left the squad looking way up at the teams in front of them in the newly-created West Division. (The NAHL added two expansion teams in 1975, pushing the league to ten teams. They split into two divisions: Beauce, Syracuse, Mohawk Valley, Cape Cod and Maine in the East Division and Johnstown, Philadelphia, Erie, Buffalo and Broome County in the West Division.) A Denis Patry hat trick on November 5 against the Buffalo Norsemen, mixed with a bench-clearing brawl that saw a club-record 108 penalty minutes handed out to the Firebirds and 190 total penalty minutes (including four game misconducts, five ten-minute misconducts and eight fighting majors), sparked a four-game winning streak that propelled the Firebirds out of the league's basement. But inconsistency was again the name of the game as the year progressed. They failed to win or lose more than two consecutive games until February.

The Philadelphia Firebirds and the Binghamton Broome Dusters drop the gloves during a typical NAHL brawl (courtesy Bruce "Scoop" Cooper).

At the beginning of the month they sat at 25–23–0, a respectable record but not quite good enough.

What was good enough, though, was the offensive firepower on the Philadelphia roster. The team could score at will, which bailed them out of many holes in which they continuously found themselves throughout the season. In late December they trailed Buffalo, 5–3, before scoring six straight third-period goals to win handily in a 9–5 decision. In January, against the Erie Blades, they scored nine goals in the second period and had 67 shots on goal—both NAHL records. (The teams also set a league record with a combined 117 shots on goal.)

In February, the team's offense took off to new levels, sparking the squad to a record eight-game winning streak. In the record-breaking game against Buffalo at the Civic Center, Collyard broke his own club record of the previous year with his 64th assist, while Michel Plante broke Collyard's previous goal record, ultimately finishing the season with 52. The win put the team in second place, 12 points behind Johnstown with 18 games remaining (six of them against the Jets). Though they would win their last five games (and win four of the six against Johnstown), the Firebirds would finish in second place with a 45–29–0

## 10. The Firebirds

record. The team potted 373 goals in their second season, leading the East Division.

Their opening round playoff series saw them matched up against Erie in a best-of-five series. After taking the entire squad to a Flyers game to get in the proper mindset for the postseason, Pilling nervously stepped behind the bench with expectations sky high. His boys met those expectations and then some, demolishing the Blades by a 10–5 score. The game marked the team's 17th consecutive win at the Civic Center, a marvelous achievement for a team that was still, at times, struggling to find its way. Those struggles resurfaced when the Blades took the next two games by a combined 11–5 score, including Game 3 in Philadelphia, breaking the team's home winning streak.

Facing elimination on the road, the Firebirds pulled themselves together. "The last two games weren't our style," Pilling said before the game. "We scored 373 goals during the season and we've only had five in the last two games. We'll score more goals Thursday night." The team came through on Pilling's prophecy and whipped the Blades, 7–4, sending the series to a fifth and deciding game.[18]

"I've never seen a team that's been down to the last game and was so confident of winning the game they had to," said Crozier. "It was quiet in the dressing room before the game. We weren't overconfident, but we knew if we stuck to hockey, we could win."[19]

Returning home for the deciding game, the Firebirds seemed focused in a way the fans hadn't seen for two seasons. With a rejuvenated offensive attack, the team potted six goals, with Patry leading the way with four points of his own, to down the Blades, 6–4, and clinch a spot in the Lockhart Cup semifinals. The team they were up against? The Johnstown Jets, their cross-state rival.

The teams split the first two games, but Game 3 is what seemed to set the tone for the rest of the series. The Firebirds launched over 40 shots on goal at the Jets, scoring seven, and taking a 2–1 lead in the best-of-seven series. The game was hard fought, with the game-winning goal coming with just 1:50 remaining, followed by an empty-net goal to ice the game.

Game 4 in Johnstown was to be a fierce test. Throughout the season, the Firebirds had managed to win in Johnstown just once. In one of the closest and toughest games of the season for either team, the Firebirds came out on top, squeaking by with a 4–3 victory. The win set up an opportunity to clinch the conference championship at home in front of the Philadelphia fans and secure a spot in the league finals.

When the team arrived for the game, they saw over 7,500 fans in attendance—the largest crowd to ever witness an NAHL semifinal

The Firebirds and Johnstown Jets, fierce rivals, take the ice at the Civic Center during the 1976 NAHL semifinals (courtesy Bruce "Scoop" Cooper).

game. It quickly turned into a circus. The Jets scored the opening two goals, but the explosive Firebirds didn't panic. Instead, they scored six of the next seven, jumping out to a 6–3 lead by the end of the first period, a frame that was filled with rough play and 25 penalty minutes. The squad scored five more goals in the second period to take an 11–6 lead, before finishing the job in the third period and completing a circus-like 14–10 victory to move on to the final round and play for the Lockhart Cup. The game was described by the *Inquirer* as "the kind of performance that made Barnum and Bailey famous" and "slapstick comedy."[20] Even the Firebirds defensemen were disgusted at the messy performance. Nonetheless, they came away with the much-needed win, dispensing of their Pennsylvania rivals and earning a date with the Beauce Jaros for the league championship. Pilling recalls being so stressed out by the back and forth play that, at one point in the middle of the action, he sat down on the bench and pulled out a cigarette. "Sudsy," he said, motioning to his equipment manager, "Change the lines, I need to have a smoke for a minute."

Beauce was by far the league's best team in the regular season, winning the East Division with a 54–18–2 record and scoring an astonishing

## 10. The Firebirds

The Philadelphia Firebirds and the Beauce Jaros face off during the 1976 NAHL final at the Civic Center (courtesy Bruce "Scoop" Cooper).

462 goals in the process (along with posting over 2,000 penalty minutes, the only team in the league to surpass that mark). Coached by NHL veteran Joe Hardy, who potted an incredible 208 points during the regular season, the Firebirds were up against perhaps their most difficult challenge since their inception—a seven-game series against arguably the strongest team in the league. The teams split the first four games: in Beauce, the Firebirds opened with a 7–5 win and the Jaros responded with a 7–4 win. In Philadelphia, the Firebirds took Game 3 by a 6–1 score, followed by the Jaros taking Game 4, 7–6.

Back in Quebec for a crucial Game 5, the Firebirds knew they would need to catch a break in order to pull ahead of the offensive juggernaut against whom they were matched. The arena, the Palais des Sports, was sold out to standing room only. (The arena, which exists today as the Center Sportif Lacroix-Dutil, had an extremely low ceiling, causing the top level of the arena to be covered in thick cigarette smoke rising from the patrons. On top of that, the Firebirds had three shots hit the rafters during the game.) The Jaros fired 47 shots at Firebirds goalie Gaye Cooley, but he was calm as could be, turning away nearly all of them and making some show stopping saves in the process. (Cooley spent the entire season with the Charlotte Checkers of the SHL, leading them to the league championship just a few weeks earlier. He joined the Firebirds for the playoffs after Lemelin was injured.) On top of that, the Firebirds' power play, which ranked eighth of ten during the season, connected on two opportunities that resulted from a five-minute major to Beauce left wing Gilles Bilodeau. Mike Penase scored a shorthanded goal while the Firebirds were two men short to give them a 5–2 lead they would not relinquish. The Firebirds put one more goal past Jaros goalie Yves Archambault (who, coincidentally, also served as the Blazers' playoff goalie a few years prior) to make the final score 6–4 and set up a championship-clinching game on home ice two nights later.

All the while, the Firebirds were hanging on by the skin of their teeth. The team was admittedly exhausted and they were struggling to get through each game. With a 14-hour bus ride separating the two cities, Pilling booked a flight home from Quebec to give the team a chance to rest. Unfortunately, the trip turned into a nine-hour charade, including three-hour layovers in two airports. "Nobody slept much last night again," said Randy Osburn before Game 6. "Right now, your body just

During a rough 1976 NAHL final, members of the Beauce Jaros were pushing past each other to get out of the penalty box (courtesy Bruce "Scoop" Cooper).

## 10. The Firebirds

takes over and the stored-up energy that you didn't know you had just started coming."[21]

"They don't know how tired they really are," said Pilling. "And I couldn't get most of them in bed last night. Their bodies are operating on automatic right now."[22]

The team was readying to play their 30th game in 42 days. Pilling, to take the edge off, took his family on a picnic that morning. Minor league hockey, he said, was tougher than major league hockey. "You say minor league and right away people automatically think bush league," he said. "But these guys, hey, they sweat as much, they bleed as much, they try as hard as the guys in the bigtime. Maybe, they even try harder. 'Cause they don't have it made yet. They're still trying to prove themselves. They can't coast."[23]

"Obviously, we don't do it for the money," said forward Peter Cahill before the game. "It's pride. And being able to live the rest of your life and not wonder whether you could have made it or not. At least, you gave yourself the chance. I guess that makes it all worthwhile."[24]

With an astonishing 9,227 in attendance at the Civic Center, the Firebirds took the ice determined to end the season right then and there. The game started ominously, with the Jaros scoring just 13 seconds into the game. But Collyard and Brooks took immediate control, scoring twice in the next 57 seconds to stun the Jaros and take an early lead. The game boiled down to another rough-and-tumble affair, with 30 minutes of fighting, 202 penalty minutes, in a three-hour game of hard-hitting hockey. In the midst of the first period, Beauce's Mike Busniuk and Firebird Ray Schultz dropped the gloves. While that fight was going on, Beauce's John Von Horlick jumped on Dean Boylan, causing Collyard, normally calm and collected, to fly in with a high hit that knocked Von Horlick to the ground. Collyard was joined by Crozier and the two laid a beat down on the Beauce player for a few seconds before the two were dragged off by an official. The rough style of hockey, which the Firebirds were thrilled to exhibit, seemed to bring the Jaros down. "They were better off when they were trying to play hockey," Pilling said after the game with a wry smile.[25]

Late in the third period, with the Firebirds leading, 3–2, Howie Heggedal took a pinpoint pass from Collyard and snuck it past the goal line, causing the arena to erupt. With just a few seconds remaining, the 'Birds potted one more insurance marker, clinching the championship for Philadelphia with a 5–2 win.

The crowd broke out in deafening cheers as the trophy was brought out to the team, but the team's celebration was surprisingly muted. With barely any energy left to rejoice, the players simply smiled, marveling at their achievement. Dean Boylan explained it best: "I was hurt, everyone was hurt," he said after the game. "Between the second and third periods we said we didn't know how many of us could make it back to Beauce [for a possible seventh game] and just decided to end it tonight."[26]

As the fans continued to cheer, Pilling took the microphone and spoke eloquently to the crowd. "We're the champions," he said, "But we're also tired. We want to get the hell out of here. Get the **** off the ice." The crowd began a chant of, "Off the ice! Off the ice!" eventually letting the Firebirds into their dressing room.[27]

Minutes later, Pilling was standing on a table in the center of the dressing room, holding a broken champagne bottle, his right thumb bleeding. "I'd be a liar if I said I didn't have disagreements with management and that thought [of resigning] didn't cross my mind," he said. "But you don't bail out on the people who back you. I pulled the team off the ice last season and I never heard a word about it. How could I be a quitter? Mr. Piszek isn't. Let's face it, the Firebirds could have been dead last summer after the bath they took. But they honestly believe there's a place in this city for the Firebirds."[28]

As the calm celebration continued, he went on: "Hockey players play above pain more than any other athlete. They not only want to show how good they are but how good they are when hurt. They sacrifice."

"These finals were worth more to me than the whole year in Charlotte," said an exasperated Cooley, who was celebrating his second championship of the *season*. "I have never seen a team in my life with more harmony. I would like to play right here the rest of my life."[29]

Collyard, who the *Inquirer* dubbed the playoff MVP (the actual award didn't exist), was described by the paper as having "as much drive as Mario Andretti and Jack Nicklaus combined." The star forward was exhausted, but not too much to miss the party. "A lot of us haven't been sleeping good," he said, "Getting three hours here, a couple more there. How am I going to celebrate? I'll get drunk and go sleep for a few days."

With the team ready to pack up, Pilling stood in front of his squad one more time. "You gave blood for this," he said, "This is ours. We are Philadelphia's first championship team in the Bicentennial."[30]

The team retired across the street to the Hilton hotel, while Pilling and other members of the organization sat in the hotel bar quietly celebrating the successful ending to their season. In the midst of their fun, Beauce owner Andrew Veilleux approached the group and stuck out his hand with respect. "You have a wonderful team," he said. "You're very deserving champions. Congratulations." Pilling never forgot the gesture.

The Firebirds coach had become a minor league legend in Philadelphia. His personality mirrored that Philadelphia tough, never-give-up

## 10. The Firebirds

attitude. His antics angered the opposition but endeared himself to the crazy NAHL fans who supported the team. Early in the season a fan hung a rubber chicken over the Firebirds' bench. Pilling took out his lighter and set it on fire.

Another time, en route to a game against Erie, he began writing his initials on the inside cover of his rulebook. Just before he wrote the "G," he realized that he would be coaching against Nick Polano, and decided to write Polano's name into the book. When, in the middle of the game, Polano complained to the referee one too many times, Pilling tossed the book on the ice while the play was at the other end. When the referee saw it on the ice, he screamed at his linesmen to find out who threw the publication on the playing surface. They opened the book, saw Polano's name, and pointed him out. The referee made a beeline toward the Erie bench, and gave Polano a bench minor—much to Polano's surprise, since he had no idea what he had done. The Firebirds scored on the ensuing power play and went on to win by one goal. After the game, Polano walked by Pilling, screaming, "You son of a bitch, you can't do that!" "Oh, we were just beside ourselves laughing," Pilling remembered.

But perhaps his best antic was when, with his team down a goal late in a game, he pulled his goalie and sent out an extra skater. As the linesman flew by, Pilling feigned shock, yelling, "Hey, wait, we got too many guys out there! Oh no, I forgot, we pulled the goalie." The linesman immediately stopped and began counting players. He counted six skaters and nobody in net, then continued up the ice. As he skated away, Pilling sent a seventh player over the boards, causing the opposing coach to scream at the ref.

"They've got seven guys out there!" he screamed. "C'mon, dummy, open your eyes!"

The linesman stopped and snapped back. "They've got six players and they pulled their goalie. I just counted, now shut up."

Just then, the linesman turned around and began counting again, for good measure. One ... two ... three.... A few seconds later, the Firebirds tied the game, whereupon the Philadelphia bench emptied, mobbing the seven players on the ice, preventing the officials from completing their count. "I saw it coming," the opposing coach later said, "But couldn't get the officials ready for it, no matter how I warned them."

Stories about Pilling have become legend in Philadelphia hockey circles, with former players sitting around, laughing about their coach's antics—most of them surrounding frustrations with the officials. One game, he told his guys not to move after the puck was dropped, in order to mess with the referee. When play began, all five players remained motionless. It confused the opposing team, who thought they didn't hear a whistle, causing them to remain motionless as well, with the clock still running. The referee, stunned, yelled at everyone to move. The Firebirds players remained motionless. The official skated over to the bench and gave Pilling a bench minor. Pilling didn't send anyone to the penalty box, causing the referee to yell at him, "Get someone over there right now or I'm running you." Pilling responded, "Who do you want?" "I don't care, just get someone over there," the referee responded.

Pilling turned to his equipment manager and said, "Sudsy, go serve that penalty," causing the Greensboro, North Carolina, native to slink across the ice toward the penalty box. When the scorekeeper noticed, he motioned to the referee, who turned to Sudsy and said, "What the hell are you doing here?" To which Sudsy, with a calm, weak voice, said, "I'm here to serve the penalty." The referee, already noticing that he was now the butt of the joke, could hardly contain his laughter as he skated back over to Pilling and said, "Get a player over there before I run you!"

Another time, when walking across the ice to the bench after the intermission, he donned a referee's jersey, cut down a hockey stick, put sunglasses on, and crossed the ice as if he were blind, to the hooting and hollering of crowd approval. And when the NAHL mandated that the players wear helmets, Pilling walked onto the ice surface before the season opener with an army helmet atop his head, took it off and gave the crowd a thumbs down, to the pleasure of the thousands in attendance.

One game in Maine saw Pilling being honored for his service to hockey. As Maine's mascot, a snowman, skated around the ice, the

A Philadelphia Firebirds game program from their time in the North American League.

public address announcer turned to the bench and introduced the Philadelphia coach. When everyone looked toward the Firebirds, Pilling was nowhere to be seen. The announcer repeated his name—"Gregg Pilling!"—and again, there was no coach. Suddenly, the mascot stopped next to the mat laid out on the ice and removed the head to reveal Pilling, who had given the actual mascot performer a few bucks to borrow his costume for the prank. The prank was pre-planned, it was later known, a publicity stunt for both teams. "You're just trying to put asses in the seats, you know?" Pilling reminisced.

Pilling's antics weren't just reserved for the officials and the fans. In one game, with Lemelin in net, Pilling warned him that he was going to switch goalies to backup Danny Sullivan at the first whistle. After the two swapped, Pilling told Lemelin that he was going back in the following whistle. The goalies switched places about three or four times, before Lemelin got frustrated and yelled to Sullivan, to the backup goalie's utter surprise, that if Pilling wanted to play games, he would do the same thing. They were going to do an on-the-fly goalie change. "We break out, a pass here, a pass there, and as soon as the puck gets to the neutral zone, I come toward the bench," Lemelin reminisced with a laugh. "[Sullivan] jumps and goes into the net. Pill's at the other end [of the bench] and goes, 'Reggie! That was fucking awesome!'"

The NAHL as a whole was filled with incredible stories from the road. A league that helped spawn the famous *Slap Shot* movie (the camera crew actually followed the Firebirds around for part of their inaugural season for research and footage), it was far from opulent. Minor league hockey, as the *Inquirer* eloquently and accurately described it once, was "about as glamorous as a dirty clothes hamper.... There aren't many roses in the NAHL and when you do bend over to sniff them what you're liable to come up with is a face full of thorns.... Your companion is exhaustion, and after seven months your legs no longer believe the lies you tell them. You play in rinks where the ice in the corners is four inches of water, in a game where the contact, if it was committed on the streets, would get you five-to-18. Years, that is."[31]

Some of the players recalled a night in which forward Tom Young fell asleep in one of the team bus's bunk beds. When the bus arrived, no one bothered to wake him up, and the driver, not knowing there was still someone on board, parked the bus in the depot, locked the door and left. When Young woke up, he realized he was alone, with no way out of the bus. Thinking quickly, he smashed through the bus window to escape, but not before a police car coincidentally drove by just as he did it. The cop didn't believe his story, which caused Young to be arrested, all while his wife tried and failed to get in touch with him through his teammates.

Firebirds goaltender Reggie Lemelin and coach Gregg Pilling had a great relationship that included some memorable on-ice antics (courtesy Bruce "Scoop" Cooper).

Another night, before a game in Buffalo, Pilling realized the team was short players—some players were sick with a bug going around the locker room, while others got stuck in a snowstorm and couldn't make it to the rink in time. NAHL rules dictated that a team had to dress at least ten players and a goalie. He only had nine. Pilling put on his equipment and put the team bus driver, Tony Gabriel, and Sudsy on a five-game tryout. By puck drop, the team had just three defensemen and eight forwards.

But simply dressing for the game wasn't enough for the eccentric head coach. He got into a fight that carried over to the parking lot. Paying him back for being lumbered earlier in the game, Pilling hit the opposing player with a hockey stick outside his locker room. Very quickly, a couple of policemen ran to the scene and attempted to arrest Pilling, who was still in full equipment. The coach convinced the policemen to allow him to change back into his street clothes, and then joined the officers in a drive to the local precinct. Gordie Brooks, who was nicknamed "Roadhog" because he often subbed for Gabriel (who also occasionally did radio color commentary with play-by-play broadcaster John McAdams), behind the wheel on the way back from road games,

10. *The Firebirds* 171

All it took was a little spark... (courtesy Bruce "Scoop" Cooper).

...to start a brawl between two rivals, such as this one between the Firebirds and the Erie Blades (courtesy Bruce "Scoop" Cooper).

The Philadelphia Firebirds team photograph in the 1976–77 season. Top row: Dave "Sudsy" Settlemyre (trainer), Richard "Pez" Campeau, Mike Bradbury, George "Swarby" Swarbrick, Peter Cahill, Michel "Itchy" Plante, Jim "Turk" Evers (equipment manager). Middle row: Bruce "Scoop" Cooper (PR), Don "Hayser" Hay, Dan Nelson, Ray "Shooter" Schultz, Mark "Bosco" Bousquet, Les "J.C." Crozier, Mike "Kono" Penasse. Bottom row: Rejean "Reggie" Lemelin, Gordie "The Roadhog" Brooks, Bobby "B.C." Collyard, Gregg "Pill" Pilling (GM/coach), Dean "Deano" Boylan, Randy "Wizzard" Osburn, Loren "Mooner" Molleken (courtesy Bruce "Scoop" Cooper).

chartered the vehicle toward the station to pick up their head coach. (Gabriel would often leave in the middle of the third period, mentioning on the broadcast that he had to go warm up the bus.) Not knowing the height of the bus, he powered toward an overpass that, incidentally wasn't tall enough to allow the bus to pass. The vehicle smashed into the bridge, taking off the lights on the top of the bus and causing the team to get stuck under the overpass.

Despite the team winning a championship, the city's second ever minor league crown (after the Ramblers won in 1936), the Firebirds still struggled financially. No matter what the team did on the ice, short of a championship-clinching game, they still couldn't manage to fill the seats. "When we started this team, we thought it would be like opening an air conditioning store on the equator," Piszek said. "I don't know why people don't come to see us play. It's discouraging." Every time Piszek went into the locker room after a game, players would ask him how many fans were in the stands, leaving him to find a legitimate excuse as to why the number is low—the Flyers are playing, the weather, a local event. Anything to kick the can up the road. It was difficult for the players as well. They would consistently see empty seats at the Civic Center, yet they would visit towns a fraction the size of Philadelphia and see a sold-out arena.[32]

As the team began its championship defense in the club's third season, the issues did not dissipate. After the team was eliminated in the first round by Erie in 1977, Piszek came out and announced disturbing news: the team had lost so much money that he was not sure they would return to operate for the 1977–78 season. Regular season attendance was simply too weak and inconsistent. "Tuesday night we could play the Red Army team and not draw anybody," Piszek said. "Friday we could play the *Inquirer* pickup team and we'd draw."[33]

On top of that, at the end of the 1977 season, Pilling and the Firebirds parted ways. The team, according to Pilling, had an understanding with him that he wanted to move his way up the ladder toward an NHL coaching gig—though there is no doubt that the owners may have tired of his antics. Either way, the two sides parted amicably, as Pilling took a job in the International League and the Piszeks searched for a new coach.

The team troubled its fans throughout the summer, refusing to sell tickets until they were certain they would operate the following season. The summer was also filled with rumors about the NAHL's imminent demise, which forced the Firebirds to seek a backup plan in case they had no league to play in come Fall. The Piszeks attempted to quell the rumors by claiming the league was as strong as ever, but everyone knew that it was hyperbole. The Firebirds were without a coach, without a schedule, and possibly without a league.

In the middle of September, the Beauce Jaros withdrew from the league, leaving the NAHL with just five teams. The league announced its intention to put a team in Baltimore or Cape Cod to strengthen the circuit, but those plans went nowhere. Danny Belisle, the Firebirds new GM-coach, was extremely unhappy with the uncertainty. "Sitting here dangling like this makes me sick," he told the *Philadelphia Daily News*. "I have a contract, but I don't know if it stipulates whether I get paid if the club goes out of existence.... It's an awful mess."[34]

The *Daily News* continued to report the league's imminent death, even as league officials claimed otherwise. All the while, commissioner Jack Timmins disappeared. No one could reach him and the only statements made were by president William Rocheleau, Jr. He announced on a conference call that the league agreed to operate in the upcoming season with just five franchises. That shocked Keenan, who was not aware of any conference call. Teams were told by the league to go ahead with ticket sales and season promotion, but the organizations weren't buying it. They knew there were legitimate issues not being addressed. All the while, the Firebirds were reportedly attempting to join the American League, but the NAHL refused to release them. The team was stuck. Perhaps Bill Fleischman of the *Daily News* said it best: "The Bugs Bunny Follies are scheduled to open October 4 at the Civic Center.... The NAHL's antics have been a fitting preview for Bugs and friends."[35]

Just four days later, the inevitable happened. The NAHL folded, claiming that the Utica franchise needed financial help from the other four teams, who refused to pitch in. Either way, the move finally freed up the Firebirds' commitments, allowing them to, on September 28, officially join the AHL, giving Philadelphia their first franchise in the top minor-league circuit since the Rockets. The team joined the Southern Division and would play alongside Hershey, New Haven, Hampton, and Rochester. They would play in the opposite division as the Flyers' farm team, the Maine Mariners.

The team immediately encountered their first challenge—putting together a competitive team in just a few weeks. "I've always liked challenges, but this is the biggest of my hockey career," said Belisle. "I have an awful task ahead of me. There are a lot of hockey players in the country without contracts right now."[36] Belisle brought with him a few members of the NAHL roster: Collyard, Brooks, Osburn, and Plante. "The time element is against me. We'll just have to work harder, faster and longer than anyone else. I will personally guarantee that any player who plays for me will work for 60 minutes—not 40 or 30."[37]

In addition, the Piszeks were still worried about the financial feasibility of the franchise. On top of the reported $125,000 franchise fee they had to pay to the AHL, the team needed to draw an average of 4,000 fans per game just to break even on operating costs—yet, they had never come close to that in their short existence—they averaged about 2,800 in the NAHL. The bosses hoped that the higher caliber of the AHL would draw more fans to their games.

The opening game of the season saw 4,026 fans show up to see the Firebirds play the Mariners. Philadelphia shocked the AHL by winning their opening game with a thrown-together roster by a 5–1 score. "The odds on us winning tonight had to be 95 to 1," said defenseman Terry Murray. Unfortunately, that was perhaps the only bit of good news over the next two seasons. The team finished with a 35–35–11 record in 1977–78 but lost in the first playoff round to New Haven. Four days before the 1978–79 season, Belisle was offered the Washington Capitals coaching job and left the Firebirds without anyone to lead the team. That season, the Firebirds won just 23 games and finished in last place. Attendance never improved, putting the team in an even greater bind.

Toward the end of the 1978–79 season, the media reported that the Firebirds would relocate to Syracuse at the end of the campaign. On April 8, 1979, the team played their last ever game in Philadelphia, losing to New Brunswick, 8–5. The team gave Bob Collyard a special award recognizing him as the franchise's all-time leader in games played and scoring. Just a few days later, George Piszek held a news conference officially announcing the move. "We're bringing to Syracuse a hockey team that fans can rally around and call their own," he said. "Back in the 1960s, Philadelphia took away Syracuse's pro basketball team, the Nats of the NBA, and now we're giving Syracuse something back."[38]

Just like that, the Firebirds were gone, only five years after their inception. After losing over $400,000 in their first season, the team lost $200,000 in the second and $150,000 in the third for a total loss of $770,000. They continued losing money in their two AHL seasons, reportedly totaling over $1,000,000 through the team's existence. Their operation was being completely funded by Mrs. Paul's $100 million of annual gross sales. Attendance was growing, but the bottom line was that the team needed to make it to the finals each year if the they even had a hope of turning a profit.

There were many factors in the Firebirds' struggles over the years. Their roster was at the mercy of the Flyers and Capitals for the first few seasons, and after the relationships were severed, the team was unable to properly recruit players. On top of that, their schedule was far from favorable. The Civic Center was often committed to other events—trade shows, ice shows, etc.—sometimes causing the Firebirds to go out of town for weeks at a time. In the opening season, for example, they played 12 home games in November, and then spent weeks at a time on the road. It is difficult, to say the least, to get fans interested when it's impossible to keep track of the team.

In a post-mortem for the *Daily News*, Jay Greenberg gave a troublingly-adept analysis of the Firebirds failures over the years. Calling them "a bastard child of a hockey fan," he pointed out their front office issues: two ownerships, three coaches, two leagues, in just five years. He bemoaned the team's lack of diehard fans, claiming, "George would have needed a gun and a mask to talk anybody off the streets to see his sorry team."³⁹

Most troubling to Greenberg was that it appeared "nobody was ever out there trying" within the organization. They failed to market the team appropriately, a constant criticism in their five years. They did nothing to get the team in the newspapers more often at a time when everyone was fighting for column space. He accused Piszek of reportedly turning down the Flyers' early offer of making the Firebirds the top farm team for their NHL roster. "A franchise that needed a transfusion simply sat back and waited to die," he wrote. "If this was the way the Firebirds were going to do business, then there should be no tears shed Sunday night. We don't mourn the Firebirds' passing, but we'll miss having another hockey team in town."

"I'm not saying I did everything right," said George Piszek at the end. "But nobody can say we're running out without giving it a fair test. We hung in for five years, but I'm convinced we're just not going to make it here. I know they've had some teams in Syracuse that have failed, but I think we'll have a better chance there. There we don't have to worry about the Flyers being on TV, or the boat show traffic. We'll be the only game in town."⁴⁰

Years later, the legacy of the NAHL's Firebirds is that of a family. The players are still very close, even decades later. (In fact, the team held a 40-year reunion of their championship team in Arizona in 2016. Dozens of players, along with George Piszek and Pilling, traveled from across the continent to see each other and celebrate old times.) They speak highly of each other and of their time in Philadelphia. "It was a family," Pilling said. "That had to come down to our team from the Piszek family. Mrs. Paul's kitchen, Mr. Piszek, George, George's brother, Eddie—they operated that business as a family, and so did our hockey team. Everybody liked one another and everybody went to bat for each other." Even the Flyers, who had no ownership stake in the team, but simply assigned some of their minor league players to the Firebirds, exuded that same culture. "We had wonderful cooperation from [Flyers GM] Keith Allen, [Flyers coach] Freddie Shero, and [Flyers assistant coaches] Mike Nykoluk and Barry Ashbee," Pilling continued. "They just treated us, again, like family ... that trench was manned by a family."⁴¹

The demise of the Firebirds was a true shame for those that supported the team. The NAHL had the potential to create the same cult-following that the EHL enjoyed before it. Many still look back fondly on those days. Perhaps the biggest disappointment in the disappearance of the Firebirds was the fact that the minor-league team provided an outlet for those to see a hockey game who couldn't otherwise get their hands on Flyers tickets—and now that option was gone. The working-class Philadelphians who wanted to take their children to a hockey game to share their love of the sport often found themselves unable to do so. Major league hockey was all that was left in Philadelphia for the foreseeable future.

# 11

# The Phantoms

*American Hockey League (AHL), 1996–2009*

In 1995, Comcast-Spectacor, the parent company of the Flyers, was at a crossroads. With a brand-new arena under construction across the parking lot from the Spectrum and the Flyers scheduled to move in by the Fall of 1996, the organization was left with a building problem. The Spectrum was, for the first time since its opening in 1967, without a full-time tenant. The company was not yet ready to tear down a piece of Philadelphia history, but business was still business. They partially filled the holes with the addition of the Philadelphia Kixx indoor soccer team, the Philadelphia Soul of the Arena Football League, and various concerts and shows. But they were still missing a bona fide, full-time team to fill the schedule.

The Philadelphia Phantoms, AHL, 1996–2009.

While on a train ride to New York for an NHL Board of Governors meeting, Comcast-Spectacor Chief Operating Officer Peter Luukko was sitting next to Ed Snider, reading *USA Today*. He was perusing the sports section and happened upon the scoresheets for the International Hockey League, a competitor to the American League at the time. He noticed the attendance numbers were respectable in many small towns that he felt didn't necessarily have the same love of hockey that Philadelphia fans had in their blood. He leaned over to his longtime boss and posed a simple question.

"Hey Ed," he said, "If we're planning on keeping the Spectrum, we might want to consider putting our farm team there."

"Well, okay," Snider responded, "But why would we do that? Wouldn't it be competition with the Flyers?"[1]

The two began an extensive discussion—two power brokers of Philadelphia hockey casually chatting about the future of professional hockey in one of the country's largest cities. At the time, an affordable Flyers ticket was around $40, while a minor-league ticket could be had for as low as ten dollars. The competition wasn't a major league hockey team, but cheap family entertainment like the movies and Dave and Buster's. A minor league franchise could be a great way to introduce fans to the sport at a low entry cost. The two were intrigued with the idea and brought it back to the organization's higher-ups to get their feedback.

So, in November 1995, it wasn't much of a shock when the Flyers announced that they would apply for an expansion franchise in the American League to be housed in the Spectrum. The team, whose cost was estimated to be $1.5 million, would become the Flyers' new minor-league affiliate, replacing Hershey, which had been the Flyers' top farm team since 1984. The Flyers, at the time, claimed they spent up to $1 million a year simply to execute their affiliate agreement with Hershey. They felt that they could easily operate a team that not only would ease their operating expenses, but even turn a profit.[2]

The business side of it made perfect sense, from both a revenue-generating and an expense perspective. Besides the cost savings of owning their own AHL affiliate, the two teams would operate just a short walk from each other. Previously, calling up or sending down a player caused a logistical mess, especially when the transaction had to be made quickly (to get a player in a specific spot in time for a game). But with the new team operating so closely, players could literally walk across the parking lot to their new locker room. On top of that, the deal would create easy revenue-sharing opportunities, in that the Flyers could oblige their corporate sponsors to also contribute to sponsorships for the new team, quickly filling up the AHL team's coffers. And, most importantly, the price point (extraordinarily less expensive than Flyers tickets) would allow a new group of hockey fans to see a hockey game— the logic of the NAHL's Firebirds with the support and financial backing of a multi-billion-dollar corporation. It was a recipe for guaranteed success.

When the organization officially submitted their application to the

AHL, the league was jovial. The AHL was in the process of seeking out larger markets for their franchises, and the idea of minor league hockey in Philadelphia for the first time in nearly twenty years had them smiling from ear to ear. "Ed had always been a big supporter of the American League," said AHL President Dave Andrews. "They had a team in Quebec City long before my time. Ed would always remind me that he was an American League guy long before I was."[3]

The league was in a much different position in the early 1990s than they are today. Competing with the International League for the world's second-tier players, the AHL was trying to establish itself as the main farm system for the NHL. When he first took over the reins of the league, Andrews established his major goal: he wanted to get the AHL into more cities and attract deeper-pocketed owners. "We were a provincial league," he said, "We needed to expand. We needed to attract better owners." When the opportunity arose for an AHL team owned by the Flyers (read: Comcast) to enter competition, Andrews jumped for joy at the news.

The AHL quickly accepted the application, with a start date of Fall 1996. The Flyers notified Hershey of their plans and immediately began building the organization from the ground up. "Our fans will have the unique opportunity to see the Flyers of tomorrow develop today," Flyers GM Bob Clarke told the press. "AHL hockey is a fast-paced, exciting game that is a great family entertainment."[4]

Immediately, the Flyers began putting in place a business team to run the new franchise. They took staff from the existing organization and transferred them over to the AHL club, along with hiring staff to man the phones and ready the team. They placed Frank Miceli, a Flyers executive and longtime employee of Ed Snider, in charge as the Chief Operating Officer of the team. But it fell to Clarke to find the team's new coach. A former Flyers assistant and long-time pro scout, Bill Barber was Clarke's linemate in their playing days and had already replaced Jay Leach as the Bears head coach midway through the 1995–96 season. When he found out Comcast was going to place a new team in Philadelphia, he sat down with Clarke. In a chat that lasted just a few minutes, Barber expressed his desire to continue coaching, while Clarke ecstatically agreed with the sentiment. Barber was named the first head coach in team history. After a fan contest to help select the team's name, the organization decided on the Phantoms. The team's colors would be purple and black.

Now that the staff was taking shape, Miceli was tasked with travelling around the region to create awareness for the Phantoms to garner fan support and, hopefully, season tickets. But a business executive wasn't going to bring people out. For that, he needed Barber, a legend of Philadelphia hockey. Barber was implored to do speaking engagements, go to restaurants and diners, and find any way to connect with potential fans—all tasks that are usually not in a head coach's job description. "We'd put him in a lot of positions where he was like, 'Do I really need to do another one of these?'" Miceli reminisced. But Barber toughed it out and was a team player. He would take pictures with fans and autograph their various items. The fans came out in droves to see what this new hockey team was about. "No one wants to hear from the business guy," said Miceli. "I wasn't a Hall-of-Famer. I didn't have the hockey credibility that Bill did."[5]

Fortunately for Barber, filling the roster was one thing he did not need to worry too much about. Since the Flyers owned the majority of the Hershey Bears' players, they simply transferred them to Philadelphia, then added a few more players to fill out the roster. The Phantoms started their history on October 4, 1996, defeating the Springfield Falcons by a 6–3 score. The next day, 9,166 fans watched them make their debut at the Spectrum, as they defeated the Rochester Americans, 3–1. By the end of the month, after a five-game winless streak that took their record to a paltry 3–3–1–2 (W-L-T-OL), the team finally began to gel. With career minor-leaguer Peter White leading the team offensively, the Phantoms went on an AHL-record 19-game home winning streak and didn't lose again at the Spectrum until February 12. (The game that set the record, their 18th, was a 5–3 win over the Adirondack Red Wings in front 13,260 at the Spectrum.)

At that point, the team had an impressive 32–11–7–2 record and were among the league's top teams. They continued their winning ways, putting together four- and five-game winning streaks to keep themselves in the top tier of the league. A mediocre ending to the regular season knocked some reality into the squad, but they managed to finish with a 49–18–10–3 record, good for first place in the league. After sweeping the Baltimore Bandits in three games in the first round of the AHL playoffs, they faced off, ironically, against the Hershey Bears team that the Flyers abandoned at the start of the season.

Continuing the story from previous Philadelphia and Hershey teams, the Phantoms and Bears had one of the deepest rivalries in hockey at any level. With 12 regular season meetings between the two clubs, plus preseason games, plus inevitable playoff matchups, there was ample time for the seeds of animosity to plant themselves within each locker room. In the 1996–97 regular season, the two teams combined for an astounding 915 penalty minutes in their meetings. In fact, a September 1997 preseason game saw the teams combine for 413 penalty minutes.

Hershey took the first game in Philadelphia, and when the series moved to Game 2, the bad blood took over. In the midst of a 7–4 Phantoms victory, the two teams took part in one of the fiercest battles in AHL playoff history. They combined for an AHL-record 350 penalty minutes, including 181 from one second period 6-on-6 brawl. The game lasted nearly three-and-a-half hours. The brawls featured eight game misconducts, including one each to Neil Little and Bears goalie Sinuhe Wallenheimo, both of whom joined in the festivities. The league suspended Hershey's Wade Belak and Philadelphia's Frank Bialowas two games for their on-ice actions, in addition to fining each team. (The matchup was also notorious for featuring five different goalies utilized by the teams.) The teams split the first four games, alternating wins, but the Phantoms took a 3–2 series lead with a 3–0 win in Game 5. They fell to the Bears in a triple-overtime Game 6 and couldn't pull off the win at home in Game 7. The Phantoms were sent home much earlier than the organization hoped, while the Bears would go on to win the Calder Cup. "You couldn't ask for a better scene in hockey than what this series has been," Bill Barber said before the final game. "I've scouted for a lot of years and I've never seen hockey played with such intensity."[6]

Nonetheless, the team's inaugural season was very successful, to say the least. White led the AHL (for the second time in his career) with 105 points, while center Vaclav Prospal finished fourth in the league with 95 points, despite playing just 63 games (due to a 17-game call up with the Flyers). Little proved to be an adept minor league goaltender, leading the team through the season and playoffs (with help from backup goaltender Dominic Roussel). Barber was extremely optimistic going into the team's second season.

The Philadelphia Phantoms handed this coin out as a souvenir to fans to honor their inaugural game at the Spectrum in October 1996 (courtesy Bruce "Scoop" Cooper).

As in their inaugural, the Phantoms ripped through the 1997–98 regular season, compiling a 47–23–10–2 record and again finished with the best record in the league. White led the league in points for

## 11. The Phantoms

the second consecutive year (with an identical 105 points), while the fans responded accordingly to the team's success. The Spectrum was sold out for numerous games throughout the season as the Phantoms posted the best attendance in the AHL, announcing a total season attendance of 472,392.[7]

The season again included intense matchups against the Bears, to the benefit of both teams. Four of the six Phantoms-Bears matchups in Philadelphia drew sellout crowds of 17,380—an astonishing number for an AHL club. Every matchup in Hershey drew sellout crowds at Hersheypark Arena. The average crowd for a Phantoms-Bears game was 120 percent higher than the average AHL game elsewhere. When the teams played in Hershey, attendance was 27 percent higher than the average Bears' home game. When they played in Philadelphia, attendance was 41 percent higher than the Phantom's home average. The fans loved the brutal rivalry and rewarded both teams for their intensity.[8]

Emotions also erupted behind the benches, as Bears coach Bob Hartley would constantly jab at Barber, and the former Broad Street Bully refused to be beaten in a test of wills. In one game at the Spectrum in the 1997–98 season, amidst an on-ice brawl, Hartley yelled over to Barber and pointed to his Calder Cup championship ring that he received the previous year, after defeating the Phantoms. Barber then pointed up to the Flyers' Stanley Cup banners and his jersey retirement banner hanging in the rafters. "That was my shot back," Barber reminisced with a laugh. In another game that season, in Hershey, Barber noticed that Hartley was only dressing 16 players of the 17 allowed. An AHL rule required the away team to dress the same number as the home team and Barber was not a fan of playing short a man. When he approached Hartley before the game, the Bears coach smirked and said, "We're hurt," which Barber knew was just a cover-up for an attempt to cripple the Phantoms offensive power. The mind games went back and forth all season, much to the delight of the fans.[9]

After dispensing the Rochester Americans in four games in the first round of the 1998 Calder Cup playoffs, the Phantoms welcomed back the Bears for a rematch of their grueling playoff battle from the previous season. This time, however, the Phantoms were not playing around, as they swept their cross-state rivals in four games, with Neil Little allowing just seven goals in the entire series. In the third round, they defeated the Albany River Rats in a six-game battle, closing them out with a 3–0 shutout in Albany on May 25, 1998.

In the Calder Cup final, a first for a Philadelphia team, the Phantoms were matched up against the Saint John Flames, the minor-league affiliate of the Calgary Flames. (The Flames also featured a young rookie winger named Martin St. Louis, who would score 20 points in 20 playoff games.) With the Flyers having been eliminated from the NHL playoffs just days earlier, the Philadelphia media was all in on the minor-league squad. "Viewers who haven't seen the Phantoms play this season will notice one marked difference between them and the Flyers," wrote Bill Fleischman in the *Philadelphia Daily News*. "The Phantoms play with emotion. And the Phantoms fans are into the games the way Flyers fans used to be." With apathy growing around the Flyers' continued failure to win another Stanley Cup, fans were thrilled at the possibility of their farm team getting the job done.[10]

The final series proved to be one of the toughest the Phantoms would ever face, with the first three games decided in overtime. The Phantoms took Games 1 and 3, while the Flames stole Game 2 in Philadelphia. The Phantoms took Game 4 with a 6–4 win, setting up a potential championship-clinching game in St. John. With everyone expecting the dominating Phantoms to win Game 5, Miceli received a call at 10:00 a.m. the day of the game from Flyers Chief Operating Officer Ron Ryan: Ed Snider was coming to the game and he was flying up the team's brass in his private plane. (Attendees included Ed Snider and his wife, Ron Ryan, Peter Luukko, Fran and Sylvan Tobin [minority owners of the Flyers], and Comcast SportsNet president Jack Williams and his wife.) Ryan instructed Miceli to reserve the following: a suite at the St. John's arena, an entertaining room at the hotel with food and a full bar, and a reservation for the entire group at the best restaurant in St. John before the game.

Miceli got to work, reserving the room at the hotel and contacting St. John COO Stew MacDonald. The problem was, the St. John arena had only two suites and since the ownership structure of their team included nearly a dozen people, both suites were already full. Miceli begged MacDonald to help him out and, under duress, he convinced the St. John owners to pile into one suite, opening up the other for Snider and his crew. Coincidentally, one of the team's owners owned one of the top Italian restaurants in New Brunswick and penciled Snider's group in for a reservation that night. Two birds killed with one stone, for Miceli. Unfortunately, the Phantoms failed to close out the series on the road, with Saint John winning Game 5 by a 6–1 score.[11]

(A funny side story: that night featured the largest 50–50 raffle in St. John's hockey history. When they picked the winning ticket, it had Ron Ryan's name on it. When he refused to walk up to the stand in the middle of the arena, just above the ice level, Ed Snider dragged him down and the two claimed the prize together.)

As the team traveled home for Game 6, the Phantoms had a minor off-ice issue: the fans expected the team to close out the series on the road, so very few people had purchased tickets to Game 6. Suddenly, with the team able to win a championship on home ice, nearly 12,000 tickets sold overnight. "We had the largest will-call in Spectrum history that night," Miceli said. The next morning, fans lined the Spectrum steps and queued all the way down Pattison Avenue, waiting to pick up their tickets. With just six windows present to hand out tickets, even the top executives came down to street level to help out. They gathered piles of ticket envelopes in their hands and went down the line, handing out tickets as quickly as possible until the line was empty.[12]

With a chance to close out the series, the fans filled the Spectrum to the brim—17,380—for the team's ninth sell out of the year, an extraordinary feat for an AHL franchise playing in an arena designed for NHL hockey. On June 10, the Phantoms dominated the game from puck drop to the final buzzer, winning the game, 6–1, and securing the city's first-ever Calder Cup championship. Neil Little carried the team on his back the entire way, posting a 15–5 record in the postseason and allowing just 48 goals in those 20 games. Mike Maneluk won the playoff MVP award after leading the playoffs with 34 points. Sixty-two years after AHL hockey had first landed in Philadelphia in the form of the Ramblers, the Calder Cup finally belonged to the City of Brotherly Love. The championship was the city's first in hockey since the Firebirds secured the NAHL title in 1976.

"It has been a long time," said Barber, "So long that I forgot some things about winning.... This is a hockey town." On the other side of the ice, captain John Stevens welled up with tears. "It's so beautiful," he said, watching his teammates parade the silver trophy around the Spectrum, the same ice where the Flyers paraded the Stanley Cup over 20 years earlier.[13]

The team discussed holding a parade down Broad Street, but decided against it, unsure that they would be able to draw enough fans on a weekday for a minor league championship parade. Instead, they announced a celebration the next day at the Spectrum, open to all fans. The morning of the event, though, Miceli received a call from one of the team's top brass. The boys had been out all night partying with the trophy and it was a little banged up from having been dropped multiple times. Miceli went to a friend's body shop, whereupon they attempted to fix the trophy. The futile attempt simply made it worse. With no more time to spare, they brought the mangled trophy to the Spectrum for the celebration. "It was a very misshapen Calder Cup," Miceli said.[14] (When the team returned the trophy to the league, they were charged $1,500 by the AHL to repair the Cup back to its original form.)

The 1998 season began with the team raising their championship banner to the Spectrum rafters, and was followed a couple months later by the club welcoming their 1,000,000th fan to a Phantoms game—an impressive feat for a minor league team just starting their third season. The team continued to see success on the ice and in the box office. Fans responded to the on-ice success, as the Phantoms set an AHL record with an average attendance of 12,002 fans per home game that year. The league rewarded the success by naming Philadelphia as the host of the 1999 AHL All-Star Classic. When the organization began planning the event, Snider suggested they make a big splash and put the game in the Center, a state-of-the-art NHL building. "We're putting on a show for the entire league," Snider said to his staff, "Let's put on the best show we can." He invited every team governor from the AHL to a surf and turf dinner in his director's lounge in the Center, something that stunned those around the league and even his own employees. "I was watching nickels and dimes, from a budget standpoint," Miceli said, laughing at the memory.[15]

(One of the obligations of the host city was to have a big auction on the day of the game. The Phantoms booked the Philadelphia Center City Marriott for the event and announced Ed Snider as the keynote speaker. Already one of the biggest names in the NHL, he commanded massive respect from the major league, let alone the AHL and their top brass. But the morning of the game, Snider was rushed to the hospital with a stomach issue and had to cancel. Panicking, Miceli called AHL President Dave Andrews and begged him for help finding a suitable replacement. Andrews made one call to the NHL front office in New York, whereupon Commissioner Gary Bettman immediately took a car down to Philadelphia and replaced the Flyers chairman as the marquee guest. Such was the respect the entire hockey world had for both the Phantoms and Snider.)

The Bill Barber era of Phantoms hockey was an extremely successful stretch in AHL history. With the cast of characters, the support from the management team above him, and a fan base that consistently supported the minor league squad, Barber's job was, on some nights, quite easy. "Nothing needed to be said," Barber remembered. "Just do your job. It was pretty cool, all the way around." Despite the team needing some prodding here and there to avoid complacency, the leadership, both on and off the ice, made the Phantoms a highly-respected organization throughout the entire league.[16]

In 2000, with Bill Barber being promoted to the Flyers as an assistant coach, recently-retired captain John Stevens was named the Phantoms' new head coach. He would lead the team to a Division Crown in the 2003–04 season, one in which the team was upset in the second round of the playoffs by the Wilkes-Barre/Scranton Penguins. That season was highlighted by a bizarre episode in the final game of the season against the Hershey Bears. With the Bears needing a win to make the playoffs, coach Paul Fixter pulled his goalie in overtime. When the Bears inadvertently shot the puck into their own net, it not only clinched the win for the Phantoms, but goalie Antero Niittymaki, being the last Phantom to touch the puck, was credited with the game-winning, shorthanded goal.

The following season would see an odd compilation of players on the AHL roster. With the NHL locked out for the entirety of the 2004–05 campaign, the Phantoms had unusual access to top-tier players that would have otherwise been with the Flyers: R.J. Umberger, Patrick Sharp, Joni Pitkanen, Dennis Seidenberg, and Niittymaki, among others. After dropping their first two games of the season, the team kicked things into gear and won an AHL-record 17 consecutive games to launch themselves into first place in the league. Though they would show some inconsistency for the remainder of the season, their second-place East Division finish was good enough to secure a playoff spot for the hungry team.

When the playoffs arrived, the team saw their odds improve even more when they added two future stars to the roster. Jeff Carter and Mike Richards had each seen their junior clubs eliminated from the playoffs just as the AHL regular season ended. Seeing the upside of getting the players professional experience before their inevitable jump to the NHL the following season, the organization added them to the Phantoms roster to help give a postseason boost to the squad. With the circus in town, the Phantoms moved across the street to the vacant Wachovia Center, whose ice was still empty due to the NHL lockout.

In the first round, the team fought through a six-game series win against the Norfolk Admirals, who had beaten the Phantoms in the season series in six out of the ten games. In the second round, the team faced off against the Wilkes-Barre/Scranton Penguins, their cross-state rival. The Penguins were no match for the powerful Phantoms, as Philadelphia dispensed of their opponent in five games, including a Game 5 victory in which they trailed, 4–1, before scoring six unanswered goals in the game's final ten minutes to send the Penguins home. (The Penguins were backstopped by a young goalie named Marc-Andre Fleury.) In round three, against the Providence Bruins, the Phantoms took the first two games at home and managed to win one out of the three road games to return to the Center with a 3–2 series lead. With a chance to return to the Calder Cup final for the first time since 1998, the Phantoms played a near-perfect game and defeated the Bruins, 4–1, to clinch the series.

Going into the final round against the Chicago Wolves, and with no NHL hockey, the Phantoms were the talk of the hockey world. A perfect 9–0 at home at that point in the postseason and with perhaps the strongest AHL roster in recent memory, the expectations were sky-high. Anything less than a Calder Cup championship would be a disappointment for the Flyers organization. Richards and Carter were tearing up the league in their professional debuts, and Niittymaki was stopping just about everything that came his way. Nonetheless, the team would be shooting against Kari Lehtonen, the Atlanta Thrashers' number two overall draft pick from 2002. Another player who would probably have made the NHL roster if there was one, Lehtonen dominated the AHL's regular season with a 38–17–2 record, along with a 2.27 goals against average and a .929 save percentage. There was no doubt the matchup would turn into a goaltending battle.

That prophecy came true in Game 1, as the teams couldn't seem to put the puck into the opposing net. The game featured fantastic defense and a tight-checking matchup, along with stellar goaltending. However, the Phantoms found a way to break through, taking a 1–0 lead and then hanging on for dear life as they closed out the low-scoring shutout. (With the Flyers coaching staff not working due to the lockout, Ken Hitchcock joined the executives in Chicago for the two games. At the end of one period, Hitchcock, who had been making notes the entire time, tore a sheet from his notebook, handed it to Miceli and instructed him to get it down to John Stevens as quickly as possible. Miceli ran through the back hallways of the Chicago arena and found Stevens just before the start of the next period. Thus was the preferred, if not inefficient, communication method before cell phones were prominent.)[17] In Game 2, Niittymaki was the star, allowing just one goal through five periods of play, as the Phantoms took the second game on the road with a 2–1 double-overtime victory. Game 3 was no different, as the Phantoms returned home and Niittymaki posted yet another career-defining game, keeping the Wolves again to one goal and leading his team to a 2–1 victory, giving the Phantoms a commanding 3–0 series lead with the chance to win the Calder Cup on home ice.

When the puck dropped for Game 4 a couple nights later, the Phantoms were out for blood. The sold-out crowd of 20,103 (an AHL record for a playoff game) were decked out in "Purple Reign" t-shirts, cheering their team on to another championship. Jon Sim and Patrick Sharp came out flying with their team behind them, each scoring two goals. Niittymaki made 28 saves and held the Wolves back just enough to allow the Phantoms to coast to the end of the game. When the final buzzer sounded, the Phantoms won, 5–2, sweeping the Wolves and clinching another Calder Cup championship for the city of Philadelphia.

Niittymaki was awarded the Jack Butterfield Trophy as the playoff MVP after giving up just four goals in the Calder Cup final. "I think we played great defense the whole series," he said amidst the celebration, "And I think we were the better team."[18] (Niittymaki would join the Flyers the following season and backstop the Finnish Olympic hockey team to a silver medal, posting three shutouts in six games and winning the tournament MVP in the process.)

Stevens raised his second Calder Cup as a Phantom, this time as the team's head coach. "Philly loves a champion," he said in the locker room, gushing over his team. "I went through it as a player and it's really exciting, but as a coach you just never relax. All I wanted was to see the excitement in my players' faces, see them win the Cup. These guys worked so hard. They're unbelievable."[19] (As an aside, the assistant coach of the Phantoms in their 2005 run was Craig Berube, now a Stanley Cup-winning head coach.)

Carter led the team offensively, posting 12 goals and 23 points in 12 postseason games, while Richards potted 15 points in 14 games. Sharp scored 21 points while playing in all 21 playoff games. The three would see major-league promotions coming their way the following season as a reward for their development and talent.

Amidst the celebration, Philadelphia never showed any care that it was "only" a minor-league team bringing a championship to the city. With no NHL team to cheer on, the city went nuts. And if there's anything that all Philadelphia athletes learn quite quickly upon coming to the city, it's that the city has one simple mantra.

"Philly likes champions," said Eric Meloche. "Right now, we're the champs. Who cares if it's minor league?"[20]

Stepping into the locker room during the celebration, Snider noticed that, with no one wearing their jerseys, he couldn't recognize most of the players. He leaned over to Miceli and asked him which one was Niittymaki. After the MVP goaltender was pointed out, Snider ran over to him, giving him a big hug and a pat on the back.

A few years after their celebration, Comcast-Spectacor encountered another business issue. The Spectrum, as a building, was nearing the end of its useful life. The infrastructure was in desperate need of updating, and it was determined that, in order to continue operating properly, the building would need a full renovation. On top of that, the work would all be behind the scenes and not even noticed by the public—plumbing, wiring, structural work, etc. The cost of the job would

The Philadelphia Phantoms played their last regular season home game at the Spectrum on April 10, 2009, against their lifetime rivals, the Hershey Bears (courtesy Bruce "Scoop" Cooper).

be in the millions—money the organization was not wont to invest in a building that wasn't pulling in nearly that much in profit. "The amount of money it took to do that, just the earnings alone from the Phantoms and secondary events we were doing, would never service the debt on that kind of investment," said Luukko.[21]

The Spectrum was not pulling its weight and the company, which had the ability to exercise development rights on a portion of the Center's parking lot, determined that they could make more money by tearing down the Flyers' first home and replacing it with something else. The only problem was that the organization had nowhere to put the Phantoms. The Center, which at this point was one of the premier arenas in the Northeast, did not have 40 open slots per season to add the AHL squad to their event schedule. And there wasn't another arena large enough to hold the number of fans needed to keep the team profitable.

Simultaneously, Comcast-Spectacor embarked on three different major business ideas: a new home for the Phantoms, tearing down the Spectrum, and finding a new development project to replace the original Flyers' home. Of those three, the third idea was the most difficult. "People had come to us with movie theaters, maybe a Bass Pro Shops, and other types of things," Luukko said. "But when you have all the

The Spectrum was home to the Philadelphia Flyers for nearly 30 years, and then became home to the Philadelphia Phantoms for over a decade (courtesy Bruce "Scoop" Cooper).

combined events of the venues there, and the fact that you charge for parking, it had to fit in with the events and facilities in the sports complex. A movie theater wouldn't work, because who would want to go to the movies, pay to park, and then be in traffic with 15,000 people?"[22]

The organization decided that whatever building was erected on the opposite side of the parking lot from the Center had to be remotely related to the stadiums surrounding it. Enter the Cordish Company, a Baltimore-based developer, who came to the organization with the idea to construct a dining and entertainment complex at the corner of 11th and Pattison Avenue, smack in the middle of the three active stadiums— the Center, Lincoln Financial Field, and Citizens Bank Park. The project, originally called "Philly Live!" was designed to have five restaurant and entertainment venues, along with an outdoor plaza. It would allow thousands of fans who didn't have tickets to the games to congregate and cheer on their Philadelphia teams as a city. From a financial perspective, it had the potential to be a gold mine. But it still left a vast question of what to do with the Phantoms.

The organization looked to other parts of the region to house the

Phantoms. They considered the possibility of putting the Phantoms in Atlantic City, but the city had a weak history in the East Coast League and Comcast-Spectacor was not confident that the area would support an AHL squad. They considered building an arena in Cherry Hill, New Jersey, but decided not to incur the expense. They looked into the rumors that Pennsauken, New Jersey, was going to build a 6,000-seat arena, but the idea never came to fruition.

It was at that point that Luukko was contacted by the Brooks family, owners of the Brooks Group out of Pittsburgh—a financial company that also owned part of the Pittsburgh Penguins, the Wilkes-Barre/Scranton Penguins, the Pittsburgh Pirates and three minor-league baseball teams. They pitched Luukko an idea that included purchasing the Phantoms and developing a state-of-the-art minor league arena in Allentown, Pennsylvania, where the team would eventually land. With no other viable option, Luukko engaged Snider and the two worked through the details of a potential deal. "Well, I wasn't thrilled," Andrews said with a chuckle as he recalled hearing the news for the first time that the Phantoms would be leaving Philadelphia. "As it's turned out, the reemergence of the Phantoms ... has been awesome."[23]

Despite the move being described as a "setback" to the Flyers by the media, knowing that there was no way the team would be able to stay in Philadelphia and continue using the Flyers' Skate Zone practice arena, the move made perfect business sense for the organization. Comcast-Spectacor was still working on growing their three subsidiary companies: Global Spectrum, a venue management company; Ovations, a food service and hospitality company; and Paciolan, a ticketing and fan engagement company. (These companies operate today under the brand name Spectra, but perform the same services to hundreds of arenas around the country.) A deal was quickly cut to sell the team to the Brooks Group for what was rumored to be close to $4 million. Also part of the deal was that the new Allentown arena would utilize all three of Comcast-Spectacor's subsidiaries to manage the team. In exchange for selling the Phantoms, the organization would see a rise in their revenue, along with adding another big-name venue to their portfolio.

"We will miss having them share the same sports complex and the same training facility, which was an incredible advantage to us," said Luukko at the time. Luukko described the sale as "a very difficult decision for us to make. When we decided to close the Spectrum, we explored many alternatives for relocating the Phantoms, and this really became the best scenario. We looked locally very hard.... Every business venture has a viable lifespan and it was becoming less and less viable," said Luukko, "And over the next 10 years it was going to require millions of dollars to operate."[24]

The Brooks Group announced their long-term plan to land the team in Allentown, but the city was lacking an AHL-ready arena. In the meantime, the group relocated the team to Glens Falls, New York, where they operated as the Adirondack Phantoms. The move worked out for all sides—Global Spectrum managed the Glens Falls Civic Center, allowing the company to keep their hands in the Phantoms pot. The team was invited by many other cities to relocate elsewhere, but each offer had hints of a city hoping to keep the team in the long run. The Brooks family did not want to stray from their ultimate plan of going to Allentown.

"We decided we'd rather go dark than mislead the fans of another city," said Brooks years later. "We knew we were going to Allentown." Glens Falls Mayor Jack Diamond approached Brooks and offered the use of his arena with no strings attached. He didn't want them to hide the fact that they would only be a temporary tenant. He wanted his city to prove that they could support an AHL team, so that when the Phantoms inevitably left for greener pastures, the city would be considered for a permanent franchise.[25]

However, the short-term relationship lasted a bit longer than expected, mostly due to political and legal challenges in Allentown. The city utilized a downtown taxing district to raise funds to publicly finance the arena, along with a $40 million contribution from the State of Pennsylvania to help cover the cost of a downtown building. Put into action in 2009, the arena did not even start construction until 2012, after the city sold $224.3 million in bonds in less than four hours. After clearing the city block, the building was erected in just a few years, opening its doors in October 2014. The final cost of the building was about $177 million and the team, with a new, permanent home, began play that month as the Lehigh Valley Phantoms.[26] (Adirondack hosted the Calgary Flames' AHL affiliate for the 2014–15 season, before receiving their permanent franchise in the form of the East Coast League's Thunder in 2015, where they still operate today.)

"Well, we've signed a deal for 29 years, plus an option for two 10-year extensions," said Jim Brooks. "So, I'm thinking we're good for the next 49 years."[27]

While the Phantoms still exist and operate successfully to this day, the Philadelphia Phantoms' life ended in 2009 upon their relocation to Glens Falls. Through their decade at the Spectrum, the Phantoms were a huge success by any measure. The team consistently sat at or near the top of the league in attendance. They won the same number of championships as the Flyers in a quarter of the time. They progressed countless players to the Flyers roster over the years, while also becoming the home of many career minor-leaguers who shaped the Phantoms over their short life span in Philadelphia. The team even established a Hall of Fame, which consists of seven people: Bill Barber, Frank Bialowas, Neil Little, John Stevens, Bob Clarke, Peter White, and Frank Miceli.

Their time in Philadelphia helped set the standard for the rest of the league. "They developed a terrific culture within their organization," said Andrews. "Ed set the tone for everything—and Peter—they set the tone for the quality of customer service, the way in which the franchise would be run, the investment that they made in staff. Bringing Frank [Miceli] over there was, I think, a bold stroke for both the organization and for Frank. He did a remarkable job there. They just had a great culture around them. If we look back to how the league has developed since that time, bringing the Phantoms into the league when we did was really valuable. It helped attract more owners and it helped us grow the league."[28]

Interestingly enough, the Phantoms organization had a deep respect for the history of Philadelphia hockey. Each year the team hosted a "Turn Back the Clock" night, in which the team wore a retro jersey from a current or former Philadelphia team. Jerseys worn included the Quebec Aces, Maine Mariners, the Richmond Robins (the team which replaced the Aces), the Blazers, Firebirds, Arrows, and even old Flyers jerseys. (The team even wore Flin Flon Bombers jerseys in honor of Bob Clarke's junior team. When Clarke found out, he called Miceli, gave him his credit card number and told him to get 50 additional jerseys for himself so he could give them out to all of his friends. "He's the most generous guy I know," Miceli said.) Over the course of their tenure, they always respected those who came before them, good and bad, and did their best to educate the fans about those squads. And they created a lasting impression on the hockey world. "Some of my best memories of the time I've been on this job were in the Spectrum and in the [Center], when they won the Cup in the new building," said Andrews. "That was one of the largest crowds in the history of Philadelphia hockey. That was an unbelievable experience. And the Cup that was won in the Spectrum, that was a memory that will stick in my mind forever. I mean, the party in the parking lots and what was happening, that was an event. It was really a very special memory.

"I remember the energy in the Spectrum, how exciting the games were in there, how great the fans were. It was a really special place to see a game, and in those formative years, for me as president of the league, it was one of those places where, when you went there, you felt good about the league, about where we were headed."[29]

## 11. The Phantoms

The picture of the last professional team to be born to the Philadelphia hockey scene, celebrating over 100 years of Philadelphia hockey history, is one that should bring a smile to any hockey fan's face. Though the city has had an up and down relationship with the sport, from Stanley Cups to teams faltering in bankruptcy, from minor league championships to franchise relocations, the history of the game in this city is so crucial in telling the story of the only remaining team—the Flyers. While minor league hockey has technically left Philadelphia, most likely for the last time, the Phantoms were a culmination of over 80 years of minor league hockey, starting with the Arrows and progressing through multiple teams of varying successes over the 20th century. "You have to be able to point to success stories to grow, you have to have a story to tell," said Andrews. "And the Philadelphia story was a very good one."

# Epilogue

It is very easy to look at the Philadelphia Flyers and marvel at the success of hockey in Philadelphia since 1967. But doing that skips a major step in understanding why the Flyers have reached their current level of popularity. By the time the first puck dropped in the Flyers inaugural season, it had already been 70 years since hockey was first introduced to Philadelphia and 40 years since the Arrows first set up shop in the Arena on 45th and Market. Philadelphia may not have fully supported all of the teams that came before, but those teams contributed a priceless piece to the city: they educated the fans on the sport, they excited the media about the sport, and they opened the door for the proper recipe to be utilized for a major league team—a recipe that was visibly absent when the Quakers showed up in 1930.

At face value and without looking deeper into the story, Philadelphia's hockey history appears sporadic before the Flyers came into being—no organization lasted more than ten years until the Flyers did so. But a closer look shows a rich history that led up to the rousing success that is hockey in Philadelphia. What started with George Orton in the 1890s and perpetuated by the Arrows, Quakers, Comets, AHL's Ramblers, Falcons, Rockets, EHL's Ramblers, Flyers, Blazers, Firebirds, and Phantoms, was a city's passion for a new sport that was faster, rougher, and more exciting than perhaps any other sport ever played in the City of Brotherly Love.

The city saw a striking pattern through each of the teams that eventually folded: poor facilities mixed with improper management, and a shaky ownership group. The number of times someone came marching into Philadelphia swearing to construct a new, state-of-the-art building for hockey is endless: Tex Rickard, Benny Leonard, Leonard Peto, Pete Tyrell, Walter Annenberg, and more. Yet, until Ed Snider and Jerry Wolman came along, no one was able to follow through with their promise. Each team's failure was mostly blamed on their home building, be it the Arena or the Civic Center. And while there is no doubt that facilities played a role in each team's eventual struggles to draw a crowd, it wasn't the only factor.

Even the Flyers, playing in a brand-new building, didn't see financial success from day one. It took many years of community outreach, roster management, and patience, to grow their organization and its foothold in the community. The Arrows saw similar success for much of their life. In a new building, with solid ownership, and a team that played their hearts out night after night, the Arrows saw great success, which gave the New York Rangers the opportunity to come in and lay claim to their own team in the city. As early as the 1930s, even New York City recognized what a great hockey town Philadelphia was!

Those outside the city give Philadelphia fans a lot of grief. But those inside the city know better. What Philadelphia sports fans want is a team that works as hard as they do—a team that leaves it all on the ice, field, or court, regardless of the result. Philadelphia has and will support a losing team, so long as the effort is there. The Arrows, the AHL's Ramblers, the EHL's Ramblers, the Firebirds, and the Phantoms all saw their own levels of success in attracting fans to their games. That was no coincidence. Those teams regularly wore their hearts on their sleeves, even if the wins weren't piling up as quickly as the players or fans would have liked. Every Philadelphia sports team sees the same thing. Philadelphia fans boo not when the team loses, but when they feel the team hasn't given the effort that the blue-collar Philadelphians give every day.

Whether it was an organization that saw on-ice and off-ice success, or whether it was one that failed spectacularly, what is inarguable is the hunger Philadelphians developed for hockey through these squads. The city has seen its share of characters, both on the ice and behind the bench, that helped grow the game. They may now be relegated to history, but the stamp they have left for hockey history will remain forever.

And to all of those that led Philadelphia to fall in love with the game of hockey, the city owes an endless amount of gratitude.

# Appendix
*The History of the Philadelphia Arena*

The history of hockey in Philadelphia goes in hand in hand with the history of the buildings that housed the sport since it was first introduced to the city in the 1800s. Being a unique sport, requiring temperatures and conditions that are only present in the Philadelphia climate for a few months each year, the city needed to provide a suitable place for teams to convene if the sport were to garner any broad support over the years.

The city's first choice of buildings was the West Park Ice Palace, which was built in 1897. That building lasted just four years before being destroyed by fire. The Philadelphia Auditorium and Ice Palace, later referred to as simply The Arena, was constructed in 1920 and stood for over 60 years before also being destroyed by a fire. The Philadelphia Convention Hall and Civic Center was built in 1931, but was not outfitted with an ice rink until the 1970s. The last time it was used for professional hockey was for the Firebirds in 1979, before the building was eventually demolished in 2005. The Spectrum was the state-of-the-art, NHL-caliber arena that Ed Snider and Jerry Wolman built, per NHL guidelines, to convince them to place an expansion team in Philadelphia. That building stood until 2010, when Flyers parent company Comcast-Spectacor decided to tear it down. The Center (known originally as CoreStates Center, and known currently as the Wells Fargo Center) was built in 1996 as a sparkling new home for the Flyers and still remains their headquarters to this day.

The West Park Ice Palace hosted the Quaker City Hockey Club. The Arena hosted the Arrows, the Quakers, the Comets, the AHL's Ramblers, the Rockets, the Falcons, and the EHL's Ramblers. The Civic Center was home to the Blazers and Firebirds. The Spectrum housed the Flyers for nearly thirty years, before welcoming the Phantoms. And the Center, of course, has been the home of the Flyers since 1996. These buildings, despite being motionless structures, mostly made of wood, steel, and concrete, have endless stories of their own and weave together the teams that comprise Philadelphia's hockey history.

The plan to construct the Philadelphia Arena was first made public on November 4, 1919, when the *Inquirer* announced that the city had awarded a contract to George F. Pawling & Company to build "a one-story brick ice palace" on Market and 45th Streets, along with an ice plant next door to power the refrigeration system, for a cost of $250,000. The project was pushed by George Orton, desiring a bona fide hockey arena to help grow the sport that he made so popular at the University of Pennsylvania. Orton and Pawling partnered with Hunt B. Miller, owner of Pittsburgh's Duquesne Gardens, to erect the new building.[1]

The ice rink was large, measuring 220 feet long by 101 feet wide (relative to modern NHL rinks, which are 200' × 85'), while the stands initially held about 4,000 seats for hockey games. The building had balconies on both the north and south sides, which comprised just under 2,000 of those seats. It would be constructed of arched steel, ensuring that there were no posts throughout the building that could obstruct the patrons' views of the action. The cloak room would be able to hold 4,000 coats, while an adjoining skating room would hold 3,000 pairs of skates available for public rental. The main lobby held a soda fountain and a refreshment counter, along with an athletic store, where customers could purchase skates, sweaters, "skating costumes," and more. A women's locker room at one end, opposite a men's locker room on the other side of the rink, would allow plenty of room for hockey players and public skaters to get in their fill of ice time.[2]

In February 1920, the city announced that the Arena was ready for its grand opening. The original opener, scheduled for February 11, was delayed because of problems with the ice plant. But on February 14, the Arena opened with a 7:45 p.m. college hockey game between Yale and Princeton, followed by a public skating session. The cost for public skating was 75 cents for evening sessions and 55 cents for afternoon sessions and included skate rental.[3] The first hockey game in Arena history belonged to Yale, as they defeated their collegiate rival by a 4–0 score.

Just a few months later, though, with ice difficult to make in the rising seasonal temperatures and no regular tenant, the Arena was revamped to make room for a new, up-and-coming attraction in Philadelphia: boxing. With a boxing ring that had a much smaller footprint than an ice rink, the Arena could seat over 10,000 fans for matchups. And with the Arena being one of newest sports buildings in the country, promoters were eager to schedule bouts in Philadelphia. Guests were taken on tours of the newly-refit building to show off the amenities and the potential of big-money fights with sold out crowds. The reaction was swift and positive from those that walked its halls.[4]

"I have visited every city in the United States where boxing is permissible," said Sammy Harris of Baltimore. "This club cannot be even tied. Never saw anything like it."

"The greatest in the United States!" said Tommy Walsh, a Chicago resident who joined the tour. "That doesn't cover a little bit of the world. I have seen clubs in Australia, England, and France, and a few other places far and near—well, I never knew it was possible. It just only proves on how high a plane boxing is going to be placed. You can score one more victory for Philly."[5]

But, despite the crowded schedule, the building quickly went into debt. In October 1922, the building was sold to Jules Mastbaum and Fred Nixon-Nirdlinger. "New York interests were bidding for the [Arena]," said Mastbaum. "And rather than see this Philadelphia institution pass out of Philadelphia management, I entered a bid for the place and I understand through my attorney that we were successful." The *Inquirer* reported that the original investment, after refits and capital, from Pawling, was $960,000. With the Franklin Trust Company holding a first mortgage of $350,000, the new owners would likely have needed to put up upwards of $1,000,000 for the purchase—though the exact amount was never disclosed.[6]

Less than two years later, with boxing becoming the main attraction at the Arena, the building again was put up for sale. Tex Rickard, a shady, oft-indicted fight promoter and owner of a new arena being constructed in New York called Madison Square Garden, announced that he had purchased the Arena from Mastbaum.[7] (Rickard also founded the NHL's New York Americans and New York Rangers in the mid–1920s, who called Madison Square Garden their home.) He expressed his desire to rebuild the Arena, extending its capacity to as high as 15,000 patrons. But just a few weeks later, on May 21, 1924, Mastbaum announced that the deal was off. On the verge of signing the final papers, the two battled and Mastbaum backed out, leaving the Arena in his control and sending Rickard back to New York to deal with his own legal and political problems.[8] In January 1927, Mastbaum would finally unload his investment, selling the building to Maurice Fishman and Rudy Fried for $850,000 (including a deposit of $50,000, $200,000 at closing, and a $600,000 mortgage).[9]

Fried announced plans to enlarge the Arena to hold 17,000 fans for hockey games. "Details of the changes to be made have not been fully decided," he said in January 1929, "But by the end of the week we expect to have the plans in tip top shape to give the sports public of Philadelphia a comprehensive idea of the new building." He added that they were planning to "embrace all the excellent features of Madison Square Garden," at that time the preeminent sports arena in the United States. But the media was not convinced of the idea's merits.[10]

"If the new garden is to be a near replica of the New York edifice," wrote Stan Baumgartner in the *Inquirer*, "The side and end walls of the building will have to be torn down, the balconies rebuilt, a new lighting system installed and hundreds of other changes which will reduce the building to a mere shell before it is rebuilt."[11]

But perhaps the most influential person in early 20th century Philadelphia sports was a young man who joined the Arena crew in the 1920s. A 29-year-old accountant named Pete Tyrrell was hired away from his firm to be an aide to boxing manager Al Lippe. He honed his craft as a promoter and manager, before being named the head of the Arena in 1934, a position he would hold for decades, thereby controlling the fate of hockey in Philadelphia, along with other sports and entertainment that would pass through the city. Under Tyrrell's watch, the Arena saw countless events, hockey teams, changes of ownership, and more. On top of that, Tyrrell held the keys to the city, from a sporting perspective. He had the influence to control what happened in Philadelphia with regards to other buildings and potential hockey teams.

In the midst of his operation of the International-American League's Ramblers in 1939, the media began reporting that an unidentified financier was attempting to build a $4,000,000 skating rink in order to attract an NHL franchise to Philadelphia, either through relocation or expansion. Tyrrell immediately put the kibosh on it, pulling strings behind the scenes to ensure his hockey team had no local competition. "If any National League franchises are being handed out, we'll get it at the Arena," he said. "We hold the first option and we certainly wouldn't stand by and

Pete Tyrrell ran the Philadelphia Arena, and thereby the Philadelphia hockey world, for decades.

see somebody else jump in and ruin a business we have spent years in establishing."[12]

A few years later, in 1946, with Leonard Peto attempting to move the Montreal Maroons to Philadelphia and construct a $2,500,000 sports arena that would seat 20,000 fans for hockey games, Tyrrell and the Arena Corp. took the Montreal sportsman to Federal Court, claiming an infringement on their territorial property. Peto laughed off the injunction, saying, "It appears to be only a nuisance; you know how those mosquitoes buzz around."[13] The suit named as defendants Peto, NHL President Red Dutton, the Bruins' Art Ross, the Black Hawks' William Tobin, the Canadiens' Donat Raymond, the Rangers' J.B. Kilpatrick, the Red Wings' James Norris, and the Maple Leafs' Conn Smythe. Tyrrell took on the entirety of the NHL and won.

Just weeks later, Peto's attempt vanished, leaving Tyrrell as the victor. "During its entire history, the National Hockey League never has granted a franchise to anyone not having a building in which to play hockey, nor has the league ever attempted a territorial steal," he said. "We have a bonafide franchise in the American League and were granted a leave of absence for the duration of the war."[14] Despite his clear attempt to keep the NHL out of Philadelphia—unless he ran the team—he denied having anything to do with it. "We have never attempted and are not now attempting to deprive Philadelphia of major league ice hockey," he told the *Inquirer*. Tyrrell was a master at manipulating those around him to get the press coverage he wanted. After again explaining to reporters that the NHL does not award teams unless a building already exists, he was asked if that means he believed any NHL club coming to Philadelphia should have to play in the Arena. "I didn't say that," he replied with a smirk. "But if you want to put it that way...."[15]

The next year, Walter Annenberg, owner of Triangle Publications (which also owned the *Philadelphia Inquirer*) purchased the Arena and, on top of that, moved the offices of WFIL-TV next door to more easily broadcast the events held there. With Annenberg recognizing the value he brought and the influence he held in the city, Tyrrell was again named the general manager of the Arena. "This is a pioneering venture in the television field," Annenberg said upon his announcement of the acquisition. "Opening up an entirely new approach which will assure television viewers of Philadelphia the best in the city's sports events ... visitors to the Arena will be able to witness television shows and productions as they are originated not only from the floor of the Arena, but from the studio itself through specially constructed observation windows."[16] (Today, a historic sign, one of hundreds around the city of Philadelphia, remembers the WFIL–TV offices at its former location. No such marker exists for the Philadelphia Arena.)

A couple years later, rumors began to spread that the NHL was considering placing a major league franchise in Philadelphia, to which Tyrrell added fuel to the fire. "We plan to build a brand-new arena to seat about 15,000 for hockey," he said. "We're only waiting for building material and labor costs to drop within reason."[17] NHL President Clarence Campbell acknowledged that he personally favored league expansion and admitted that he would love to see Philadelphia added as a seventh team.

But the idea never came to fruition. Building plans stalled, and Philadelphia was left with an Arena that was starting to seem antiquated and outdated. By 1958, the building was nearly 40 years old and had not received a proper refit in quite some time. Annenberg moved away from arena management in the '50s and put the building up for sale. With no immediate takers and Tyrrell wanting to remain in control, the general manager put together an ownership bid, formed the Tyrrell Group and purchased the building, along with a few other investors from the region. Tyrrell now owned the empire which he had spent decades growing.

Over the years, the Arena's halls were regularly filled. The building hosted superstars, such as the night Elvis Presley performed. The building welcomed Bob Hope, Doris Day, Nat (King) Cole, and Duke Ellington, among others. It hosted championships, with the NBA's Philadelphia Warriors winning the 1947 title. Some of the most famous boxing matches of the early 20th century occurred at the Arena. It hosted one of the first ever Ice Follies shows, helping to launch it from obscurity into a modern staple at ice arenas across the country.

But there were many events that made the public scratch their heads. In the 1930s, the Arena staged an endurance race, pitting men against horses around a track. "The horses, with jockeys, of course, ran around on a dirt track," Tyrrell reminisced in the 1960s. "The idea was to see who lasted longer." The idea was squashed pretty quickly, with the American Society for the Prevention of Cruelty to Animals saying that the Arena could not run horses until they dropped. Instead, they would have to switch animals every four hours. The Arena management simply made behind the scenes swaps so that fans thought the same horses were still running—not that there were many fans in attendance for the ridiculous event. "We lost money," said Elsie Tyrrell, Pete's wife, years after his death. "Nobody came, but we still had to feed the horses."[18]

Years later, the Arena held a six-day bicycle race, another endurance

The Arena was home to thousands of events over the years, ranging from hockey games to tennis matches, from horse races to concerts (Special Collections Research Center, Temple University Libraries, Philadelphia, Pennsylvania).

test, for which few fans showed up. The Arena floor was constantly turned into various outfits for events: a ski slope, a swimming tank, a billiard parlor, a concert hall, a furniture showroom, and more. Anything that Tyrrell thought would bring people to the building and fill an open slot in the schedule was acceptable to him.

Another time, a dancing competition was held just across the river, in Camden, New Jersey. The rule was that the attendees were not allowed to stop dancing the entire night. In the midst of the event, two attendees wanted to get married, but there wasn't enough room in the building to cater to the number of guests wanting to watch. The two lovers were loaded into the bed of a truck and, still dancing, were slowly driven across the Ben Franklin Bridge and into Philadelphia. The vehicle stopped at the Arena, where the two danced out of the truck, into the building, and into the boxing ring where, still dancing, they were wed in front of thousands of people. The ceremony complete, they danced back to the truck, across the bridge, and back to Camden.[19]

In 1946, the Arena was even host to a funeral. During a performance of the Roy Rogers Rodeo, a cowgirl died in an unfortunate

In 1977, the Arena went up for auction yet again, as the city tried desperately to find someone to refurbish the run-down building (Richard Rosenberg, Special Collections Research Center, Temple University Libraries, Philadelphia, Pennsylvania).

accident. The following Sunday, her casket was placed in the center of the Arena floor, with thousands attending to mourn her loss.

But in 1965, the 69-year-old Tyrrell announced his desire to retire. With no potential buyers for his building and a claim that the building needed a $2,500,000 facelift in order to keep it functioning properly, he put the Arena up for auction. A few weeks later, boxing promoter Jimmy Toppi outlasted former NBA president Maurice Podoloff in a bidding war to secure the Arena for a $351,000 price tag. Toppi had previously been involved with the Arena in the 1940s in arranging some boxing matches and even attempted to build an outdoor boxing stadium in South Philadelphia. Now, he finally had his own building. With the close of the sale, Tyrrell left the Philadelphia sports scene, marking the end of an era.[20]

Toppi planned to hold all of the same attractions at the Arena, but chose not to renovate and improve the building, leaving it in a poor state that troubled many that would have otherwise chosen to attend events. Two years later, Toppi passed away, leaving his estate to manage the property until his next of kin could garner a plan to sell it.

In 1977, the building went up for auction again, this time selling for just $165,000 to three men, Ronald Wright, Carlton Wright, and Al Thomas, who hoped to turn the building into a profitable establishment. That plan failed, with the trio selling the Arena to businessman Mark Stewart in June 1980 for a reported $350,000. (Coincidentally, Stewart was also the representative for Fred Shero, the former Flyers coach and at that time coach of the New York Rangers, though Shero had nothing to do with the purchase of the Arena.) "There's a misconception over what sort of condition this place is in," Stewart said, hoping to convince the media and the public that the 60-year-old building was in great shape. "Aside from the décor and the security, it's fine. To me, that means— with a little work—we can have it ready for boxing cards, music concerts, wrestling, whatever."[21]

But the plan was not meant to be. After renaming the building Martin Luther King, Jr. Arena, the building went up in flames—a two-alarm fire—on October 4, 1981. The blaze took down most of the roof and caved in one of the entrances. Stewart held ownership but did not rebuild. The building remained partially standing until August 25, 1983, when an even larger fire was started after a drunk passerby threw a lit cigarette into the abandoned property. This blaze became a four-alarm

By 1980, the Arena was merely a dilapidated former home to so many Philadelphia hockey organizations (Michael J. Maicher, Special Collections Research Center, Temple University Libraries, Philadelphia, Pennsylvania).

fire, breaking through the roof and most of the walls and causing two other fires on the same street. "I don't know if the building can be saved," said Captain Robert Drenner from the fire commissioner's office. "If the walls are okay, they can always put on a new roof but, we won't know until after we've gone through it thoroughly."[22]

After an investigation, the perpetrator was arrested and indicted for three counts of arson. Despite initially admitting to accidentally causing the fire, after conviction he mysteriously changed course and claimed he was innocent. Regardless, in 1985, he was sentenced to 11.5 to 23 months in prison. At that point, the Arena had already been demolished, thereby ending the story of the longest-standing hockey arena in Philadelphia.

"It was the spot in Philadelphia," said 76ers announcer Dave Zinkoff at the time of the fire. "Everything was held there…. All of the major indoor sporting events were held there then, and I'm thankful that I had a small part in announcing most of them."[23]

With the Spectrum's construction in 1967, hockey was a thing of the past in the Arena now that the Flyers entered the picture and were the stars of the Philadelphia hockey world. But the story of the Arena is one that requires telling, as it set the stage for the Philadelphia sports

The Philadelphia Arena was demolished in the 1980s, finally putting an end to the building that housed more Philadelphia hockey teams than any other in the city (courtesy Bob Busser).

scene that the city now enjoys. Today, the site of the old Arena is covered by a row of townhouses and The Enterprise Center, a non-profit that specializes in helping small businesses and creating jobs in low income communities. Across the street from a beautiful park, the area now has baseball fields, a soccer field, a football field, tennis courts, basketball courts, and biking trails—an irony that the site of thousands of sporting events from decades ago now hosts Philadelphia residents wanting to take part in sport. The building may no longer exist, but its contribution to Philadelphia sports is still visibly evident.

# Chapter Notes

## Introduction

1. NHL Archives, November 1, 1924 letter from Irwin Wener to NHL Board of Governors (cited via email by Stuart McCommish).
2. "Phila. May Get Pro Hockey," *Altoona Tribute (Associated Press)*, 1 February 1946, 12.
3. NHL Archives, Board of Governors Meeting Notes, February 14, 1946 (cited via email by Stuart McCommish).
4. NHL Archives, Correspondence from December 14, 1945 (cited via email by Stuart McCommish).
5. "Maroons Moving to Philly?" *The Ottawa Citizen (CP)*, 18 August 1947, 29.
6. Coleman, Charles, *The Trail of the Stanley Cup, Volume 2* (Toronto, ON: NHL, 1969), 523.

## Chapter 1

1. "Ice Sports," *Amateur Athlete*, 4 March 1897, 17, as cited in Hebscher, Mark. *The Greatest Athlete (You've Never Heard Of): Canada's First Olympic Gold Medallist.* (Toronto, ON: Dundurn, 2019), 87.
2. Ibid., 86.
3. "A paradise for skaters," *The Times (Philadelphia)*, 14 December 1897, 4.
4. "Ice Palace Opening," *The Philadelphia Inquirer*, 15 December 1897, 3.
5. Hebscher, Mark. *The Greatest Athlete (You've Never Heard Of): Canada's First Olympic Gold Medallist.* (Toronto, ON: Dundurn, 2019), 88.
6. "Odds and Ends of Many Sports," *The Times (Philadelphia)*, 3 December 1898, 8.
7. Ibid.
8. "Yale to Play Here on Tuesday and Wednesday Evenings at the Ice Palace," *The Philadelphia Inquirer*, 25 December 1898, 11.
9. "The Game of Hockey," *The Times (Philadelphia)*, 12 February 1899, 8.
10. "Yale to Play Here on Tuesday and Wednesday Evenings at the Ice Palace," *The Philadelphia Inquirer*, 25 December 1898, 11.
11. "Brooklyns Beat Quakers," *The Brooklyn Daily Eagle*, 10 March 1899, 12.
12. "Orton to Try Fast Skating," *The Philadelphia Inquirer*, 19 January 1899, 4.
13. "Hockey for Championship," *The New York Times*, 2 December 1900, 9.
14. "New York Hockey Players Prove To Be Hot Stuff," *The Philadelphia Inquirer*, 12 January 12, 1901, 6.
15. "Tailenders Defeat Hockey Champions in a Fast Game at Philadelphia," *The Brooklyn Daily Eagle*, 9 March 1901, 6.
16. "West Park Ice Palace Destroyed By Fire," *The Philadelphia Inquirer*, 25 March 1901.

## Chapter 2

1. Baumgartner, Stan, "Philadelphia to Have First-Class Team in New Ice Hockey Loop," *The Philadelphia Inquirer*, 20 October 1927, 24.
2. Ibid.
3. "Ice Hockey Contest Closes

Tonight," *The Philadelphia Inquirer*, 26 October 1927, 21.

4. Baumgartner, Stan, "Lightheavy King Would Fight Gene," *The Philadelphia Inquirer*, 13 November 1927, 53.

5. Baumgartner, Stan, "Pesek Tossed Bull Now Meets Lutze," *The Philadelphia Inquirer*, 15 November 1927, 24.

6. "Arrows Pry Open Hockey Season Wednesday With Boston As Opposing Foes," *The Philadelphia Inquirer*, 27 November 1927, 47.

7. Baumgartner, Stan, "Ungentle Ice Hockey Pastime Makes Local Debut Here Tonight," *The Philadelphia Inquirer*, 30 November 1927, 24.

8. "Lowrey Shines Out in Locals' Triumph," *The Philadelphia Inquirer*, 17 November 1927, 23.

9. Baumgartner, Stan, "Boston Hockeyists Send Arrows Tumbling in Rink Inaugural at the Arena," *The Philadelphia Inquirer*, 1 December 1927, 28.

10. Baumgartner, Stan, "Five Players Hurt in Rough House Tilt As Arrows Triumph," *The Philadelphia Inquirer*, 18 December 1927, 45.

11. Ibid.

12. Ibid., 47.

13. Baumgartner, Stan, "Ice Hockey Scrambles Not New, Says President," *The Philadelphia Inquirer*, 19 December, 1927, 17.

14. Baumgartner, Stan, "Arrows' Pilot Protests Hockey Game at Quebec," *The Philadelphia Inquirer*, 25 December 1927, 35.

15. Baumgartner, Stan, "Local Hockey Club Head Makes $7500 Offer for Release of Harrington," *The Philadelphia Inquirer*, 31 December 1927, 20.

16. Ibid.

17. Baumgartner, Stan, "President Wener's Offer of Bonus Spurs Arrows on to Greater Efforts," *The Philadelphia Inquirer*, 15 January 1928, 47.

18. "Philadelphia Seeks Big League Hockey," *The Morning Call*, 27 January 1929, 14.

19. Baumgartner, Stan, "Shay Released As Arrows' Manager; Fynan New Pilot," *The Philadelphia Inquirer*, 6 February 1929, 18.

20. Dilello, Ty, *Golden Boys: The Top 50 Manitoba Hockey Players of All Time* (Winnipeg, MB: Great Plains Publications, 2017), 252–255.

21. "Herb Gardiner Is Voted Most Useful Player in League," *The Montreal Gazette*, 26, March 1927, 21.

22. "The Old Sport's Musings," *The Philadelphia Inquirer*, 4 January 1932, 12.

23. "Cude Best Goalie, Maroons Best Team, Gorman Thinks," *The Windsor Star*, 19 February 1935, 25.

24. Baumgartner, Stan, "Arrows and Cubs Collide in Titular Series," *The Philadelphia Inquirer*, 5 April 1933, 18.

25. "Pratt's Goal Gives Arrows Playoff Victory," *The Philadelphia Inquirer*, 6 April 1933, 18.

26. Baumgartner, Stan, "Runge's Four Goals Ruin Red Hockeymen," *The Philadelphia Inquirer*, 22 January 1933, 23.

27. "Pratt's Goal Gives Arrows Playoff Victory," *The Philadelphia Inquirer*, 6 April 1933, 18.

28. Baumgartner, Stan, "Arrows Again Defeat Boston in Play-off, 3–2," *The Philadelphia Inquirer*, 9 April 1933, 29.

29. Baumgartner, Stan, "Cubs Beat Arrows to Win Can.-American Title," *The Philadelphia Inquirer*, 16 April 1933, 32.

30. Ibid.

31. "The Old Sport's Musings," *The Philadelphia Inquirer*, 22 January 1935, 17.

32. Ibid.

## Chapter 3

1. Yong Chae Rhee, and John Wong. "Knocked Out! Marketing the Philadelphia Quakers." *Journal of Sport History* 45, no. 1 (2018): 48. doi:10.5406/jsporthistory.45.1.0041.

2. Christman, Paul, "Philly's 1st NHL Team—Philadelphia Quakers," accessed May 9, 2019, https://quakers.flyershistory.net.

3. Rhee and Wong, 42.

4. Davis, Ralph, "Local Hockey Outlook," *The Pittsburgh Press*, 4 March 1930, 30.

5. Fitzpatrick, Frank, "The Quakers: An NHL Team Worth Forgetting," *The Philadelphia Inquirer*, 31 May 1987, 64.

6. Christman, Paul, "1930–31 Pittsburgh Pirates convert to Quakers," accessed May 9, 2019, https://pittsburghhockey.net/other-teams/pirates-nhl/1930-31-pittsburgh-pirates-convert-to-quakers.
7. "Former Pittsburgher for Quaker Hockey," *The Indiana Gazette*, 21 October 1930, 8.
8. Christman, Paul, "Philly's 1st NHL Team—Philadelphia Quakers," accessed May 9, 2019, https://quakers.flyershistory.net.
9. Rhee and Wong, 51.
10. NHL Archives, Various correspondences (as cited via email by Stuart McCommish).
11. Baumgartner, Stan, "Just a Moment," *The Philadelphia Inquirer*, 25 October 1930, 14.
12. Christman, Paul, "1930–31 Pittsburgh Pirates Convert to Quakers," accessed May 9, 2019, https://pittsburghhockey.net/other-teams/pirates-nhl/1930-31-pittsburgh-pirates-convert-to-quakers.
13. Rhee and Wong, "Knocked Out! Marketing the Philadelphia Quakers." 53.
14. *Ibid.*, 54.
15. *Ibid.*
16. Christman, Paul, "Philly's 1st NHL Team—Philadelphia Quakers," accessed May 9, 2019, https://quakers.flyershistory.net.
17. Christman, Paul, "1930–31 Pittsburgh Pirates Convert to Quakers," accessed May 9, 2019, https://pittsburghhockey.net/other-teams/pirates-nhl/1930-31-pittsburgh-pirates-convert-to-quakers.
18. Rhee and Wong, "Knocked Out! Marketing the Philadelphia Quakers." 56.
19. *Ibid.*
20. "Benny Leonard Seeks to Strengthen Quakers," *The Morning Call*, 12 December 1930, 38.
21. Baumgartner, Stan, "Just a Moment," *The Philadelphia Inquirer*, 20 December 1930, 16.
22. *Ibid.*
23. *Ibid.*
24. Christman, Paul, "1930–31 Pittsburgh Pirates Convert to Quakers," accessed May 9, 2019, https://pittsburghhockey.net/other-teams/pirates-nhl/1930-31-pittsburgh-pirates-convert-to-quakers.
25. Rhee and Wong, "Knocked Out! Marketing the Philadelphia Quakers." 57.
26. Ritt, Bill, "Spying on Sports," *The Courier-News*, 20 January 1931, 19.
27. Christman, Paul, "1930–31 Pittsburgh Pirates Convert to Quakers," accessed May 9, 2019, https://pittsburghhockey.net/other-teams/pirates-nhl/1930-31-pittsburgh-pirates-convert-to-quakers.
28. Shapiro, L. S. B., "Canadiens Held to 4-All Deadlock by Philadelphia Six," *The Montreal Gazette*, 23 March 1931, 21.
29. Rhee and Wong, "Knocked Out! Marketing the Philadelphia Quakers." 56.
30. Ross, J. Andrew, *Joining the Clubs: The Business of the National Hockey League to 1945* (Syracuse, NY: Syracuse University Press, 2015): 209.
31. Fachet, Robert, "It Takes a Quaker to Know the Feeling," *The Washington Post*, 25 March 1975.
32. Stubbs, Dave, "Quakers Made Wrong Kind of History in Philadelphia Decades Before Flyers," NHL.com, 22 February 2019, https://www.nhl.com/news/philadelphia-quakers-made-wrong-kind-of-history-after-leaving-pittsburgh/c-304995730.

## Chapter 4

1. "Tri-State Hockey League Schedule," *The Evening Sun*, 31 October 1932, 26.
2. Linthicum, Jesse A., "Bird Goalie Star of Game," *The Baltimore Sun*, 12 December 1932, 10.
3. "Sea Gulls Overwhelm Comets in League Tiff," *Courier-Post*, 24 December 1932, 15.
4. "Hershey Team Has Two Games," *Harrisburg Telegraph*, 27 December 1932, 11.
5. "Hershey in a League Tiff on Saturday," *The Daily News (Lebanon)*, 29 December 1932, 7.
6. "Baltimore Defeats Comet Skaters, 3–2," *The Philadelphia Inquirer*, 30 December 1932, 14.

7. "Hershey in a League Tiff on Saturday," *The Daily News (Lebanon)*, 29 December 1932, 7.
8. "Sea Gulls Win By Whirlwind Finish," *The Philadelphia Inquirer*, 6 January 1933, 18.
9. "Players Clash at Close of Contest," *Harrisburg Sunday Courier*, 22 January 1933, 2.
10. *Ibid.*
11. Sparrow, C. Edward, "Quaker Sextet Is Outclassed," *The Baltimore Sun*, 10 February 1933, 12.
12. "Hershey Team to Meet Philadelphia in Saturday Game," *Harrisburg Telegraph*, 14 February 1933, 9.
13. "Comets Are Blanked by Oriole Ice Rivals," *The Philadelphia Inquirer*, 20 February 1933, 9.

## Chapter 5

1. "The Old Sport's Musings," *The Philadelphia Inquirer*, 9 November 1935, 13.
2. "Ramblers Will Depend on Speed," *The Philadelphia Inquirer*, 11 November 1935, 14.
3. "The Old Sport's Musings," *The Philadelphia Inquirer*, 7 December 1935, 17.
4. Dilello, Ty, *Golden Boys: The Top 50 Manitoba Hockey Players of All Time* (Winnipeg, MB: Great Plains Publications, 2017), 252.
5. Cooper, Bruce, "The Philadelphia-Hershey Hockey Wars on 1938," 1996, http://hockeyscoop.net/hpa/index1.html.
6. *Ibid.*
7. Baumgartner, Stan, "Barton Stars as Blues Rout Hershey's Six," *The Philadelphia Inquirer*, 9 February 1939, 19.
8. "Ramblers Rally Late in Contest," *Harrisburg Sunday Courier*, 26 March 1939, 2.
9. "Hershey Wins and Deadlocks Series," *The Gazette and Daily (Associated Press)*, 29 March 1939, 10.
10. "Ramblers Ice Team Disbanded by Rangers," *The Brooklyn Daily Eagle*, 3 September 1941, 16.
11. "14 Ranger Rookies Sold in 72 Hours," *Daily News (New York)*, 12 September 1941, 58.

## Chapter 6

1. "Philly to Have Own Entry in Hockey League," *The Courier-News (Associated Press)*, 20 June 1941, 20.
2. Baumgartner, Stan, "Danny Cox Is Named Pilot of Ramblers Hockey Team," *The Philadelphia Inquirer*, 20 July 1941, 29.
3. "Rockets Offered Bonus for Wins," *Courier-Post*, 10 December 1941, 22.
4. "Rockets Hockey Squad Disbanded For Duration," *Harrisburg Telegraph (Associated Press)*, 16 September 1942, 20.
5. "Amateur Hockey on Arena Ice," *The Philadelphia Inquirer*, 12 October 1942, 35.
6. Baumgartner, Stan, "Youths Will Keep Sports Rolling Throughout War," *The Philadelphia Inquirer*, 13 December 1942, 37.
7. *Ibid.*
8. "Pics Win Twice, Game, 4 to 1, and Impromptu Fight," *The Boston Globe*, 9 January 1944, 21.
9. "Falcons Quit Ice in Row, Then Lose to Boston, 8–2," *The Boston Globe*, 21 February 1944, 15.
10. Morrow, Art, "Desson, Falcons' Defense Man Studious, But All Other League Teams Respect Him," *The Philadelphia Inquirer*, 10 March 1944, 26.
11. *Ibid.*
12. "Joe Desson Fined After Hockey Row," *The Philadelphia Inquirer*, 18 December 1945, 24.
13. Baumgartner, Stan, "5500 See Falcons Tie Olympics, 3–3," *The Philadelphia Inquirer*, 31 January 1946, 22.
14. "Falcons Fall Into Cellar," *Delaware County Daily Times*, 7 March 1946, 27.
15. "Falcons Score Over Rovers, 9–4," *Delaware County Daily Times*, 14 March 1946, 30.
16. Lurie, Dora, "6799 Watch Falcons Win; Tied for Lead," *The Philadelphia Inquirer*, 24 March 1946, 32.
17. "Falcons Need 11–0 Victory To Take Title," *The Philadelphia Inquirer*, 26 March 1946, 26.
18. "Falcons Triumph, 6–5, But Pics Take Title," *The Philadelphia Inquirer*, 27 March 1946, 32.
19. "Pro Hockey Returns To Quaker

City," *The Daily American (Associated Press)*, 6 May 1946, 3.
20. "Arena Will Not Operate AHL Franchise in '49–'50," *The Philadelphia Inquirer*, 21 March 1949, 25.
21. "Kaminsky Boss of New Falcons," *The Philadelphia Inquirer*, 2 May 1951, 48.
22. Baumgartner, Stan, "Jets Trounce Falcons, 9–3," *The Philadelphia Inquirer*, 16 December 1951, 65.
23. Baumgartner, Stan, "Arena to Disband Falcons Because of Poor Attendance," *The Philadelphia Inquirer*, 20 December 1951, 32.
24. "Falcons Cancel Final Two Games," *The Gazette and Daily (Associated Press)*, 21 December 1951, 27.

## Chapter 7

1. "Quaker City Gets Hockey," *The Plain Speaker (Associated Press)*, 7 September 1955, 17.
2. Daniels, Don, "Frantic Fans Flip for Rocky Hockey," *The Philadelphia Inquirer*, 22 January 1957, 30.
3. "New Ramblers Sign 1st Player," *The Philadelphia Inquirer*, 14 October 1955, 43.
4. Klein, Edward, "Ramblers' 6 in Third Beats Baltimore, 10–7, As Hockey Returns," *The Philadelphia Inquirer*, 2 November 1955, 43.
5. "Ramblers Beat Lions, Referee Floors Player," *The Philadelphia Inquirer*, 6 November 1955, 87.
6. Inkpen, Gregg, *Broph: On and Off the Ice with John Brophy, One of Hockey's Most Colorful Characters* (Independently Published, 2018), 36.
7. Ibid., 39.
8. Rukavina, Nik, Personal Interview, 20 June 2019.
9. "Ramblers Host to New Haven," *Courier-Post*, 1 March 1957, 25.
10. "Soviet Hockey Coach Praises U.S. Goalie," *Wilkes-Barre Times Leader, The Evening News (Associated Press)*, 15 January 1959, 5.
11. "Philadelphia Ramblers File for Bankruptcy," *The Evening Sun (Associated Press)*, 28 May 1960, 10.
12. "Bud Dudley Picks Up Rambler Membership," *The Philadelphia Inquirer*, 8 July 1960, 27.

13. Callaway, Ben, "Anyone for Hockey? Fans Can Take Pick," *Philadelphia Daily News*, 8 July 1960, 57.
14. Dolson, Frank, "Bud's High Hopes Shifted to Hockey," *The Philadelphia Inquirer*, 9 July 1960, 18.
15. Callaway, Ben, "Adam Agrees: Ramblers Hottest Team in League," *Philadelphia Daily News*, 23 February 1961, 50.
16. Dolson, Frank, "In the Spring a... Well, Take a Guess!" *The Philadelphia Inquirer*, 8 March 1961, 44.
17. Fachet, Bob, "Jets Win, 4–2, Take 2–0 Lead Over Ramblers," *The Philadelphia Inquirer*, 11 March 1961, 17.
18. Zabitka, Matt, "It's December in April for Bud Dudley," *Delaware County Daily Times*, 17 April 1961, 14.
19. "Pleased Coach Greets Eager Ramblers," *Philadelphia Daily News*, 11 October 1961, 72.
20. "O'Brien Quits Ramblers," *Philadelphia Daily News*, 31 May 1962, 62.
21. Inkpen, Gregg, *Broph: On and Off the Ice with John Brophy, One of Hockey's Most Colorful Characters*, 53.
22. Ibid., 55–56.
23. Ibid., 57.
24. Forbes, Gordon, "Dudley Quits Ramblers; City May Lose Club," *The Philadelphia Inquirer*, 18 August 1964, 27.
25. Crudden, George C., "American Hockey League to Keep Same Entry List," *Intelligencer Journal*, 12 April 1963, 36.
26. Forbes, Gordon, "Dudley Quits Ramblers; City May Lose Club," *The Philadelphia Inquirer*, 18 August 1964, 27.
27. "Tyrrell Steps in to Save Ramblers, Signs Up Adam," *Philadelphia Daily News*, 19 August 1964, 67.
28. Good, Herb, "Arena Rebuffed As Cherry Hill Gets EHL Berth," *The Philadelphia Inquirer*, 21 August 1964, 33.
29. "Blame Is Placed on Attorney For Ramblers' Exit," *The Philadelphia Inquirer*, 19 August 1964, 40.
30. Rukavina, Nik, Personal Interview, 20 June 2019.

## Chapter 8

1. Bass, Alan, *The Great Expansion: The Ultimate Risk That Changed the*

*NHL Forever* (Bloomington, IN: iUniverse, 2011), 17.
  2. *Ibid.*, 17.
  3. *Ibid.*, 18.
  4. *Ibid.*, 18.
  5. *Ibid.*, 20.
  6. *Ibid.*, 20.
  7. *Ibid.*, 20.
  8. *Ibid.*, 20–21.
  9. "Charter-Business Corporation," *Philadelphia Daily News*, 16 February 1966, 46.
  10. Bass, Alan, *The Great Expansion: The Ultimate Risk That Changed the NHL Forever*, 23.
  11. Merchant, Larry, "The Iceman Cometh," *Philadelphia Daily News*, 10 February 1966, 55.
  12. Weir, Frank H., "'Nobody Makes It By Himself,' Says Jerry Wolman," *The Philadelphia Inquirer*, 24 April 1966, 248.
  13. *Ibid.*, 249.
  14. *Ibid.*, 249.
  15. Bass, Alan, *The Great Expansion: The Ultimate Risk That Changed the NHL Forever*, 119–120.
  16. *Ibid.*, 120.
  17. *Ibid.*, 120.
  18. Snider, Ed, Personal Interview, November 12, 2010.
  19. Scheinfeld, Lou, Personal Interview, August 10, 2019.
  20. *Ibid.*
  21. Snider, Ed, Personal Interview, November 12, 2010.
  22. "New Hockey Arena Will Be Built in Philly," *Lebanon Daily News (United Press International)*, 10 February 1966, 56.
  23. Scheinfeld, Lou, Personal Interview, August 10, 2019.
  24. Bass, Alan, *The Great Expansion: The Ultimate Risk That Changed the NHL Forever*, 122.
  25. *Ibid.*, 123.
  26. *Standard-Speaker*, 6 April 1967 (no headline), 28.
  27. "'Iron Man' Came to NHL at 35," *Philadelphia Evening Bulletin*, 1 December 1966, 16.
  28. Snider, Ed, Personal Interview, November 12, 2010.
  29. *Ibid.*
  30. *Ibid.*
  31. Scheinfeld, Lou, Personal Interview, August 10, 2019.
  32. *Ibid.*
  33. Weir, Frank H., "'Nobody Makes It By Himself,' Says Jerry Wolman," *The Philadelphia Inquirer*, 24 April 1966, 249.
  34. Chevalier, Jack, "Wolman Sells Share of Flyers to Snider," *The Philadelphia Inquirer*, 27 August 1967, 76.
  35. Conrad, Ed, "Tight Dollars That Make Sense," *Philadelphia Daily News*, 29 August 1967, 58.
  36. *Ibid.*
  37. *Ibid.*
  38. Scheinfeld, Lou, Personal Interview, August 10, 2019.
  39. Byrod, Fred, "Snider Fired By Wolman in Struggle Over Eagles," *The Philadelphia Inquirer*, 20 October 1967, 1.
  40. Scheinfeld, Lou, Personal Interview, August 10, 2019.
  41. Bernstein, Ralph, "Kuharich-Snider Riff Was Cause of Firing," *Associated Press*, 21 October 1967.
  42. Padwe, Sandy, "'May Be Your Party Next,' Snider Tells Joe Kuharich," *The Philadelphia Inquirer*, 21 October 1967, 26.
  43. Byrod, Fred, "'Wolman Money' Didn't Buy the Flyers," *The Philadelphia Inquirer*, 3 November 1967, 37.
  44. *Ibid.*
  45. Scheinfeld, Lou, Personal Interview, August 10, 2019.
  46. *Ibid.*

## Chapter 9

  1. "Form New Group to Rival NHL Ottawa Proposed," *Ottawa Journal (United Press International)*, 26 June 1971, 14.
  2. Parent, Bernie and Hochman, Stan, *Unmasked: Bernie Parent and the Broad Street Bullies* (Chicago, IL: Triumph Books, 2012), P#.
  3. Brown, Sidney, Personal Interview, 10 September 2019.
  4. "WHA Plans Battle Against Flyers," *Philadelphia Daily News*, 23 May 1972, 61.
  5. Dolson, Frank, "Blazing: The First GM Lasted Four Hours," *The Philadelphia Inquirer*, 7 June 1972, 15.
  6. *Ibid.*

7. "WHA Blazers Lose G.M., Sign Ex-Flyer Lacroix," *The Morning News*, 7 June 1972, 27.
8. "McKenzie: Bruins at Fault," *The Herald-News (Associated Press)*, 15 June 1972, 50.
9. Heisler, Mark, "Blazers Name Creighton, Sign Five Players," *The Philadelphia Inquirer*, 30 June 1972, 33.
10. Courtney, Gene, "Blazers Sign to Play in Civic Center," *The Philadelphia Inquirer*, 20 July 1972, 27.
11. Hochman, Stan, "Blazers' 'Policeman' on Trial Already," *Philadelphia Daily News*, 28 July 1972, 35.
12. Ibid.
13. Sanderson, Derek and Shea, Kevin, *Crossing the Line: The Outrageous Story of a Hockey Original* (Chicago, IL: Triumph Books, 2012), 180–184.
14. Fitzpatrick, Frank, "A Debut That Went Up in Blazers," *Philadelphia Inquirer*, 6 October 2017, https://www.inquirer.com/philly/sports/a-debut-that-went-up-in-blazers-franks-place-20171006.html.
15. Bertucci, Frank, "Biggest Faceoff: WHA vs. NHL," *Philadelphia Daily News*, 13 September 1972, 42.
16. "Blazers-Flyers Face-Off: The 50 Winnahs!!!" *Philadelphia Daily News*, 4 October 1972, 56.
17. Fleischman, Bill, "Strength in Middle Nucleus for Blazers' Run at Pennant," *Philadelphia Daily News*, 11 October 1972, 38.
18. Sanderson and Shea, *Crossing the Line: The Outrageous Story of a Hockey Original*, 201–202.
19. Ibid., 203.
20. "Blazers Idled By Unsafe Ice," *Pittsburgh Post-Gazette (Associated Press)*, 14 October 1972, 12.
21. Sanderson and Shea, *Crossing the Line: The Outrageous Story of a Hockey Original*, 210.
22. Brown, Sidney, Personal Interview, 10 September 2019.
23. "James Cooper Quits Blazers," *The Philadelphia Inquirer*, 19 November 1972, 78.
24. Sanderson and Shea, *Crossing the Line: The Outrageous Story of a Hockey Original*, 210.
25. Keidan, Bruce, "3,391 (or 750) See Blazers Burn Raiders," *The Philadelphia Inquirer*, 9 December 1972, 21.
26. Keidan, Bruce, "Businessman Dick Olson Named Blazers President," *The Philadelphia Inquirer*, 3 January 1973, 21.
27. Conrad, Ed, "McKenzie: Blazers Edge Flyers in Certain Areas," *Philadelphia Daily News*, 17 February 1973, 30.
28. Forbes, Gordon, "Blazers Romp, Clinch Playoff Spot As Lacroix Wins Scoring Crown," *The Philadelphia Inquirer*, 1 April 1973, 39.
29. Summers, Steve, "Blazing Finish for the Blazers," *Intelligencer Journal*, 3 April 1973, 17.
30. Brown, Sidney, Personal Interview, 10 September 2019.
31. "Blazers Have to 'Wait 'Til Next Year,'" *Delaware County Daily Times*, 12 April 1973, 30.
32. "WHA to Remain in Philadelphia," *Delaware County Daily Times (Associated Press)*, 12 April 1973, 30.
33. Plaisant, John, "Parent Earns His Paycheck," *Delaware County Daily Times*, 16 April 1973, 15.
34. Forbes, Gordon, "Owner Sees Blazers Staying for Awhile; Rips Bernie Parent," *The Philadelphia Inquirer*, 9 May 1973, 29.
35. Brown, Sidney, Personal Interview, 10 September 2019.
36. Forbes, Gordon, "Good-by, Blazers," *The Philadelphia Inquirer*, 12 May 1973, 21.
37. "Vancouver May Get Blazers," *The Morning Call (Associated Press)*, 12 May 1973, 17.
38. Dolson, Frank, "Bad Joke Struck Blazer Workers," *The Philadelphia Inquirer*, 15 May 1973, 33.
39. Doria, Vince, "Fans Aren't Sorry," *The Philadelphia Inquirer*, 12 May 1973, 21.
40. Newman, Bruce, "Man on the Move," *Sports Illustrated*, 23 October 1978, https://www.si.com/vault/1978/10/23/823080/man-on-the-move-andre-lacroix-is-the-whas-alltime-leading-scorer-but-a-pox-on-league-franchises-he-has-played-for-five-teams-and-all-five-have-gone-broke-will-new-england-be-next.
41. Flesichman, Bill, "Blazers Bold and Brash for 'Top Drawer Hockey,'"

*Philadelphia Daily News*, 23 August 1972, 58.
42. Fleischman, Bill, "Parent, THE 'Phantom,' on Way Back," *Philadelphia Daily News*, 1 June 1972, 56.
43. Sanderson and Shea, *Crossing the Line: The Outrageous Story of a Hockey Original*, 214.

## Chapter 10

Unless otherwise cited, all "stories" are gleaned from a compilation of interviews from various members of the team, including Bruce Cooper, Gregg Pilling, Gord Brooks, Reggie Lemelin, and Dave Settlemyre.
1. Michener, James A., "Robin Roberts: Great Record But No Color," *Sunday News (Lancaster)*, 24 November 1974, 49.
2. Pilling, Gregg, Personal interview, 18 September 2019.
3. *Ibid.*
4. Livingston, Bill, "'Name' Game for Hockey Team," *The Philadelphia Inquirer*, 6 August 1974, 18.
5. Newman, Chuck, "New Icers to Open on Oct. 18," *The Philadelphia Inquirer*, 13 July 1974, 24.
6. Livingston, Bill, "'Name' Game for Hockey Team," *The Philadelphia Inquirer*, 6 August 1974, 18.
7. McKee, Don, "Firebirds Have Line with Flyers," *The Philadelphia Inquirer*, 13 September 1974, 34.
8. "Roberts Throws Curve at His Coach," *Philadelphia Daily News*, 27 November 1974, 56.
9. NAHL Press Release, 7 March 1975.
10. McKee, Don, "Firebirds Triumph on 3-Goal Flurry," *The Philadelphia Inquirer*, 26 March 1975, 34.
11. Newman, Chuck, "Ill Wind Blows Firebirds No Good," *The Philadelphia Inquirer*, 5 April 1975, 19.
12. *Ibid.*, 20.
13. Jasner, Phil, "Fishy Firebird Biz Wasn't Roberts' Cup of Tea," *Philadelphia Daily News*, 13 June 1975, 74.
14. Livingston, Bill, "Firebirds Promise They'll Stagger Back in Fall," *The Philadelphia Inquirer*, 13 June 1975, 24.
15. *Ibid.*

16. *Ibid.*
17. "Firebirds Have Few Positions to Fill," *Bucks County Times*, 7 September 1975, 31.
18. "Firebirds Rediscover Offense to Reject Elimination," *Courier-Post*, 24 March 1976, 59.
19. *Ibid.*
20. Dent, Jim, "Firebirds Win, Gain Finals," *The Philadelphia Inquirer*, 3 April 1976, 19.
21. Dent, Jim, "Firebirds, Tired But Eager, Can Win It All Tonight," *The Philadelphia Inquirer*, 14 April 1976, 33.
22. *Ibid.*
23. Lyon, Bill, "Life No Picnic for Firebirds," *The Philadelphia Inquirer*, 15 April 1976, 21.
24. *Ibid.*
25. Dent, Jim, "Firebirds Win Title, 5–2; Blood and Champagne Flow," *The Philadelphia Inquirer*, 15 April 1976, 21.
26. Knight, Michael, "Another Cup on Philly's Shelf," *Philadelphia Daily News*, 15 April 1976, 60.
27. *Ibid.*
28. *Ibid.*
29. Dent, Jim, "Firebirds Win Title, 5–2; Blood and Champagne Flow," *The Philadelphia Inquirer*, 15 April 1976, 21.
30. Knight, Michael, "Another Cup on Philly's Shelf," *Philadelphia Daily News*, 15 April 1976, 60.
31. Lyon, Bill, "Life No Picnic for Firebirds," *The Philadelphia Inquirer*, 15 April 1976, 21.
32. Dent, Jim, "Winning Can Be Frustrating When Only 2,279 Fans Turn Out," *The Philadelphia Inquirer*, 20 February 1976, 22.
33. Forbes, Gordon, "The Firebirds: From Bubbles to Bust," *The Philadelphia Inquirer*, 31 March 1977, 38.
34. Fleischman, Bill, "Is NAHL Caving In on Firebirds," *Philadelphia Daily News*, 19 September 1977, 69.
35. Fleischman, Bill, "Firebirds Alive in Slimmed-Down NAHL," *Philadelphia Daily News*, 22 September 1977, 63.
36. Pray, Rusty, "AHL Firebirds Must Begin Player Search," *Courier-Post*, 1 October 1977, 32.
37. *Ibid.*
38. "Firebirds to Syracuse," *Philadelphia*

Daily News (United Press International), 13 April 1979, 69.
39. Greenberg, Jay, "Firebirds' Leaving Means Lockout for Fans," Philadelphia Daily News, 3 April 1979, 61.
40. Ibid.
41. Pilling, Gregg, Personal interview, 18 September 2019.

## Chapter 11

1. Luukko, Peter, Personal interview, 15 July 2019.
2. Bowen, Les, "Flyers Likely to Run AHL Team in Philly," Philadelphia Daily News, 27 November 1995, 78.
3. Andrews, Dave, Personal interview, 17 September 2019.
4. Bowen, Les, "Flyers Likely to Run AHL Team in Philly," Philadelphia Daily News, 27 November 1995, 78.
5. Miceli, Frank, Personal interview, 22 August 2019.
6. Miles, Gary, "Phantoms Loaded for Bears," The Philadelphia Inquirer, 14 May 1997, E6.
7. Cooper, Bruce, "A Concise History of the American Hockey League & Minor League Pro Hockey in Philadelphia: 1927–2009," 2009, http://hockeyscoop.net/ahlphl/.
8. Zeigler, Howard, "Bears-Phantoms Rivalry Is Still at a Fever Pitch," Lancaster New Era, 16 January 1998, C1.
9. Barber, Bill, Personal interview, 22 August 2019.
10. Fleischman, Bill, "Phantoms' playoffs Can Feed Hockey Habit," Philadelphia Daily News, 15 May 1998, 45.
11. Miceli, Frank, Personal interview, 22 August 2019.
12. Ibid.
13. Smith, Marcia C., "Triumphant Phantoms Drink from Calder Cup," The Philadelphia Inquirer, 11 June 1998, E1.
14. Miceli, Frank, Personal interview, 22 August 2019.
15. Miceli, Frank, Personal interview, 22 August 2019.
16. Barber, Bill, Personal interview, 22 August 2019.
17. Miceli, Frank, Personal interview, 22 August 2019.
18. Parillo, Ray, "Ice Princes: Phantoms Hoist Calder Cup After Finishing Sweep," The Philadelphia Inquirer, 11 June 2005, E6.
19. Ibid.
20. Ibid.
21. Luukko, Peter, Personal interview, 15 July 2019.
22. Ibid.
23. Andrews, Dave, Personal interview, 17 September 2019.
24. Carchidi, Sam, "Phantoms' Sale Likely Means a Move Out of the Area—and a Blow to the Flyers," The Philadelphia Inquirer, 5 February 2009, D1.
25. Assad, Matt, "The Phantoms Are Coming Home," The Morning Call, 10 March 2013, Y1.
26. Ibid.
27. Ibid.
28. Andrews, Dave, Personal interview, 17 September 2019.
29. Ibid.

## Appendix

1. "Ice Palace Costing $250,000 to Be Erected at Forty-fifth and Market Streets," The Philadelphia Inquirer, 4 November 1919, 15.
2. "Ice Palace at Last Is Assured," The Philadelphia Inquirer, 9 November 1919, 22.
3. "The Show Place of Philadelphia," The Philadelphia Inquirer, 10 February 1920, 14.
4. Jaffe, Louis H., "New Boxing Club is Magnificent Arena," Evening Public Ledger, 19 May 1920, 20.
5. Ibid.
6. "Ice Palace Bought By Theatrical Men," The Philadelphia Inquirer, 4 October 1922, 3.
7. MacKay, Gordon, "Rickard Admits His Purchase of Arena," The Philadelphia Inquirer, 8 May 1924, 23.
8. MacKay, Gordon, "Rickard Deal is Off; Arena to Hold Bouts," The Philadelphia Inquirer, 21 May 1924, 20.
9. Lewis, Perry, "$200,000 More to be Paid to Swing Deal in Arena Sale," The Philadelphia Inquirer, 23 January 1927, 49.
10. Baumgartner, Stan, "To Enlarge Arena to Seat 17,000 for Winter Activities," The Philadelphia Inquirer, 31 January 1929, 20.

11. *Ibid.*, 20.
12. "New Rink Rumor Denied by Tyrrell," *The Philadelphia Inquirer*, 9 February 1939, 20.
13. "Federal Court May Be Needed to Stop Hockey War, Phila.," *Pottsville Republican*, 14 February 1946, 16.
14. *Ibid.*
15. Morrow, Art, "Is Arena Trying to Keep Big League Hockey Out?" *The Philadelphia Inquirer*, 15 February 1946, 28.
16. "Inquirer Interests Purchase the Arena," *The Philadelphia Inquirer*, 12 June 1947, 4.
17. "Philadelphia Sports High Hopes for Entering Hockey League," *The Mercury (Associated Press)*, 29 January 1949, 11.
18. Dolson, Frank, "Arena Survived It All—Rodeos, Circuses, and Elvis," *The Philadelphia Inquirer*, 14 February 1960, 81.
19. *Ibid.*
20. Fox, Joe, "'New' Arena: More of Same," *Philadelphia Daily News*, 2 March 1965, 4.
21. Roberts, Chris, "Arena Sold for $165,000," *Pottsville Republican (Associated Press)*, 23 June 1977, 35.
22. Lounsberry, Louis T., "Blaze Heavily Damages Philadelphia Arena," *Courier-Post*, 25 August 1983, 3.
23. Williams, Edgar, "The Arena: 50 Years of Memories," *The Philadelphia Inquirer*, 25 August 1983, 27.

# Bibliography

## Books and Articles

Assad, Matt. "The Phantoms Are Coming Home." *Allentown (PA) Morning Call*, March 10, 2013.

———. "Power Play: Allentown Hopes Flyers Fever Infects the Valley and Attracts New Fans for Minor League Phantoms." *Allentown (PA) Morning Call*, May 30, 2010.

"Baltimore Defeats Comet Skaters, 3–2." *The Philadelphia Inquirer*, December 30, 1932.

"B'ars, Comets to Clash." *Philadelphia Daily News*, January 25, 1933.

Bass, Alan. *The Great Expansion: The Ultimate Risk That Changed the NHL Forever*. iUniverse, 2011.

Baumgartner, Stan. "Arena to Disband Falcons Because of Poor Attendance." *Philadelphia Inquirer*. December 20, 1951.

———. "5000 Fans See Ramblers Play at Fast Clip." *Philadelphia Inquirer*, November 28, 1935.

———. "5500 See Falcons Tie Olympics, 3–3." *Philadelphia Inquirer*, January 31, 1946.

———. "Ice Hockey Scrambles Not New, Says President." *Philadelphia Inquirer*, December 19, 1927.

———. "Just a Moment." *Philadelphia Inquirer*, October 25, 1930.

———. "Just a Moment." *Philadelphia Inquirer*, December 20, 1930.

———. "Local Hockey Club Head Makes $7500 Offer for Release of Harrington." *Philadelphia Inquirer*, December 31, 1927.

———. "President Wener's Offer of Bonus Spurs Arrows on to Greater Efforts." *Philadelphia Inquirer*, January 15, 1928.

———. "Ungentle Ice Hockey Pastime Makes Local Debut Here Tonight." *Philadelphia Inquirer*, November 30, 1927.

Bockol, Joseph, and Richard Bockol. *Jerry Wolman: The World's Richest Man*. Arnold, MD: American Literary Press, 2010.

Bowen, Les. "Flyers Likely to Run AHL Team in Philly." *Philadelphia Daily News*, November 27, 1995.

"Bud Dudley Picks Up Rambler Membership." *Philadelphia Inquirer*, July 8, 1960.

Byrod, Fred. "'Wolman Money' Didn't Buy the Flyers." *Philadelphia Inquirer*, November 3, 1967.

Callaway, Ben, "Anyone for Hockey? Fans Can Take Pick," *Philadelphia Daily News*, July 8, 1960.

"Can Philadelphia Accommodate the Quakers?" *Philadelphia Inquirer*, October 20, 1930.

Carchidi, Sam. "Phantoms' Sale Likely Means a Move Out of the Area—And a Blow to the Flyers." *Philadelphia Inquirer*, February 5, 2009.

Christman, Paul. "1930–31 Pittsburgh Pirates Convert to Quakers." Pittsburgh Hockey (website). Accessed May 9, 2019. https://pittsburghhockey.net/other-teams/pirates-nhl/1930-31-pittsburgh-pirates-convert-to-quakers.

———. "Philly's 1st NHL Team—Philadelphia Quakers." Accessed May 9, 2019. https://quakers.flyershistory.net.

Coleman, Charles L. *The Trail of the Stanley Cup: Volume 1, 1893–1926*. Quebec: Sherbrooke Daily Record Company, National Hockey League, 1966.

———. *The Trail of the Stanley Cup: Volume 2, 1927–1946*. Quebec: Sherbrooke

Daily Record Company, National Hockey League, 1969.

———. *The Trail of the Stanley Cup: Volume 3, 1947–1967*. Quebec: Sherbrooke Daily Record Company, National Hockey League, 1976.

"Comets Are Blanked by Oriole Ice Rivals." *Philadelphia Inquirer*, February 20, 1933.

Cooper, Bruce. "A Concise History of the American Hockey League & Minor League Pro Hockey in Philadelphia: 1927–2009." Hockey Scoop (website), 2009. http://hockeyscoop.net/ahlphl/.

———. "The Philadelphia-Hershey Hockey Wars on 1938." Hockey Scoop (website), 1996. http://hockeyscoop.net/hpa/index1.html.

Daniels, Don. "Frantic Fans Flip for Rocky Hockey." *Philadelphia Inquirer*, January 22, 1957.

Davis, Ralph. "Local Hockey Outlook." *Pittsburgh Press*, March 4, 1930.

Dent, Jim. "Firebirds Win Title, 5–2; Blood and Champagne Flow." *Philadelphia Inquirer*, April 15, 1976.

Dilello, Ty. *Golden Boys: The Top 50 Manitoba Hockey Players of All Time*. Winnipeg, MB: Great Plains Publications, 2017.

Dolson, Frank. "Arena Survived It All— Rodeos, Circuses, and Elvis." *Philadelphia Inquirer*, February 14, 1960.

———. "Bad Joke Struck Blazer Workers." *Philadelphia Inquirer*, May 15, 1973.

———. "Blazing: The First GM Lasted Four Hours." *Philadelphia Inquirer*, June 7, 1972.

———. "In the Spring A…Well, Take a Guess!" *Philadelphia Inquirer*, March 8, 1961.

Fachet, Robert. "It Takes a Quaker to Know the Feeling." *Washington Post*, March 25, 1975.

Fitzpatrick, Frank. "The Quakers: An NHL Team Worth Forgetting." *Philadelphia Inquirer*, May 31, 1987.

Forbes, Gordon. "Dudley Quits Ramblers; City May Lose Club." *Philadelphia Inquirer*, August 18, 1964.

"The Game of Hockey." *New York Times*, February 12, 1899.

Greenberg, Jay. "Firebirds' Leaving Means Lockout for Fans." *Philadelphia Daily News*, April 3, 1979.

———. *Full Spectrum: The Complete History of the Philadelphia Flyers Hockey Club*. Chicago: Triumph, 2016.

Hebscher, Mark. *The Greatest Athlete (You've Never Heard Of): Canada's First Olympic Gold Medalist*. Toronto: Dundurn, 2019.

"Hershey Team to Meet Philadelphia in Saturday Game." *Harrisburg (PA) Telegraph*, February 14, 1933.

"Ice Palace Costing $250,000 to Be Erected at Forty-fifth and Market Streets." *Philadelphia Inquirer*, November 4, 1919.

Inkpen, Gregg. *Broph: On and Off the Ice with John Brophy, One of Hockey's Most Colorful Characters*. N.p: self-published, 2018.

Linthicum, Jesse A. "Bird Goalie Star of Game." *Baltimore Sun*, December 12, 1932.

Lyon, Bill. "Life No Picnic for Firebirds." *Philadelphia Inquirer*, April 15, 1976.

Merchant, Larry. "The Iceman Cometh." *Philadelphia Daily News*, February 10, 1966.

Morrow, Art. "Desson, Falcons' Defense Man Studious, but All Other League Teams Respect Him." *Philadelphia Inquirer*, March 10, 1944.

———. "Don't Look Now, But—Wide-Open Hockey." *Philadelphia Inquirer*, February 24, 1944.

Newman, Bruce. "Man on the Move." *Sports Illustrated*, October 23, 1978. https://www.si.com/vault/1978/10/23/823080/man-on-the-move-and-re-lacroix-is-the-whas-alltime-leading-scorer-but-a-pox-on-league-franchises-he-has-played-for-five-teams-and-all-five-have-gone-broke-will-new-england-be-next.

"The Old Sport's Musings." *Philadelphia Inquirer*, January 4, 1932.

Parent, Bernie and Hochman, Stan. *Unmasked: Bernie Parent and the Broad Street Bullies*. Chicago: Triumph Books, 2012.

"Philadelphia Blazers Hockey Club Season Preview." *Philadelphia Daily News*, September 13, 1972.

Rhee, Yong Chae, and John Wong. "'Knocked Out!' Marketing the Philadelphia Quakers." *Journal of Sport History* 45, no. 1 (2018), 41. doi:10.5406/jsporthistory.45.1.0041.

Ross, J. Andrew. *Joining the Clubs: The Business of the National Hockey League to 1945.* Syracuse, NY: Syracuse University Press, 2015.

Sanderson, Derek and Shea, Kevin. *Crossing the Line: The Outrageous Story of a Hockey Original.* Chicago: Triumph Books, 2012.

"Soviet Hockey Coach Praises U.S. Goalie." *Wilkes-Barre (PA) Times Leader,* January 15, 1959.

Stellick, Gord. *Stellicktricity: Stories, Highlights, and Other Hockey Juice from a Life Plugged into the Game.* Mississauga, ONT: Wiley Canada, 2011.

Stubbs, Dave. "Quakers Made Wrong Kind of History in Philadelphia Decades Before Flyers." NHL.com. February 22, 2019. https://www.nhl.com/news/philadelphia-quakers-made-wrong-kind-of-history-after-leaving-pittsburgh/c-304995730.

"Tri-State Hockey League Schedule." *Baltimore Evening Sun,* October 31, 1932.

Weir, Frank H. "'Nobody Makes It by Himself,' Says Jerry Wolman." *Philadelphia Inquirer,* April 24, 1966.

"West Park Ice Palace Destroyed by Fire." *Philadelphia Inquirer,* March 25, 1901.

Westcott, Rich. *Century of Philadelphia Sports.* Philadelphia: Temple University Press, 2001.

Willes, Ed. *The Rebel League: The Short and Unruly Life of the World Hockey Association.* Toronto: McClelland & Stewart, 2005.

Williams, Edgar. "The Arena: 50 Years of Memories." *Philadelphia Inquirer,* August 25, 1983.

Zabitka, Matt. "It's December in April for Bud Dudley." *Delaware County (PA) Times,* April 17, 1961.

Zeigler, Harold. "Bears-Phantoms Rivalry Is Still at a Fever Pitch." *Lancaster (PA) New Era,* January 16, 1998.

Zweig, Eric, Duplacey, James, and Diamond, Dan. *Total Hockey: The Official Encyclopedia of the National Hockey League.* Kingston, NY: Total Sports, 1998.

## Interviews

Andrews, Dave. September 17, 2019.
Barber, Bill. August 27, 2019.
Brooks, Gord. July 31, 2019.
Brown, Sidney. September 10, 2019.
Cooper, Bruce C. July 26, 2019.
Hebscher, Mark. August 19, 2019.
Kitrinos, Bob. September 8, 2019.
Lemelin, Rejean. July 23, 2019.
Luukko, Peter. July 15, 2019.
Miceli, Frank. August 21, 2019.
Pilling, Gregg. July 26, 2019
Rukavina, Nick. June 20, 2019.
Sanderson, Derek. August 12, 2019.
Scheinfeld, Lou. August 10, 2019.
Snider, Ed. November 12, 2010.

# Index

Numbers in **_bold italics_** indicate pages with illustrations

Adam, Doug  **_98_**, 101, 103–105
Adams, Weston, Sr.  137
Allen, Keith  117
American Amateur Hockey League (AAHL)  17
American Basketball Association  **_130_**, 133
American Hockey League (AHL)  77, **_90_**, 174, 179–180, 185
Andrews, Dave  180, 186, 192, 194–195
Andrews, Lloyd "Shrimp"  28
Annenberg, Walter H.  89, 203
The Arena  *see* Philadelphia Arena
Atlantic City Sea Gulls  **_58_**, 60–62
Auerbach, Red  108

Ballard, Harold  108, 131
Baltimore Orioles (hockey)  **_57–58_**, 60–62
Barber, Bill  180–183, 186, 194
Beauce Jaros  **_163_**, 165–166, 173
Belisle, Danny  173
Bettman, Gary  186
Bialowas, Frank  **_182_**, 194
Binghamton Broome Dusters  160
Binkley, Les  97
Blake, Hector "Toe"  67
Boston Bruins  108, 134, 136–137
Boston Celtics  108, **_113_**
Boston Cubs  34–38
Boston Olympics  **_82_**, 84–**_85_**, 87–88
Boylan, Dean  166
Brenchley, Edgar "Chirp"  94, 97–**_98_**
Brennan, Tommy  81
Brickman, Gordon  **_58_**, 60
Briden, Archie  25
Brimsek, Frank "Mr. Zero"  86
Brooklyn Athletic Club  16–17
Brooks, Gord  **_158_**–159, 165, **_170_**, 174
The Brooks Group  192–193
Brophy, John  96, 102–103
Brown, Bernie  131, 141–142, **_145_**–148
Buckles, Vern  **_33_**, 58, 63
Buffalo Bisons  71
Byrne, Paddy  67–68

Calder, Frank  29, 42, 44, **_47_**, **_51_**, **_69_**
Calder Cup  **_182_**, 185, 187–189
Calgary Tigers  **_30_**
Campbell, Clarence  8, **_106_**–107, 109, 115, 119–120
Campbell, Dave  23–24, 26
Canadian-American Hockey League (CAHL)  22–**_23_**, 29, 36, **_69_**
Carson, Gerold "Stub"  25–26
Carter, Jeff  187–189
The Center  187
Charlotte Clippers  97
Chicago Wolves  188–189
Civic Center  134–**_135_**, 139–**_140_**, **_143_**, 147–148, 154–155, 157, 161, 165, 173, 175, 199
Clarke, Bob  180, 194
Cleveland Barons  76–**_77_**
Cleveland Crusaders  **_145_**
Clinton Comets  103
Clothier, William Jackson "Bill"  **_18_**
Collyard, Bobby  155, 157, 159–**_160_**, 165, 174–175
Colville Brothers (Mac and Neil)  65, 68–**_69_**
Comcast-Spectacor  **_178_**, **_189_**, 192, 199
Connelly, Bert  68
Cooke, Jack Kent  **_113_**–115
Cooley, Gaye  **_163_**, 166
Cooper, Jim  131–137, **_140_**–141
Cooper, Joe  67
CoreStates Center  *see* The Center
Cox, Danny  65–66, 68–**_69_**, **_71_**
Creighton, Dave  134, 141
Crozier, Les  155, 161, 165
Cude, Wilf  **_33_**–37, 52–54

Dandurand, Leo  **_30_**
Davis, George  **_93_**–94, **_98_**–99
Desson, Joe  **_83_**–84, 86–87
Dextraze, Bob  155–156
Dixon, Fitz Eugene  36
D'Ortona, Paul  115
Drury, Herb  **_49_**
Dudley, Ambrose "Bud"  99–101, 103–**_104_**
Duquesne Gardens  42, **_48_**

225

Dutton, Mervyn "Red" 7, *30*
Dwyer, William "Big Bill" *43*, 55–*56*

Eastern Amateur Hockey League (EAHL) 63, 91

First Union Center *see* The Center
Fishman, Maurice 201
Fleury, Marc-Andre 187
Fontaine Cup 67, 69–70
Fontana, Al 95
Foreman, Earl *113*, 123–124
Frederickson, Frank *34*, 44–45
Fried, Rudy 201
Fynan, Percy "Spider" 23–24, 25, 28–29

Gardiner, Bert *64*–65, 67–69, 72, *74*–*75*, *77*–78
Gardiner, Herb 29–34, 37–38, 40, *64*–65, *69*, *77*, 86, 117–*118*

Harrington, Leland "Hago" 28
Hartley, Bob 183
Hergesheimer, Phil 76
Herriman, Don *144*
Hershey Bears *57*, *59*–62, 71–76, 179, 181–183, 187, *189*
Hextall, Bryan *70*–71
Hitchcock, Ken 188
Hockey Hall of Fame 9, *31*, 65, *70*
Howe, Syd *46*, *56*
Hutchinson, Dave 135

International-American Hockey League (I-AHL) *69*

Jennings, Bill, 107, 114–116, 119
Johnstown Jets 97, 100–101, 155, *160*–*162*

Kaminsky, Max 91
Kerr, Dave *35*–36, *75*
Kilrea, Wally *75*, 89
Kirk, Bobby 65–66, *74*–*75*
Kuharich, Joe 124

Lacroix, Andre 134, *143*- *145*, 147
Lawson, Danny *143*–*144*
Lehtonen, Kari 188
Lemelin, Rejean "Reggie" 154, 156, *164*, 169–*170*
Leonard, Benny *43*–49, *51*–54, *56*
Levinsky, Alec *77*
Little, Neil *182*–183, 194
Lockhart Cup 161–*162*
Long Island Cougars 155–156
Lowrey, Frederick "Frock" 25–27
Luukko, Peter *178*–179, 184, *189*, 192–193

MacDonald, Kilby 71, *74*, 76
MacKenzie, Redvers 81–*83*, 86
Maneluk, Mike 185

Mastbaum, Jules 6, 201
McClenaghan, Russ 96, 102
McCormack, Hugh 54
McKenzie, John 134, 138, 141, *143*, 146
McLaughlin, Frederic *51*
McManus, Sammy 65
Melville Millionaires *33*
Meserve, Reggie 95, 102
Miceli, Frank 180–181, 184–186, 194
Miller, Joe *50*
Molyneaux, Larry 65
Montreal Canadiens *30*–*31*, *35*, 53
Montreal Maroons 6–7, 66
Moore, Alfie 72, *75*, 80
Morenz, Howie *30*
Muckler, John 96, 102–103
Mulcahy, Charlie 137

New Haven Eagles 28, 36
New York Americans *43*
New York Rangers 6, 40, *49*–*50*, *64*, 69–70, 78–80
Niittymaki, Antero 187–189
Norris, Bruce 109
Norris, James 109
North American Hockey League (NAHL) 150–151, 159, 174

O'Brien, Obie 101–102
O'Hara, Jack 81
Olson, Dick 142, 146
Orton, George Washington 11–*18*, *20*, 200
Osburn, Randy 159, *164*, 174

Parent, Bernie 131, *144*–148
Patrick, Lester 65, *69*, 78
Patry, Denis *158*–159
Pattison, Jim 147
Peto, Leonard A. 7–*8*, 89, 203
Philadelphia Arena 20, 22, 27, 37, 42, 45, *48*, 53–54, 65, 67, *73*, *75*–76, 78, 81, 86–88, 92, 96, 101, 199–*209*
Philadelphia Arrows 22–30, 32, 35–41
The Philadelphia Auditorium and Ice Palace *see* Philadelphia Arena
Philadelphia Blazers *130*–149
Philadelphia Comets *57*–62
Philadelphia Eagles 110, 112, 114–115, 123
Philadelphia Falcons *79*, 81–88, 91
Philadelphia Firebirds *150*–177
Philadelphia Flyers 5, *106*, 110, 119, 121, 125–*128*, 132, 134–*135*, 137, *143*, 153, 178–179, 184, *191*
Philadelphia Hockey Club, Inc. 114–129
Philadelphia Phantoms *178*–195
Philadelphia Quakers 5, *34*, 42–*43*, 45–*56*
Philadelphia Ramblers (AHL) *64*–78
Philadelphia Ramblers (EHL) *93*–105
Philadelphia Rockets 80, 89–91
Phymister, William *15*
Pilling, Gregg 152–159, 161, 165–*170*, 173

## Index

Piszek, Ed 151–152, 156–157, *172*–176
Piszek, George 151–152, 156–157, *172*–176
Pittsburgh Pirates *34*, 42, 44–45, 55
Plumb, Ron *144*
Poile, Bud 117
Polano, Nick 167
Pratt, Jack 37
Pratt, Walter "Babe" 65, *69*
Providence Reds 40, 67–68, 134
Putnam, Bill *113*–117, 119, 125

Quaker City Hockey Club 11–19, 21
Quebec Beavers 38–*39*

Richards, Mike 187–189
Rickard, Tex 197, 201
Roberts, Robin 151–152, 154–155, 157–158
Robinson, Earl 24, 26
Rochester Americans 181, 183
Rukavina, Nick "Rocky" 96–99, 105

Saint John Flames 183–184
St. Louis, Martin 184
Sanderson, Derek 136–137, 139–142, 149
Scheinfeld, Lou 116, *118*–120, 123–125, *127*–*128*
Schiff, Jerry 115–117, 121
Scott, Joe 117
Settlemyre, Dave "Sudsy" 153, *162*, *168*
Sharp, Patrick 188
Shay, Norman 22–23, 27–29
Shibicky, Alec 65, *69*
Sim, Jon 188
*Slap Shot* (movie) 81, 95, 155, 169
Smeaton, J. Cooper 45–*47*, *51*, *56*
Smythe, Stafford 108
Snider, Ed 11, 112–129, 149, *178*–180, 184, 186, 189, 192, 199
Soviet Union hockey team 99
Specter, Arlen 126
The Spectrum 121–*122*, 124–*127*, 134–*135*,
*140*, 148, 150, 179, *182*, 185, 189–192, 194, 199, *208*
Stanley Cup 14, *33*, 183, 185
Stark, Joe 25–27
Stevens, John 185–186, 188–189
Sullivan, Dan 153–154, 169

Tarasov, Anatoli 99
Tate, Mayor James H.J. 115, 126
Teno, Harvey *74*–76
Thayer, Freddy *82*
Toppi, Jimmy 206
Toronto Maple Leafs *50*
Tri-State Hockey League (T-SHL) *57*, 63
Tyrell, Pete *79*–81, 89–92, 99, *104*–105, *202*–204, 206

University of Pennsylvania 11, 14–*15*, 21

Van Wickle, Bob *58*, 60–61
Veno, Stan "Shorty" 27

Wachovia Center *see* The Center
Walmsley, Ivan 94, 96, 99
Wares, Eddie 65, 68
Watson, Phil 65, 136, 141
Wells Fargo Center *see* The Center
Wener, Irwin 6, 27–29, 42
West Park Ice Palace 13–14, 16, 19–21, 199
White, Peter 194
Wilkes-Barre/Scranton Penguins 187
Willett, Stanley *15*
Williamson, Murray 133
Wirtz, Bill 107, 109
Wolman, Jerry 110–112, 114–*118*, 120–*127*, 199
World Hockey Association (WHA) 130–131, 138

Young, Tom 169

Ziegler, John 109